Deploying AI Models: From Research to Real-World Applications

Gilbert Gutiérrez

Artificial Intelligence (AI) has made groundbreaking progress in research and innovation, but one of the biggest challenges remains: how do we take an AI model from a research prototype and deploy it in real-world applications? Whether you're a data scientist, machine learning (ML) engineer, or AI enthusiast, Deploying AI Models: From Research to Real-World Applications provides a practical, step-by-step guide to operationalizing AI.

This book is the 13th installment in the AI from Scratch series, continuing the tradition of breaking down complex AI topics into easy-to-follow, structured guides. While many books focus on building AI models, this book emphasizes the crucial yet often overlooked phase of AI development: deployment, scaling, and maintenance.

In this comprehensive guide, we walk you through the AI model lifecycle, from preparing models for deployment to choosing the right deployment strategy, optimizing for scalability, and ensuring security and ethical considerations. You will explore cloud-based, on-premises, and edge AI deployment methods, alongside real-world case studies from industries like healthcare, finance, e-commerce, and smart cities.

By the end of this book, you will not only understand how to deploy AI models efficiently but also how to maintain, monitor, and improve them over time.

Who Is This Book For?

- AI researchers looking to transition from research to production
- Machine learning engineers and data scientists aiming to deploy and scale AI models
- Software developers who want to integrate AI models into real-world applications
- IT professionals interested in cloud-based, edge, and on-premises AI deployment
- Business leaders and product managers seeking AI deployment strategies

Whether you are deploying models for startups, large enterprises, or research projects, this book will provide the insights and hands-on knowledge you need.

What You Will Learn

1. Understanding AI Deployment

The first section of this book lays the foundation by exploring what AI deployment entails. You will understand the differences between research models and production models, the challenges faced during deployment, and the importance of MLOps. Topics include:

- **What is AI Deployment?** – Understanding the AI model lifecycle
- **Bridging the Gap Between Research and Production** – Common pitfalls and solutions
- **Managing AI Model Lifecycle** – From training and validation to monitoring and iteration

2. Preparing AI Models for Deployment

Deploying AI models is not just about coding; it requires data pipeline management, performance optimization, and model packaging. You will learn:

- **Building Scalable Data Pipelines** – Real-time vs. batch data processing
- **Optimizing Model Performance** – Quantization, pruning, and acceleration techniques
- **Model Packaging and Serialization** – Saving and loading models using TensorFlow, PyTorch, ONNX, and TorchScript

3. Deployment Strategies: Cloud, Edge, and On-Premises

Different applications require different deployment strategies. This section explores various deployment approaches and their trade-offs:

- **Cloud AI Deployment** – AWS SageMaker, Google Vertex AI, Azure Machine Learning
- **Edge AI Deployment** – Running AI on mobile devices (TensorFlow Lite, CoreML) and IoT (Raspberry Pi, NVIDIA Jetson)
- **On-Premises Deployment** – Kubernetes, Docker, and private AI infrastructures
- **Deploying AI with APIs and Microservices** – Building scalable REST and gRPC API-based AI solutions

4. Scaling and Monitoring AI Models

Once a model is deployed, monitoring and continuous improvement are essential. This section teaches you how to maintain AI models effectively:

- **MLOps: Automating AI Deployment** – CI/CD pipelines, automated model retraining
- **Monitoring AI Models** – Detecting model drift, logging, and observability
- **Security and Privacy Considerations** – Protecting AI models against adversarial attacks, compliance with GDPR, and ethical AI deployment

5. Real-World AI Deployment Case Studies

In this section, we explore how AI models are deployed in different industries. You will gain insights from real-world applications:

- **Healthcare AI** – Deploying medical diagnosis models while ensuring patient privacy
- **Finance & Fraud Detection** – Handling large-scale financial transactions with AI
- **E-Commerce & Personalization** – AI-powered recommendation engines at scale
- **Autonomous Vehicles & Smart Cities** – Deploying AI in safety-critical applications

6. Future of AI Deployment

Finally, we explore emerging trends and the future of AI deployment:

- **Serverless AI & Cloud-Native Models** – Future of AI infrastructure
- **Federated Learning & Decentralized AI** – Privacy-preserving AI at scale
- **AI Regulation & Ethical Considerations** – The impact of government policies on AI deployment

Why This Book?

1. Hands-On and Practical Approach

Rather than just theory, this book provides step-by-step implementations for deploying AI models, making it easy for you to follow along.

2. Covers the Full AI Model Lifecycle

From building scalable data pipelines to MLOps, monitoring, and security, this book covers all the crucial aspects of AI deployment.

3. Focuses on Real-World AI Deployment Challenges

Many AI projects fail due to deployment challenges. This book highlights common mistakes and best practices, ensuring you avoid deployment pitfalls.

4. Bridges the Gap Between Research and Production

If you've built AI models before but struggled to deploy them, this book will help you transition from research to production-ready applications.

Bonus Content

- **Code Examples** – Hands-on examples in Python using frameworks like TensorFlow, PyTorch, and Scikit-Learn
- **Deployment Scripts** – Ready-to-use scripts for deploying models on AWS, GCP, and on-premises servers
- **Interview with AI Practitioners** – Insights from industry leaders on best deployment practices

Final Thoughts

Deploying AI models is as important as training them, and this book ensures you master the end-to-end AI deployment process. With clear explanations, hands-on examples, and real-world case studies, Deploying AI Models: From Research to Real-World Applications is an essential guide for AI practitioners who want to bring their models into production and drive real impact.

Whether you're an AI researcher, ML engineer, or business leader, this book will equip you with the skills and knowledge to successfully deploy AI models at scale.

Get ready to turn AI research into real-world applications—let's deploy AI models efficiently and effectively! 🚀

1. Introduction to AI Deployment

Artificial Intelligence (AI) is revolutionizing industries, but building an AI model is just the beginning—the real challenge lies in deploying it for real-world use. AI deployment involves moving models from research and development to production environments where they can handle real-time data, scale efficiently, and deliver actionable insights. In this chapter, we explore the fundamentals of AI deployment, the key differences between research and production models, and the challenges organizations face in making AI operational. Understanding these concepts is crucial for ensuring that AI solutions are not just theoretical but practical, scalable, and impactful in real-world applications.

1.1 What is AI Deployment?

Artificial Intelligence (AI) has moved from research labs to real-world applications, driving innovation across industries such as healthcare, finance, e-commerce, and manufacturing. However, building an AI model is just the first step. The real challenge lies in AI deployment, which involves integrating trained models into production environments where they can generate real-time predictions, automate processes, and deliver business value. AI deployment ensures that models are not just theoretical constructs but functional, scalable, and reliable systems capable of handling real-world data and use cases.

In this section, we will explore what AI deployment entails, why it is crucial, and the challenges organizations face when operationalizing AI models.

Understanding AI Deployment

AI deployment refers to the process of making an AI model operational in a real-world environment so it can interact with users, applications, and data streams. This process involves several key steps, including:

- **Model Packaging** – Converting a trained model into a deployable format.
- **Infrastructure Selection** – Choosing where and how the model will run (cloud, edge, on-premises).
- **Integration** – Embedding the AI model into applications through APIs or microservices.
- **Optimization** – Enhancing model efficiency for speed, scalability, and cost-effectiveness.

- **Monitoring & Maintenance** – Continuously tracking model performance, retraining when necessary.

The goal of AI deployment is to ensure the model runs efficiently in real-world scenarios, maintaining accuracy, robustness, and compliance with business and regulatory requirements.

Why is AI Deployment Important?

Many AI projects fail to transition from research to production due to deployment challenges. AI deployment is essential because:

- **Bridges the Gap Between Research and Real-World Use**: A well-trained AI model is useless unless it is accessible and functional in a real-world system. Deployment ensures that AI models deliver actionable insights and automation capabilities where they are needed.
- **Ensures Scalability**: AI models need to handle high volumes of data and requests efficiently. Deployment ensures that models can be scaled to support thousands or even millions of users.
- **Improves Decision-Making and Automation**: Organizations deploy AI to automate processes, enhance decision-making, and optimize workflows, leading to better efficiency and cost savings.
- **Provides Real-Time Insights**: AI models deployed in production can process real-time data streams, enabling dynamic responses in applications such as fraud detection, autonomous vehicles, and personalized recommendations.
- **Enhances User Experience**: AI-powered applications, such as chatbots, recommendation engines, and predictive analytics, improve customer interactions by delivering faster and more personalized experiences.

Without proper deployment, AI models remain isolated experiments with no tangible impact on business operations or user engagement.

Types of AI Deployment

AI models can be deployed in different environments based on business needs, computational resources, and latency requirements. The three primary deployment types are:

1. Cloud-Based Deployment

Cloud platforms like AWS, Google Cloud, and Microsoft Azure offer powerful AI deployment services. Cloud deployment provides:

- **Scalability**: AI models can handle large datasets and high traffic.
- **Accessibility**: Models can be accessed from anywhere via APIs.
- **Managed Services**: Cloud providers handle infrastructure, making deployment easier.

However, cloud deployment may incur high costs and raise data privacy concerns, especially for sensitive applications.

2. Edge AI Deployment

Edge AI involves running models directly on IoT devices, smartphones, and embedded systems rather than in the cloud. Benefits include:

- **Low Latency**: AI models process data locally, reducing response time.
- **Privacy & Security**: Sensitive data remains on the device rather than being transmitted to the cloud.
- **Offline Functionality**: Models can operate without an internet connection.

However, edge AI deployment is resource-constrained and requires model optimization techniques like quantization and pruning.

3. On-Premises Deployment

On-premises AI deployment involves running models on local servers or private data centers, offering:

- **Full Control**: Organizations maintain complete ownership of AI infrastructure.
- **Security & Compliance**: Ideal for industries with strict regulatory requirements, such as healthcare and finance.
- **Customization**: Tailored AI solutions with specific hardware and configurations.

The downside is that on-premises deployment requires significant infrastructure investments and ongoing maintenance.

Challenges in AI Deployment

Despite its benefits, AI deployment is not without challenges. Organizations often face the following hurdles:

1. Infrastructure and Scalability Issues

Deploying AI models requires computational resources, such as GPUs and TPUs, which can be expensive. Ensuring that models scale efficiently under varying workloads is crucial.

2. Model Performance and Drift

AI models can experience model drift, where their accuracy declines over time due to shifting data distributions. Continuous monitoring and retraining are essential to maintaining model reliability.

3. Integration with Existing Systems

Many businesses rely on legacy systems that may not be compatible with modern AI frameworks. Seamless integration requires APIs, microservices, and middleware solutions.

4. Security and Privacy Risks

AI models are vulnerable to adversarial attacks, data breaches, and unauthorized access. Organizations must implement robust security measures such as encryption, access controls, and federated learning.

5. Deployment Complexity and MLOps

AI deployment involves multiple teams (data scientists, engineers, IT, DevOps). MLOps (Machine Learning Operations) helps streamline deployment but requires automation tools like Kubeflow and MLflow to manage workflows.

Best Practices for AI Deployment

To ensure successful AI deployment, organizations should follow these best practices:

- **Choose the Right Deployment Environment**: Select cloud, edge, or on-premises deployment based on performance, cost, and security needs.

- **Optimize Models for Efficiency**: Use techniques like quantization, pruning, and model distillation to improve performance and reduce latency.
- **Automate Deployment with MLOps**: Implement CI/CD pipelines for continuous model updates, version control, and monitoring.
- **Monitor Model Performance Continuously**: Use tools like Prometheus, Grafana, and MLflow to track model accuracy and detect drift.
- **Ensure Security and Compliance**: Encrypt sensitive data, apply access controls, and comply with industry regulations (e.g., GDPR, CCPA).
- **Enable API-Based Deployment**: Make AI models accessible via RESTful APIs or gRPC, ensuring easy integration with existing applications.
- **Establish a Feedback Loop**: Collect real-world data and user feedback to improve model accuracy over time.

AI deployment is the crucial link between research and real-world applications, transforming AI models from theoretical constructs into functional, scalable solutions. Whether deploying in the cloud, on-premises, or on edge devices, organizations must consider scalability, performance optimization, security, and monitoring to ensure long-term success.

As AI continues to evolve, the ability to deploy, maintain, and scale AI models effectively will become a key differentiator for businesses and industries. By understanding the principles of AI deployment, practitioners can bridge the gap between AI research and impactful real-world implementation. 🚀

1.2 Why Deployment Matters in AI Projects

Developing an AI model is only half the battle—the real challenge lies in deploying it effectively so that it delivers real-world value. Many AI projects fail to move beyond the research phase because they are not designed for scalability, real-time inference, or integration with business workflows. Deployment ensures that an AI model is accessible, efficient, and continuously improving, allowing organizations to derive actionable insights and automate complex processes.

In this section, we will explore the importance of AI deployment, its impact on business success, and the key challenges that hinder AI adoption in production.

1. AI Deployment Bridges the Gap Between Research and Real-World Use

AI projects often start as proof-of-concept (PoC) models in a controlled environment with static datasets. However, moving from research to production requires overcoming challenges such as:

- Handling real-time data streams instead of static datasets.
- Scaling the model to process thousands or millions of predictions per second.
- Integrating AI into business applications, APIs, and user interfaces.
- Ensuring low latency and high availability for mission-critical tasks.

Without proper deployment, even the most advanced AI models remain isolated experiments with no practical use. By deploying AI, organizations can unlock its full potential, making AI-powered automation, decision-making, and personalization a reality.

2. Deployment Unlocks Business Value and Competitive Advantage

AI deployment is not just a technical step—it's a business enabler. Organizations that successfully deploy AI gain a competitive edge by:

- **Automating Repetitive Tasks** – AI reduces human effort in tasks like document processing, fraud detection, and predictive maintenance.
- **Enhancing Customer Experience** – AI-powered chatbots, recommendation engines, and personalization improve user satisfaction.
- **Improving Decision-Making** – AI helps businesses make data-driven decisions with real-time analytics and forecasting models.
- **Optimizing Costs and Efficiency** – AI-driven process automation reduces manual errors, operational costs, and inefficiencies.
- **Creating New Revenue Streams** – AI-driven products, services, and insights open new business opportunities.

By deploying AI in production, organizations can move beyond experimentation and achieve tangible business outcomes.

3. AI Deployment Ensures Scalability and Performance

A common misconception is that a well-trained AI model will perform just as effectively in production as it did in a research setting. However, real-world constraints—such as unpredictable data patterns, latency requirements, and computational limitations—can significantly impact model performance.

Why scalability matters in AI deployment:

✔️ **Handling High Workloads**: AI models must support millions of requests per day in applications like e-commerce, healthcare, and finance.

✔️ **Ensuring Low Latency**: AI models deployed in autonomous systems, fraud detection, and conversational AI require responses in milliseconds.

✔️ **Optimizing Computational Costs**: AI deployment must balance accuracy and efficiency, preventing excessive cloud computing expenses.

✔️ **Maintaining Model Accuracy Over Time**: AI models degrade over time due to data drift—continuous monitoring and retraining are necessary.

AI deployment ensures that models are optimized for speed, cost, and scalability, making them reliable for real-world applications.

4. AI Deployment Supports Continuous Learning and Improvement

AI models are not static—they need continuous monitoring, retraining, and adaptation to maintain accuracy and relevance. A well-deployed AI system should:

- **Detect model drift**: AI models may become less effective due to changes in real-world data distributions.
- **Enable automated retraining**: MLOps tools (e.g., Kubeflow, MLflow, TensorFlow Extended) allow models to retrain on new data without human intervention.
- **Collect feedback for fine-tuning**: User feedback helps improve model recommendations, search results, and predictions over time.

Without deployment, AI models cannot adapt to evolving data, leading to outdated and unreliable predictions.

5. Deployment Ensures Security, Compliance, and Ethical AI Practices

AI deployment must adhere to strict security, privacy, and ethical standards to protect users and organizations. Some key considerations include:

🔒 **Data Privacy**: AI systems must comply with laws like GDPR, CCPA, and HIPAA to protect user data.

⚠️ **Security Threats**: AI models are vulnerable to adversarial attacks, where manipulated inputs trick models into making incorrect predictions.

☐ **Bias and Fairness**: AI deployment should include bias detection and mitigation strategies to ensure fairness in decision-making (e.g., in hiring, lending, and law enforcement applications).

By integrating security measures and ethical guidelines, AI deployment becomes trustworthy, safe, and legally compliant.

6. Deployment Enables AI Integration Across Platforms and Devices

A well-deployed AI model should be accessible across multiple platforms, devices, and business applications. AI deployment makes this possible by:

📱 **Powering mobile and web apps** – AI is embedded in applications for voice assistants, chatbots, and recommendation engines.

☐ **Running on cloud and edge devices** – AI models are deployed in the cloud, on-premises, or on edge devices like smartphones and IoT systems.

🔗 **Connecting with APIs and microservices** – AI services can be accessed via RESTful APIs, gRPC, and containerized microservices.

By ensuring cross-platform AI integration, organizations can reach more users and scale AI solutions seamlessly.

Challenges in AI Deployment

Despite its importance, AI deployment comes with significant challenges:

✗ **Infrastructure Complexity** – Managing servers, GPUs, and cloud resources for AI workloads can be difficult and expensive.

✗ **Model Performance Drift** – AI models degrade over time and require continuous monitoring and retraining.

✗ **Integration with Existing Systems** – Many businesses struggle to embed AI into legacy applications and workflows.

✗ Security Risks and Ethical Concerns – AI models can be vulnerable to hacking, bias, and regulatory violations.

Understanding and addressing these challenges is critical to successful AI deployment.

Best Practices for Successful AI Deployment

To ensure a smooth AI deployment process, follow these best practices:

✓ Optimize Models for Performance: Use techniques like quantization, pruning, and distillation to improve efficiency.

✓ Automate Deployment with MLOps: Implement CI/CD pipelines for continuous model updates and monitoring.

✓ Ensure Scalability: Use cloud-based services like AWS SageMaker, Google Vertex AI, and Azure ML to scale AI models dynamically.

✓ Enhance Security and Compliance: Protect AI models with encryption, access controls, and adversarial robustness techniques.

✓ Enable Real-Time Monitoring: Track AI performance with Grafana, Prometheus, and MLflow to detect model drift early.

✓ Integrate with APIs: Deploy AI models via RESTful APIs and microservices for seamless application integration.

By following these best practices, organizations can maximize the impact of AI and ensure long-term success.

AI deployment is the key to transforming research-based AI models into real-world applications that drive business value, automate decision-making, and enhance user experiences. Without proper deployment, AI models remain underutilized, failing to generate meaningful impact.

Successful AI deployment ensures that models are scalable, performant, continuously learning, secure, and ethically sound. As organizations increasingly rely on AI, mastering deployment strategies will be a crucial skill for data scientists, ML engineers, and AI practitioners.

By understanding why AI deployment matters, you are now one step closer to making AI a powerful, real-world solution rather than just a theoretical concept. 🚀

1.3 Key Challenges in Deploying AI Models

Deploying AI models into production environments is a complex process that goes beyond simply training a model. Many organizations struggle with scalability, integration, security, performance degradation, and compliance issues, which can prevent AI models from delivering real business value. Studies indicate that a significant percentage of AI projects fail to transition from research to real-world applications due to these challenges.

In this section, we explore the most common challenges in AI deployment, covering technical, operational, and strategic obstacles. By understanding these challenges, AI practitioners can develop effective strategies to overcome them and ensure smooth, reliable deployments.

1. Infrastructure and Scalability Challenges

One of the biggest hurdles in AI deployment is ensuring the model can scale efficiently to handle large workloads and high traffic while maintaining performance. AI models often require substantial computing resources, making infrastructure planning a critical factor.

🏋 Challenge: High Computational Requirements

AI models, especially deep learning models, require powerful GPUs, TPUs, or specialized hardware to process large datasets and perform real-time inference. Running AI workloads on low-resource environments (e.g., edge devices, mobile applications) can be challenging.

☐ Solution: Optimizing AI for Deployment

- Use model compression techniques like quantization, pruning, and knowledge distillation to reduce model size and improve efficiency.
- Leverage cloud-based AI services like AWS SageMaker, Google Vertex AI, and Azure Machine Learning for scalable compute power.

- Deploy AI on edge devices using lightweight models such as TensorFlow Lite or ONNX.

2. Model Performance and Drift Over Time

An AI model's performance is not static—it can degrade over time due to data drift, concept drift, and real-world variability. If not monitored, AI models can become inaccurate, biased, or irrelevant.

🔧 Challenge: Model Drift and Degradation

- **Data Drift**: The statistical properties of input data change over time, leading to incorrect predictions.
- **Concept Drift**: The relationship between input features and output labels evolves, making previous model knowledge obsolete.
- **Catastrophic Forgetting**: If a model is retrained with new data but forgets old knowledge, its predictions may become inconsistent.

☐ Solution: Continuous Monitoring & Retraining

- Implement real-time monitoring using tools like Prometheus, Grafana, and MLflow.
- Use automated retraining pipelines with MLOps frameworks (Kubeflow, TensorFlow Extended) to update models with fresh data.
- Establish a feedback loop where real-world predictions are validated and used to improve future performance.

3. Integration with Existing Systems

Deploying AI models into existing business applications, databases, and software ecosystems can be challenging, especially when dealing with legacy systems that were not designed to support AI.

🔧 Challenge: Compatibility Issues with Legacy Systems

- Many enterprises operate on monolithic architectures that lack flexibility for AI integration.
- AI models need to interact with existing databases, APIs, and third-party services, which may require major modifications.
- Organizations may struggle with data silos, preventing AI models from accessing centralized and structured data.

☐ Solution: API-Driven and Microservices-Based AI Integration

- Deploy AI models as RESTful APIs or gRPC services using frameworks like FastAPI, Flask, or TensorFlow Serving.
- Use microservices architecture to make AI components modular and easy to integrate with different systems.
- Implement ETL (Extract, Transform, Load) pipelines to structure and preprocess data efficiently before feeding it into AI models.

4. Latency and Real-Time Inference Challenges

Many AI applications, such as autonomous vehicles, fraud detection, and chatbot systems, require real-time predictions with low latency. However, AI inference can be computationally expensive, leading to slow response times.

🌾 Challenge: High Latency in AI Inference

- Cloud-hosted AI models introduce network delays due to data transmission.
- Large models take longer to process data, increasing latency.
- Edge AI devices have limited processing power, making it difficult to run complex models locally.

☐ Solution: Optimizing for Low Latency AI Inference

- Use model quantization to speed up inference without sacrificing much accuracy.
- Deploy AI models using containerized environments (Docker, Kubernetes) for efficient resource management.
- Use edge AI deployment for time-sensitive applications to minimize cloud communication overhead.

5. Security and Privacy Risks in AI Deployment

AI models are vulnerable to security threats, adversarial attacks, and data breaches, which can expose sensitive information and compromise system integrity.

🌾 Challenge: AI Security Threats

- **Adversarial Attacks**: Hackers can manipulate model inputs to trick AI into making incorrect predictions (e.g., bypassing fraud detection systems).

- **Data Privacy Violations**: AI models often require access to sensitive user data, which raises privacy concerns.
- **Model Theft**: Trained AI models are valuable intellectual property and can be stolen or reverse-engineered.

☐ Solution: Strengthening AI Security and Privacy

- Implement robust authentication and access control mechanisms to protect AI APIs.
- Use federated learning and differential privacy to train models without exposing raw data.
- Encrypt AI model parameters and use secure model deployment techniques to prevent theft.

6. Compliance and Ethical AI Challenges

AI deployment must comply with legal regulations, industry standards, and ethical AI guidelines to ensure fairness and transparency.

🚧 Challenge: Regulatory Compliance and Bias in AI Models

- **Data Protection Laws**: AI must comply with GDPR (Europe), CCPA (California), and HIPAA (healthcare) when handling user data.
- **Algorithmic Bias**: If an AI model is trained on biased data, it can reinforce unfair discrimination (e.g., in hiring or lending decisions).
- **Explainability Issues**: Many AI models, especially deep learning models, are black boxes, making it hard to justify their decisions.

☐ Solution: Deploying Ethical and Compliant AI

- Implement AI explainability tools like LIME, SHAP, and AI Fairness 360 to interpret model decisions.
- Perform bias audits and ensure diverse training data to mitigate unfairness.
- Adopt privacy-by-design principles to ensure data security throughout the AI lifecycle.

7. Cost and Resource Management

Deploying AI models at scale can be expensive, requiring substantial investment in computing power, cloud services, and maintenance.

🏃 Challenge: High Costs of AI Deployment

- Running AI models on cloud GPUs and TPUs incurs ongoing costs.
- Inefficient resource allocation leads to overuse of computing power.
- Frequent model retraining can be expensive if not optimized.

☐ Solution: Cost-Effective AI Deployment Strategies

- Use serverless AI deployment to scale up or down based on demand (e.g., AWS Lambda, Google Cloud Run).
- Apply batch inference instead of real-time inference where possible to reduce computing costs.
- Monitor resource utilization with cloud cost-management tools to prevent excessive expenses.

AI deployment is a complex process with multiple technical, operational, and ethical challenges. From infrastructure and latency issues to security threats and compliance concerns, organizations must proactively address these challenges to ensure successful AI deployment.

By implementing scalable infrastructure, robust security measures, ethical AI principles, and cost-efficient deployment strategies, AI practitioners can bridge the gap between research and production, ensuring that AI delivers real-world value with efficiency, reliability, and trustworthiness. 🚀

1.4 AI Deployment in Different Industries

AI deployment is transforming industries by automating processes, improving decision-making, and creating innovative solutions. From healthcare and finance to manufacturing and retail, AI is being used to enhance efficiency, reduce costs, and drive business growth. However, each industry has unique challenges and requirements that influence how AI models are deployed.

This section explores how AI is deployed across various industries, highlighting use cases, benefits, and key deployment challenges.

1. AI in Healthcare ⊕

Use Cases

- **Medical Diagnosis & Imaging** – AI models analyze X-rays, MRIs, and CT scans to detect diseases like cancer, fractures, and neurological disorders.
- **Predictive Analytics** – AI predicts patient disease risks, hospital readmission rates, and potential outbreaks.
- **Drug Discovery & Development** – AI accelerates new drug formulations by analyzing molecular structures.
- **AI-Powered Virtual Assistants** – AI chatbots provide medical advice and symptom assessment.

Deployment Challenges

✗ **Data Privacy & Compliance** – AI in healthcare must comply with HIPAA, GDPR, and other regulations to protect patient data.

✗ **High-Stakes Decision Making** – AI errors in diagnosis can have life-threatening consequences, requiring strict validation.

✗ **Integration with Legacy Systems** – Hospitals use outdated electronic health records (EHRs) that make AI integration difficult.

Deployment Strategies

✓ **Edge AI for Real-Time Diagnosis** – Deploy AI models directly on hospital imaging devices for instant results.

✓ **Federated Learning for Privacy** – Train AI models across multiple hospitals without sharing patient data.

✓ **Cloud-Based AI APIs** – Use Google Health, AWS HealthLake, or Microsoft Azure AI for scalable healthcare AI solutions.

2. AI in Finance and Banking 💰

Use Cases

- **Fraud Detection** – AI analyzes transaction patterns to detect credit card fraud, money laundering, and cyber threats.
- **Algorithmic Trading** – AI-powered trading bots analyze market trends, news, and investor sentiment for automated trading.

- **Loan and Credit Scoring** – AI models assess borrower risk based on historical financial data.
- **Personalized Financial Services** – AI-driven robo-advisors offer personalized investment strategies.

Deployment Challenges

✗ **Regulatory Compliance** – AI models must meet financial regulations (Basel III, GDPR, AML laws).

✗ **Explainability Issues** – AI-driven financial decisions must be interpretable for regulatory approval.

✗ **Real-Time Processing Needs** – Fraud detection models must process transactions in milliseconds.

Deployment Strategies

✓ **Hybrid AI Deployment** – Combine on-premises and cloud AI for secure, scalable solutions.

✓ **AI-Powered Risk Analysis APIs** – Use APIs from IBM Watson, Google AI, and AWS AI for fraud detection.

✓ **Edge AI for Instant Fraud Detection** – Deploy fraud detection models directly at POS (point-of-sale) systems.

3. AI in Manufacturing and Industry 4.0 🏭

Use Cases

- **Predictive Maintenance** – AI predicts machine failures before they occur, reducing downtime.
- **Robotic Process Automation (RPA)** – AI-powered robots automate assembly lines, inspections, and quality control.
- **Supply Chain Optimization** – AI forecasts demand, manages inventory, and optimizes logistics.
- **Defect Detection** – AI-powered computer vision identifies defective products in manufacturing lines.

Deployment Challenges

✗ **High Infrastructure Costs** – Deploying AI in manufacturing requires expensive sensors, IoT devices, and computing power.

✗ **Data Silos** – AI needs access to real-time machine data, but many factories lack centralized data systems.

✗ **Edge Computing Constraints** – AI models must process data directly on factory floors without cloud dependency.

Deployment Strategies

✓ **Edge AI for Low-Latency Processing** – Deploy AI models on IoT edge devices like NVIDIA Jetson.

✓ **AI-Integrated SCADA Systems** – Integrate AI with industrial control systems for real-time automation.

✓ **Cloud-Based AI Analytics** – Use AWS IoT Analytics, Google AutoML, and Microsoft Azure AI for industrial AI applications.

4. AI in Retail and E-Commerce ☐

Use Cases

- **Recommendation Engines** – AI suggests personalized products based on customer behavior.
- **AI-Powered Chatbots** – Virtual assistants handle customer queries and order tracking.
- **Dynamic Pricing Strategies** – AI adjusts product prices based on demand, competition, and customer trends.
- **Inventory and Demand Forecasting** – AI predicts stock levels and replenishment needs.

Deployment Challenges

✗ **Data Privacy Concerns** – AI systems must protect customer purchase history and personal information.

✗ **Scalability Issues** – AI must handle millions of daily transactions during peak shopping seasons.

✗ **Real-Time Processing Needs** – AI must deliver instant product recommendations with low latency.

Deployment Strategies

✓ **AI-Powered APIs** – Use Google Recommendations AI, AWS Personalize, or Shopify AI for real-time recommendations.

✓ **Cloud-Based Retail AI** – Deploy AI models on AWS, Azure, or Google Cloud for scalable e-commerce applications.

✓ **Edge AI for In-Store Analytics** – Use AI-powered cameras and sensors to analyze foot traffic and sales trends.

5. AI in Autonomous Vehicles and Transportation 🚗

Use Cases

- **Self-Driving Vehicles** – AI enables autonomous navigation and collision avoidance.
- **Traffic Prediction & Optimization** – AI predicts traffic congestion and optimizes traffic signals.
- **Fleet Management** – AI monitors vehicle health, fuel efficiency, and route optimization.
- **AI-Powered Navigation Systems** – AI-enhanced GPS provides real-time routing and hazard detection.

Deployment Challenges

✗ **High Computational Requirements** – Self-driving AI needs real-time image and sensor processing.

✗ **Regulatory Approval** – Governments impose strict safety and testing regulations.

✗ **AI Safety Risks** – AI errors in self-driving cars can cause fatal accidents.

Deployment Strategies

✓ **Edge AI for Real-Time Processing** – AI models run locally on vehicle processors like Tesla's FSD chip.

✓ **5G-Enabled AI** – Use cloud-edge hybrid deployment for faster real-time updates.

✓ **AI Simulations for Testing** – Use AI-powered simulators (e.g., NVIDIA Drive Sim) for safer AI training.

AI deployment is revolutionizing industries, making processes more efficient, data-driven, and intelligent. However, each industry faces unique deployment challenges, from regulatory compliance to real-time processing constraints.

By selecting the right AI deployment strategies—whether cloud-based, edge computing, or hybrid models—organizations can ensure scalable, secure, and high-performance AI applications. As AI continues to evolve, its deployment across industries will further accelerate innovation and digital transformation worldwide. 🚀

2. From Research to Production: Bridging the Gap

Building an AI model in a research environment is vastly different from deploying it in a real-world application. Many AI projects struggle to transition from proof-of-concept to scalable production systems due to challenges such as data inconsistencies, model performance drift, infrastructure limitations, and business constraints. In this chapter, we explore the key differences between research and production AI, common pitfalls in deployment, and strategies to bridge the gap effectively. By understanding the technical, operational, and business factors involved, you'll be better prepared to take your AI models from the lab to large-scale deployment with confidence.

2.1 Research vs. Production: Key Differences

Artificial intelligence (AI) research is focused on developing, testing, and refining new algorithms, while AI production is about deploying these models into real-world environments where they deliver value. The transition from research to production is one of the most challenging phases in AI deployment, as models need to shift from controlled, academic settings to dynamic, unpredictable real-world applications.

This section explores the key differences between AI research and AI production, highlighting the technical, operational, and strategic gaps that must be bridged for successful deployment.

1. Objective: Experimentation vs. Real-World Performance

AI Research

- Focuses on algorithm development, accuracy improvement, and theoretical advancements.
- Experiments with different architectures, hyperparameters, and datasets to find the best-performing model.
- Success is measured by benchmarks like accuracy, precision, recall, and F1-score.

AI Production

- Prioritizes scalability, robustness, and real-time performance over theoretical accuracy.
- Must handle real-world data, which is often noisy, incomplete, and constantly evolving.
- Success is measured by latency, reliability, cost-efficiency, and business impact.

✓ **Key Takeaway**: A model that performs well in a research setting may not work effectively in production due to data shifts, computational constraints, and operational challenges.

2. Data Handling: Clean & Labeled vs. Noisy & Dynamic

AI Research

- Uses preprocessed, structured, and well-labeled datasets from sources like Kaggle, OpenAI, or academic institutions.
- Experiments with balanced datasets, often curated for optimal learning.
- Assumes data remains static and follows the same distribution over time.

AI Production

- Works with unstructured, raw, and often missing data coming from real-world sources.
- Data distributions change over time, leading to data drift and concept drift.
- Requires real-time data ingestion pipelines from IoT sensors, user interactions, or live databases.

✓ **Key Takeaway**: AI models in production need continuous data monitoring, preprocessing, and retraining to stay relevant.

3. Model Performance: Maximum Accuracy vs. Efficiency and Speed

AI Research

- Focuses on achieving state-of-the-art accuracy, often using large, complex models (e.g., GPT-4, BERT, DALL·E).
- Model size and inference time are not major concerns, as computations can run on high-performance clusters.
- Evaluates models using offline testing on historical datasets.

AI Production

- Prioritizes fast inference speed and minimal latency, often requiring model compression and optimization.
- Must run on cost-effective infrastructure, sometimes on low-power edge devices.
- Needs to balance accuracy with speed and resource efficiency.

✓ **Key Takeaway**: Lighter, optimized models (e.g., quantized, pruned, or distilled versions) are often needed for real-time applications.

4. Infrastructure: Research Environments vs. Scalable Deployment

AI Research

- Runs on high-end GPUs, TPUs, or cloud-based AI training environments like Google Colab, Jupyter notebooks, and on-premises research clusters.
- Does not require real-time response or integration with live systems.

AI Production

- Needs to support scalable, distributed deployment across cloud platforms (AWS, GCP, Azure), on-premises servers, or edge devices.
- Requires integration with existing enterprise systems, APIs, and databases.
- Models must be packaged using Docker, Kubernetes, or serverless functions for efficient deployment.

✓ **Key Takeaway**: Deploying AI models requires a shift from ad-hoc research environments to production-ready infrastructures with auto-scaling, security, and monitoring.

5. Model Maintenance: Static vs. Continuous Learning

AI Research

- Models are trained once, evaluated on test data, and published in research papers.
- Does not account for concept drift or changing user behavior.

AI Production

- Requires continuous model monitoring, retraining, and performance tuning.
- Must adapt to evolving data patterns (e.g., fraud detection models must detect new fraud tactics).
- Needs MLOps pipelines to automate model retraining and deployment.

✓ **Key Takeaway**: Production AI requires a feedback loop for continuous learning and adaptation.

6. Security and Compliance: Open Research vs. Regulated Deployment

AI Research

- Models and datasets are often publicly available for experimentation.
- Security and privacy concerns are not a primary focus.

AI Production

- Must comply with data protection regulations (e.g., GDPR, HIPAA, CCPA).
- Needs secure APIs, encrypted data storage, and adversarial defense mechanisms.
- Faces risks like model theft, adversarial attacks, and biased decision-making.

✓ **Key Takeaway**: AI production requires strong security measures, compliance checks, and ethical considerations to avoid legal and reputational risks.

7. Collaboration: Individual Research vs. Cross-Functional Teams

AI Research

- Conducted by small teams of AI researchers, data scientists, and engineers.
- Focuses on publishing papers and improving algorithms.

AI Production

Involves cross-functional teams, including:

- Software Engineers (to integrate AI into applications)
- Data Engineers (to build data pipelines)

- DevOps/MLOps Teams (to manage infrastructure and monitoring)
- Business Analysts & Domain Experts (to align AI with real-world needs)

✓ **Key Takeaway**: AI deployment is a team effort that requires collaboration between technical, operational, and business stakeholders.

Conclusion: Bridging the Research-to-Production Gap

The transition from AI research to production is one of the most critical steps in AI deployment. Many organizations struggle because they fail to address the key differences between research and production, such as scalability, data complexity, performance trade-offs, security, and continuous maintenance.

To successfully deploy AI models, organizations must:

✓ Optimize models for efficiency (reduce latency, size, and computational cost).

✓ Set up scalable infrastructure (cloud, edge, or hybrid deployment).

✓ Implement MLOps best practices (monitoring, retraining, automation).

✓ Ensure security, compliance, and ethical considerations.

✓ Foster collaboration between AI researchers, engineers, and business teams.

By recognizing and addressing these key differences, organizations can turn AI research into real-world, scalable, and impactful solutions. 🚀

2.2 Common Pitfalls in Transitioning AI Models

Transitioning AI models from research to production is a complex process that often leads to unexpected challenges. Many organizations struggle with model performance, scalability, integration, and maintenance when deploying AI systems in real-world environments. Even well-trained models can fail when exposed to dynamic data, latency constraints, security risks, and operational inefficiencies.

This section explores the most common pitfalls in AI deployment and offers strategies to overcome them, ensuring a smooth and efficient transition from research to production.

1. Ignoring Real-World Data Complexity

The Pitfall

- Research models are often trained on clean, well-labeled, and balanced datasets that do not represent real-world conditions.
- In production, models face noisy, incomplete, unstructured, and evolving data, leading to performance degradation.
- Data drift (distribution changes over time) and concept drift (relationships between inputs and outputs change) make models obsolete.

How to Avoid It

✓ **Use Realistic Training Data** – Incorporate real-world noise, missing values, and adversarial examples in training.

✓ **Monitor for Data Drift** – Use automated monitoring tools (e.g., Evidently AI, DataRobot) to detect shifts in data.

✓ **Retrain Models Regularly** – Set up continuous learning pipelines to adapt to new data.

2. Overfitting to Training Data

The Pitfall

- AI researchers often optimize models to achieve high accuracy on static test datasets, but these models fail when exposed to new, unseen data.
- Overfitted models memorize patterns instead of generalizing, leading to poor real-world performance.

How to Avoid It

✓ **Use Cross-Validation** – Test models on diverse validation sets to ensure robustness.

✓ **Regularization Techniques** – Apply dropout, L1/L2 regularization, and early stopping to prevent overfitting.

✓ **A/B Testing in Production** – Deploy models in a controlled environment to evaluate real-world performance before full rollout.

3. Ignoring Model Scalability and Latency

The Pitfall

- Research models are not optimized for speed and efficiency, leading to high latency and computational costs in production.
- Large models like GPT, BERT, and ResNet require extensive resources, making real-time inference impractical.

How to Avoid It

✓ **Optimize for Efficiency** – Use model quantization, pruning, and knowledge distillation to reduce size and improve speed.

✓ **Deploy on the Right Infrastructure** – Choose cloud, edge, or on-premises deployment based on latency needs.

✓ **Use Model Caching and Batch Processing** – Reduce redundant computations and improve response times.

4. Lack of MLOps and Automation

The Pitfall

- Many organizations manually deploy AI models, leading to slow, error-prone, and inefficient workflows.
- Without proper monitoring and automation, deployed models degrade over time and require constant human intervention.

How to Avoid It

✓ **Implement MLOps Best Practices** – Automate model training, testing, deployment, and monitoring with tools like Kubeflow, MLflow, and TensorFlow Extended (TFX).

✓ **Set Up CI/CD Pipelines** – Use GitOps, Jenkins, and ArgoCD to enable continuous integration and deployment of AI models.

✓ **Use AutoML for Retraining** – Automate model selection and hyperparameter tuning with Google AutoML, H2O.ai, or DataRobot.

5. Poor Integration with Business Applications

The Pitfall

- AI models often exist as standalone projects that do not integrate well with existing enterprise software, APIs, and workflows.
- Lack of seamless integration prevents business teams from leveraging AI insights effectively.

How to Avoid It

✓ **Use Standardized APIs** – Deploy AI models via RESTful APIs, gRPC, or GraphQL for easy integration.

✓ **Collaborate with Engineering Teams** – Work closely with software developers, data engineers, and IT teams to align AI with business needs.

✓ **Deploy Microservices Architecture** – Containerize AI models using Docker, Kubernetes, or serverless functions for modular and scalable deployment.

6. Neglecting Security and Compliance

The Pitfall

- AI models handle sensitive data, making them vulnerable to security breaches, adversarial attacks, and privacy violations.
- Many organizations fail to comply with GDPR, HIPAA, CCPA, and financial regulations, leading to legal and reputational risks.

How to Avoid It

✓ **Implement Data Encryption and Access Controls** – Use TLS, SSL, and IAM policies to secure AI APIs and databases.

✓ **Defend Against Adversarial Attacks** – Use adversarial training, input validation, and anomaly detection to prevent attacks.

✓ **Ensure Compliance from the Start** – Work with legal and compliance teams to follow regulations before deployment.

7. Failure to Monitor and Maintain AI Models

The Pitfall

- Once deployed, many AI models are left unattended, leading to performance degradation over time.
- Model drift, data changes, and evolving user behavior reduce the effectiveness of AI models.

How to Avoid It

✓ **Use Real-Time Model Monitoring** – Track accuracy, latency, and error rates using tools like Prometheus, Grafana, and AWS SageMaker Monitor.

✓ **Set Up Automated Alerts** – Detect data drift, performance drops, and anomalies to trigger retraining.

✓ **Develop a Model Retraining Strategy** – Schedule periodic retraining or use online learning techniques for continuous adaptation.

8. Ignoring Explainability and Interpretability

The Pitfall

- Black-box AI models make critical decisions without explaining their reasoning, leading to lack of trust and regulatory issues.
- In industries like finance, healthcare, and legal, explainability is mandatory for compliance.

How to Avoid It

✓ **Use Explainable AI (XAI) Techniques** – Implement SHAP, LIME, and model interpretability tools.

✓ **Choose Interpretable Models** – When possible, prefer decision trees, logistic regression, or rule-based models over deep learning.

✓ **Provide Human-AI Collaboration** – Allow human oversight for AI-driven decisions in sensitive applications.

Conclusion: Building a Successful AI Deployment Strategy

Successfully transitioning AI models from research to production requires careful planning, automation, and continuous monitoring. The most common pitfalls—such as ignoring real-world data complexity, overfitting, poor scalability, security risks, and lack of automation—can severely impact AI performance and reliability.

To ensure a successful AI deployment, organizations should:

✅ Train models on realistic, diverse, and continuously updated datasets.

✅ Optimize models for speed, scalability, and real-world efficiency.

✅ Implement MLOps pipelines for automated model deployment, monitoring, and retraining.

✅ Prioritize security, compliance, and explainability to build trust in AI decisions.

✅ Collaborate across AI, engineering, IT, and business teams to ensure smooth integration.

By avoiding these common pitfalls and following best practices, AI teams can deploy robust, scalable, and high-performing models that deliver real-world value and drive business success. 🚀

2.3 The Role of Engineering in AI Deployment

Deploying AI models successfully isn't just about building accurate algorithms—it's about engineering robust, scalable, and efficient systems that integrate AI into real-world applications. While data scientists and AI researchers focus on model development, software engineers, DevOps specialists, and MLOps professionals ensure that these models work reliably in production environments.

AI deployment requires expertise in infrastructure, software development, data engineering, security, and automation. Without a strong engineering foundation, even the most advanced AI models can fail in real-world scenarios. This section explores the critical role engineering plays in AI deployment and how different engineering disciplines contribute to the AI lifecycle.

1. Software Engineering: Building AI-Ready Applications

Why It Matters

- AI models need to be integrated into applications, APIs, or services that end users can interact with.
- Poor software engineering can lead to inefficient, buggy, and unscalable AI implementations.
- AI applications must follow best practices in coding, modularity, and maintainability.

Key Responsibilities

✅ **Develop AI-Powered Applications** – Build software that connects AI models with front-end and back-end systems.

✅ **Create APIs for AI Models** – Expose AI capabilities through REST, gRPC, or WebSocket APIs.

✅ **Ensure Code Maintainability** – Use clean code principles, version control (Git), and documentation for long-term scalability.

✅ **Optimize Performance** – Implement multi-threading, caching, and load balancing to handle AI inference efficiently.

Best Practices

✔ Use modular and scalable architectures (e.g., microservices).

✔ Implement unit tests and integration tests for AI components.

✔ Ensure seamless integration with databases, cloud services, and enterprise systems.

2. Data Engineering: Managing AI Data Pipelines

Why It Matters

- AI models are only as good as the data they are trained on. Clean, structured, and real-time data pipelines are crucial for AI success.
- AI in production requires continuous data ingestion, transformation, and validation.
- Poor data engineering leads to model failures, outdated predictions, and unreliable insights.

Key Responsibilities

✅ **Design Data Pipelines** – Create ETL (Extract, Transform, Load) workflows to collect and process data.

✅ **Ensure Data Quality** – Clean and preprocess raw data to remove noise, duplicates, and inconsistencies.

✅ **Build Data Storage Systems** – Use databases (SQL, NoSQL), data lakes, and cloud storage solutions.

✅ **Enable Real-Time Data Processing** – Use Kafka, Apache Spark, or Flink for real-time AI applications.

Best Practices

✓ Implement data versioning to track dataset changes.

✓ Use feature stores (e.g., Feast, Tecton) for consistent AI feature engineering.

✓ Automate data validation and anomaly detection before feeding into AI models.

3. DevOps & MLOps: Automating AI Deployment

Why It Matters

- AI models cannot be deployed manually every time they are updated. Automation is key.
- DevOps and MLOps ensure that AI models are continuously integrated, deployed, and monitored without disrupting business operations.
- AI models degrade over time due to data drift, requiring automated retraining and updates.

Key Responsibilities

✅ **Set Up CI/CD Pipelines for AI** – Automate model testing, validation, and deployment.

✅ **Enable Model Monitoring** – Track latency, accuracy, and error rates in production.

✅ **Implement Version Control for Models** – Store different versions of AI models for rollback and comparison.

✅ **Automate Model Retraining** – Schedule regular retraining based on real-world data changes.

Best Practices

✓ Use MLOps tools like Kubeflow, MLflow, or TensorFlow Extended (TFX).

✓ Implement containerization (Docker) and orchestration (Kubernetes) for scalable AI deployment.

✓ Set up logging and alert systems for real-time monitoring of AI performance.

4. Cloud & Infrastructure Engineering: AI Scalability & Reliability

Why It Matters

- AI models need powerful computing resources for inference and training.
- Cloud platforms (AWS, Google Cloud, Azure) provide cost-effective, scalable infrastructure for AI deployment.
- AI models must be deployed on reliable, distributed systems to handle high traffic and real-time demands.

Key Responsibilities

✓ **Choose the Right Compute Resources** – Select GPUs, TPUs, CPUs, or edge devices based on workload.

✓ **Deploy AI in Cloud, Edge, or On-Premises** – Optimize deployment for speed, cost, and availability.

✓ **Ensure High Availability** – Use auto-scaling, load balancing, and distributed systems.

✓ **Manage Storage & Networking** – Optimize database access, bandwidth, and latency for AI applications.

Best Practices

✓ Use serverless AI models (e.g., AWS Lambda, Google Cloud Functions) for low-latency applications.

✓ Implement edge AI for real-time inference without cloud dependency.

✓ Monitor cloud costs and optimize resource allocation to avoid unnecessary expenses.

5. Security & Compliance Engineering: Protecting AI Systems

Why It Matters

- AI models handle sensitive data, making them a target for cyberattacks and adversarial manipulation.
- Many industries have strict regulations (GDPR, HIPAA, CCPA) for AI applications.
- Security breaches in AI systems can lead to bias, misinformation, and financial losses.

Key Responsibilities

✅ **Secure AI APIs & Services** – Implement authentication, encryption, and access control.

✅ **Defend Against Adversarial Attacks** – Detect and prevent poisoning, evasion, and model inversion attacks.

✅ **Ensure Compliance & Ethical AI** – Follow legal frameworks for privacy, fairness, and bias mitigation.

✅ **Monitor AI for Security Threats** – Use AI-specific security tools to detect anomalies.

Best Practices

✔ Implement zero-trust security for AI models in production.

✔ Use differential privacy and homomorphic encryption for sensitive data.

✔ Regularly audit AI decisions to ensure fairness and compliance.

Conclusion: Engineering as the Backbone of AI Deployment

AI deployment is not just a data science problem—it is a complex engineering challenge that requires expertise across multiple domains. From software development and data engineering to DevOps, cloud infrastructure, and security, each engineering discipline plays a crucial role in ensuring AI models are scalable, reliable, and secure.

To successfully deploy AI, organizations must:

✅ Collaborate across AI, software, and infrastructure teams for seamless integration.

✅ Automate deployment with MLOps to ensure continuous model updates and monitoring.

✅ Optimize AI performance for real-time inference, scalability, and cost efficiency.

✅ Implement strong security measures to protect AI models from adversarial threats.

By investing in a strong engineering foundation, businesses can deploy AI systems that are not just accurate but also efficient, scalable, and enterprise-ready. 🚀

2.4 Understanding Business Needs in Deployment

AI deployment is not just a technical process—it must align with business goals, industry requirements, and end-user expectations. Many AI projects fail because they focus solely on model accuracy and neglect the real-world impact and business value. To ensure a successful AI deployment, organizations must deeply understand business needs, stakeholder expectations, and operational constraints.

This section explores how businesses drive AI deployment, the importance of ROI (Return on Investment), and how AI teams can bridge the gap between technology and business strategy.

1. Why Business Needs Matter in AI Deployment

The Pitfall: Tech-First vs. Business-First Approach

- Many AI teams take a tech-first approach, focusing on model accuracy, architecture, and data science innovations without considering real-world use cases.
- A business-first approach ensures that AI is aligned with organizational goals, making AI adoption practical, valuable, and scalable.

Key Questions to Ask Before Deployment

✓ **What business problem is AI solving?** – Is it optimizing costs, improving customer experience, automating processes, or generating revenue?

✓ **Who are the stakeholders?** – Understanding C-suite executives, product managers, IT teams, and end-users helps in aligning AI with business needs.

✓ **What are the success metrics?** – AI success is measured not just by accuracy but by cost savings, efficiency improvements, and revenue impact.

💡 **Example**: A fraud detection AI model with 99% accuracy might be ineffective if it flags too many legitimate transactions, leading to poor customer experience and lost sales.

2. Identifying Business Use Cases for AI Deployment

Common AI Applications Across Industries

◆ **Retail & E-commerce** – AI-powered recommendation systems, demand forecasting, and personalized marketing.

◆ **Finance & Banking** – Fraud detection, risk assessment, and automated trading.

◆ **Healthcare** – AI diagnostics, predictive analytics, and drug discovery.

◆ **Manufacturing** – Predictive maintenance, quality control, and supply chain optimization.

◆ **Customer Support** – AI chatbots, sentiment analysis, and call center automation.

Steps to Align AI with Business Goals

1 **Define the Problem Clearly** – Identify a specific business challenge that AI can solve.

2 **Validate AI's Business Impact** – Conduct pilot projects before full-scale deployment.

3 **Set Measurable KPIs** – Define success based on business outcomes (e.g., revenue growth, cost reduction, customer retention).

4 **Ensure Cross-Team Collaboration** – Work with product managers, engineers, and decision-makers to integrate AI into business processes.

💡 **Example**: A call center AI chatbot should not only improve response times but also reduce operational costs while maintaining customer satisfaction.

3. Calculating ROI for AI Deployment

Why ROI Matters

- AI investments can be costly, so businesses must justify the cost vs. benefits of AI solutions.
- ROI helps decision-makers evaluate whether an AI model is worth deploying.

How to Calculate AI ROI

📌 **ROI Formula:**

$$ROI = \frac{\text{Net Profit from AI Implementation}}{\text{Total AI Investment}} \times 100$$

Factors Affecting AI ROI

✅ **Cost Savings** – Reduction in labor, operational costs, and process inefficiencies.
✅ **Revenue Growth** – AI-driven sales increases, personalized marketing, and customer retention.
✅ **Operational Efficiency** – Faster decision-making, automation, and reduced downtime.
✅ **Compliance & Risk Reduction** – Avoiding penalties, improving security, and reducing fraud.

💡 **Example**: If an AI-powered fraud detection system saves $5M annually in fraud losses but costs $1M to build and maintain, the ROI is 400%.

4. Understanding AI Scalability and Business Expansion

Why Scalability Matters

- AI models must handle growing data volumes, user traffic, and evolving business needs.
- An AI model that works well for 100 customers may fail when scaled to 1 million users.
- Key Considerations for Scalable AI

✅ **Cloud vs. On-Premises Deployment** – Cloud AI solutions (AWS, Azure, Google Cloud) allow easier scaling.
✅ **Infrastructure Readiness** – Ensure AI models can run on distributed systems without performance issues.
✅ **Automated Retraining** – Implement MLOps to keep AI models up-to-date as business needs change.

💡 **Example**: A small e-commerce AI recommendation engine may work well for 10,000 products, but if the company expands to 500,000 products, it needs a more scalable AI solution.

5. Managing AI Risks and Ethical Considerations

AI Risks in Business

- **Bias & Fairness Issues** – AI models may produce biased outcomes, harming brand reputation.
- **Regulatory Compliance** – AI applications in healthcare, finance, and security must follow strict laws (GDPR, HIPAA).
- **Customer Trust & Transparency** – Businesses must explain how AI models make decisions.

How to Mitigate AI Risks

✓ **Bias Auditing** – Use Fairness AI tools to test for bias in AI models.

✓ **Explainability & Transparency** – Implement Explainable AI (XAI) techniques to show how AI makes decisions.

✓ **Legal & Compliance Checkpoints** – Ensure AI solutions comply with industry regulations.

💡 **Example**: AI-powered loan approval systems must ensure fair lending practices to avoid discrimination lawsuits.

6. Collaboration Between AI & Business Teams

Why Collaboration is Critical

- AI deployment should be a joint effort between data scientists, engineers, product managers, and business leaders.
- AI solutions should be designed with direct input from business stakeholders to meet real-world needs.

Best Practices for AI-Business Collaboration

✅ **Involve Business Leaders Early** – Ensure AI aligns with strategic goals from the start.

✅ **Use Agile AI Development** – Deploy AI in small, testable iterations instead of long, isolated research projects.

✅ **Communicate AI Capabilities Clearly** – Help business teams understand AI's potential and limitations.

💡 **Example**: A finance company's AI fraud detection team should regularly collaborate with risk analysts and legal experts to refine fraud detection rules.

Conclusion: Business-Driven AI Deployment

AI deployment is not just about technical accuracy—it's about delivering real business value. To successfully implement AI, organizations must:

✅ Align AI with business goals to solve practical challenges.

✅ Define clear ROI metrics to measure success.

✅ Ensure AI is scalable and adaptable for long-term business growth.

✅ Mitigate AI risks through fairness, compliance, and transparency.

✅ Foster strong collaboration between AI, engineering, and business teams.

By focusing on business needs first, AI deployment can drive measurable impact, operational efficiency, and sustainable growth. 🚀

3. AI Model Lifecycle Management

Deploying an AI model is not a one-time task—it requires continuous management, monitoring, and optimization to ensure long-term success. The AI model lifecycle consists of several critical stages, including data collection, model training, validation, deployment, monitoring, and retraining. Each stage plays a crucial role in maintaining model accuracy, efficiency, and reliability in real-world applications. In this chapter, we dive into the end-to-end AI lifecycle, discussing best practices for version control, automation with MLOps, and handling model drift. By mastering lifecycle management, organizations can ensure that AI models remain scalable, adaptable, and high-performing over time.

3.1 Stages of AI Model Lifecycle

The AI model lifecycle encompasses the entire journey of an AI model, from its initial conception to deployment and ongoing maintenance. Understanding each stage is crucial for ensuring a successful, scalable, and maintainable AI system. Without a structured approach, AI models risk becoming ineffective, biased, or obsolete over time.

In this section, we will explore the key stages of the AI model lifecycle, from data collection and model training to deployment, monitoring, and continuous improvement.

1. Problem Definition and Business Understanding

Why It Matters

Before building an AI model, it's essential to define the problem clearly and align it with business objectives. Many AI projects fail because they focus on technology first, rather than understanding the real-world impact of AI.

Key Questions to Ask

✓ What business problem are we solving?

✓ What are the expected outcomes and success metrics?

✓ How will AI be integrated into existing systems and workflows?

💡 **Example**: A fraud detection AI model should not only identify fraudulent transactions but also minimize false positives to avoid disrupting legitimate customers.

2. Data Collection and Preparation

Why It Matters

AI models rely on high-quality data for training and prediction. Poor data can lead to biased, inaccurate, or unreliable AI models.

Key Steps in Data Preparation

✅ **Data Collection** – Gather data from databases, APIs, web scraping, IoT sensors, or user interactions.
✅ **Data Cleaning** – Remove duplicates, handle missing values, and filter out noise.
✅ **Data Labeling** – For supervised learning, label the data accurately to ensure correct model training.
✅ **Data Splitting** – Divide data into training, validation, and test sets to evaluate model performance.

💡 **Example**: In medical AI, patient data must be accurate, unbiased, and privacy-compliant (HIPAA, GDPR) to ensure ethical AI deployment.

3. Model Selection and Training

Why It Matters

Choosing the right model architecture determines the accuracy, efficiency, and scalability of AI deployment.

Key Considerations

✅ **Select the Right Model** – Choose from linear regression, deep learning, decision trees, transformers, etc. based on the problem.
✅ **Hyperparameter Tuning** – Optimize parameters such as learning rate, batch size, and regularization to improve performance.
✅ **Training & Validation** – Train models using GPU/TPU acceleration and validate performance using cross-validation.

☑ **Avoid Overfitting** – Use regularization, dropout, and data augmentation to generalize better on real-world data.

💡 **Example**: In speech recognition AI, a deep learning model trained on limited accents and dialects may struggle with diverse real-world users.

4. Model Evaluation and Validation

Why It Matters

An AI model should not only perform well in training but also generalize to unseen real-world data.

Key Metrics for Evaluation

☑ **Classification Models**: Accuracy, Precision, Recall, F1-score, AUC-ROC.
☑ **Regression Models**: Mean Squared Error (MSE), R² Score.
☑ **Clustering Models**: Silhouette Score, Davies-Bouldin Index.

Best Practices

✔ Use cross-validation to ensure the model is not overfitting.

✔ Compare models against baseline performance.

✔ Perform bias and fairness testing to detect unintended discrimination.

💡 **Example**: A facial recognition AI should be tested on diverse demographic groups to avoid racial and gender bias.

5. Model Packaging and Deployment

Why It Matters

Even the best AI models are useless if they cannot be integrated into real-world applications.

Key Steps in Deployment

✅ **Model Serialization** – Save the model using formats like ONNX, TensorFlow SavedModel, or PyTorch TorchScript.

✅ **API & Microservices Integration** – Deploy AI models as RESTful APIs, gRPC services, or embedded software.

✅ **Containerization** – Use Docker, Kubernetes, or serverless frameworks to make AI models portable and scalable.

✅ **Edge AI Deployment** – Optimize models for low-power devices (IoT, mobile, embedded systems).

💡 **Example**: A real-time recommendation engine for e-commerce should be deployed as an API microservice to handle millions of user interactions per second.

6. Model Monitoring and Maintenance

Why It Matters

AI models degrade over time due to data drift, model decay, and evolving business needs. Continuous monitoring ensures the AI system remains accurate, fair, and efficient.

Key Monitoring Metrics

✅ **Data Drift** – Detect changes in input data distribution over time.

✅ **Concept Drift** – Monitor shifts in the relationship between input and output variables.

✅ **Model Performance Decay** – Track accuracy, latency, and resource consumption.

✅ **Bias and Fairness Audits** – Regularly check for unintended biases in predictions.

💡 **Example**: An AI chatbot that learns from user conversations might develop biases over time, requiring continuous oversight and retraining.

7. Model Retraining and Continuous Improvement

Why It Matters

AI is not a one-time implementation—it requires ongoing retraining and optimization to adapt to new data and business needs.

Key Strategies for Continuous Learning

✅ **Automated Retraining Pipelines** – Use MLOps tools (Kubeflow, MLflow, TFX) to schedule regular model updates.

✅ **Active Learning** – Continuously label and incorporate new data to improve model accuracy.

✅ **Human-in-the-Loop AI** – Combine human feedback with automated learning for adaptive AI systems.

✅ **A/B Testing** – Compare new model versions with previous ones before full deployment.

💡 **Example**: A spam detection AI should continuously learn from new spam patterns and user feedback to stay effective.

8. Model Retirement and Replacement

Why It Matters

At some point, an AI model may become obsolete, inefficient, or non-compliant with regulations. Managing model retirement ensures a smooth transition to newer models.

When to Retire a Model

✅ Significant performance degradation despite retraining.

✅ New AI architectures outperform existing models.

✅ Regulatory changes require a shift in AI processes.

💡 **Example**: An AI-powered search engine might retire old ranking models as new transformer-based AI models (like GPT-based search engines) outperform them.

Conclusion: Managing the AI Model Lifecycle for Long-Term Success

The AI model lifecycle is a continuous process, requiring engineering, monitoring, and adaptation to remain valuable. Successfully managing an AI model through its lifecycle ensures:

✅ **Scalability** – AI models can handle increasing data and business needs.

✅ **Reliability** – AI predictions remain accurate and relevant.

✅ **Compliance & Ethics** – AI models follow legal regulations and fairness standards.

☑ **Business Impact** – AI solutions drive measurable improvements in efficiency, revenue, and customer satisfaction.

By mastering these lifecycle stages, AI teams can build, deploy, and maintain AI systems that are robust, responsible, and future-proof. 🚀

3.2 Managing Model Versions and Experimentation

AI model development is an iterative process where multiple versions of a model are trained, tested, and deployed before finding the optimal solution. Without proper version control and structured experimentation, teams risk losing track of changes, making it difficult to debug issues, reproduce results, and ensure consistency across deployments.

In this section, we explore best practices for managing model versions, tracking experiments, and optimizing models for deployment in real-world applications.

1. Why Model Versioning is Critical

Challenges Without Version Control

🔩 Inconsistent results between development and production environments.
🔩 Difficulty reproducing successful models for future improvements.
🔩 Lack of accountability when a model's performance degrades.
🔩 Unclear rollback strategy when a deployed model fails.

Key Benefits of Model Versioning

☑ **Reproducibility** – Ability to retrain models with the same data and parameters.
☑ **Experiment Tracking** – Compare different models and fine-tune them efficiently.
☑ **Rollback Capabilities** – Quickly revert to a previous version if a new deployment fails.
☑ **Collaboration** – Enable seamless teamwork across data scientists and engineers.

💡 **Example**: If a fraud detection AI model suddenly misclassifies transactions, versioning allows teams to quickly revert to the last stable model while debugging the new one.

2. Implementing AI Model Versioning

What Should Be Versioned?

To ensure consistency, teams should track:

✓ **Training Data** – Datasets, preprocessing steps, and augmentation techniques.

✓ **Model Parameters & Hyperparameters** – Learning rates, batch sizes, architectures.

✓ **Model Weights & Checkpoints** – Saved model files (.h5, .pkl, .onnx, etc.).

✓ **Code & Scripts** – Training scripts, feature engineering steps, and evaluation metrics.

✓ **Deployment Configurations** – API endpoints, hardware specifications, and dependencies.

Versioning Tools & Methods

📌 **Git & DVC (Data Version Control)** – Track datasets and experiments in a Git-like manner.

📌 **MLflow** – Manage the lifecycle of AI models, including tracking, versioning, and serving.

📌 **Weights & Biases** – Monitor experiments, hyperparameters, and model performance.

📌 **TensorBoard** – Visualize model training and compare versions over time.

💡 **Example**: A self-driving car AI system should maintain strict versioning of both the AI model and the sensor data it was trained on to ensure safety.

3. Best Practices for Experimentation in AI

AI development requires systematic experimentation to test different model architectures, hyperparameters, and preprocessing techniques. Without structured tracking, experimentation becomes chaotic and unmanageable.

1. Define Clear Experiment Goals

Before running experiments, teams should answer:

◆ What problem are we solving?
◆ What are the baseline metrics for comparison?
◆ What parameters or features are we modifying?

💡 **Example**: If an image classification AI achieves 85% accuracy, an experiment should focus on improving accuracy while maintaining inference speed.

2. Implement Automated Experiment Tracking

Manual tracking of experiments in spreadsheets or notebooks is prone to errors. Instead, use:

✅ **MLflow Tracking** – Logs parameters, metrics, and artifacts.
✅ **Weights & Biases** – Tracks hyperparameters and visualizes performance.
✅ **TensorBoard** – Monitors model training and loss functions.

💡 **Example**: An NLP sentiment analysis model can track how different embeddings (Word2Vec, BERT, GPT) affect accuracy over multiple experiments.

3. Use A/B Testing for Model Deployment

Deploying a new model without testing can lead to unexpected failures. Instead, use A/B testing:

◆ **A/B Testing** – Deploy two versions of a model and compare real-world performance.
◆ **Shadow Mode Testing** – Run a new model alongside an existing one without affecting users.
◆ **Canary Deployment** – Deploy the new model to a small subset of users before full rollout.

💡 **Example**: A recommendation AI system for e-commerce can run A/B tests to measure whether a new model improves conversion rates.

4. Handling Model Drift and Updating Versions

What is Model Drift?

Model drift occurs when a model's performance degrades over time due to changes in data patterns. There are two main types:

📈 **Concept Drift** – The relationship between inputs and outputs changes (e.g., customer behavior shifts).
📈 **Data Drift** – The input data distribution changes (e.g., seasonal trends).

How to Detect and Handle Drift?

✓ **Monitor Performance Metrics** – Track precision, recall, and other KPIs over time.
✓ **Set Up Alerts** – Use automated monitoring tools to detect sudden drops in accuracy.
✓ **Retrain Models Periodically** – Schedule automated retraining pipelines using MLOps.
✓ **Compare New vs. Old Models** – Run parallel inference to ensure improvements.

💡 **Example**: A financial risk prediction AI must update regularly to account for economic changes and new fraud patterns.

5. Automating Model Versioning and Experimentation with MLOps

MLOps (Machine Learning Operations) automates AI deployment, monitoring, and model management, ensuring scalability and reliability.

MLOps Best Practices for Versioning

✓ **CI/CD for AI Models** – Automate testing and deployment using GitHub Actions, Jenkins, or GitLab CI/CD.
✓ **Model Registry** – Store and manage different model versions using MLflow Model Registry or TensorFlow Model Garden.
✓ **Feature Stores** – Maintain reusable features using Feast or Databricks Feature Store.
✓ **Automated Retraining Pipelines** – Use Kubeflow, TFX, or AWS SageMaker Pipelines to manage model lifecycles.

💡 **Example**: A speech-to-text AI model in a call center should have an automated MLOps pipeline to update models weekly based on new voice data.

6. Case Study: Model Versioning in a Real-World AI System

◆ **Scenario**: A healthcare company deploys an AI model to predict patient readmission rates.
◆ **Challenge**: As medical treatments evolve, the model's performance declines.

◆ **Solution**:

✓ Model versioning with MLflow to track changes.

✓ Automated monitoring to detect performance decay.

✓ Scheduled retraining every 3 months using new hospital records.

✓ A/B testing to compare new models before full deployment.

◆ **Result**: The AI system maintains high accuracy, reducing hospital readmissions and improving patient outcomes.

Conclusion: Ensuring AI Reliability with Versioning & Experimentation

Managing AI model versions and structured experimentation is essential for long-term success. A well-defined versioning strategy ensures:

✓ **Reproducibility** – Models can be retrained consistently.
✓ **Scalability** – AI systems remain reliable even as data changes.
✓ **Faster Debugging** – Issues can be traced to specific versions.
✓ **Continuous Improvement** – Experimentation helps optimize performance over time.

By integrating versioning, experimentation, and MLOps, AI teams can deploy robust, scalable, and high-performing models in production. 🚀

3.3 Continuous Learning and Model Updates

AI models are not static; they must evolve over time to remain effective. As data distributions shift, user behavior changes, and new patterns emerge, AI systems must be continuously updated and improved. Without a robust strategy for continuous learning and model updates, deployed AI models risk becoming obsolete, inaccurate, or even biased over time.

In this section, we explore why continuous learning is essential, strategies for updating AI models, and best practices for automating the process using MLOps.

1. Why Continuous Learning is Essential in AI Deployment

Challenges of Static AI Models

📖 **Model Performance Degradation** – Over time, AI models may fail to make accurate predictions due to data drift.

📖 **Concept Drift** – Relationships between inputs and outputs may change, reducing model effectiveness.

📖 **New Data Patterns** – AI models trained on past data might not generalize well to emerging trends.

📖 **Regulatory & Ethical Concerns** – AI models must adapt to new compliance standards (e.g., GDPR, HIPAA).

💡 **Example**: A credit risk assessment AI trained on pre-pandemic financial data might fail to predict loan defaults in the post-pandemic era due to shifting economic conditions.

Benefits of Continuous Learning

✅ **Improved Model Accuracy** – AI models stay relevant by adapting to new data.

✅ **Faster Response to Changes** – AI systems react quickly to new trends and behaviors.

✅ **Bias and Fairness Monitoring** – Regular updates help detect and mitigate biases.

✅ **Competitive Advantage** – Businesses leveraging continuous AI learning maintain better customer experiences and efficiency.

2. Strategies for Continuous Learning in AI Models

1. Periodic Model Retraining

✔ Batch retraining at scheduled intervals (daily, weekly, monthly) using the latest data.

✔ Helps adapt models to new patterns while maintaining stability.

💡 **Example**: A spam detection AI retrains every two weeks to detect new phishing techniques.

2. Online Learning (Incremental Learning)

✔ AI models continuously update themselves with each new data point.

✔ Suitable for real-time applications such as recommendation systems and fraud detection.

💡 **Example**: A stock price prediction AI updates itself every second as new market data arrives.

3. Active Learning (Human-in-the-Loop AI)

✓ The model selects uncertain predictions and asks humans to label new data.

✓ Improves model performance while minimizing labeling costs.

💡 **Example**: A medical diagnosis AI asks doctors to verify borderline cases, improving accuracy over time.

4. Reinforcement Learning for Continuous Improvement

✓ Models learn from feedback and dynamically adjust their behavior.

✓ Used in autonomous systems, robotics, and dynamic pricing algorithms.

💡 **Example**: A self-driving car AI continuously improves by learning from real-world driving experiences.

3. Detecting When a Model Needs an Update

AI models do not always need frequent retraining—updating them too often can cause instability. It's essential to monitor key indicators to determine when an update is necessary.

Key Indicators for Model Updates

📉 **Performance Decay** – Accuracy, precision, recall, or other key metrics decline over time.

📊 **Data Drift** – The input data distribution changes significantly compared to training data.

☐ **Concept Drift** – The relationship between input features and target outputs evolves.

⚖️ **Bias & Fairness Shifts** – The model starts exhibiting biased predictions against specific groups.

🗄 **New Data Availability** – Additional labeled data can improve generalization.

💡 **Example**: A fraud detection AI trained on last year's transactions may start missing new fraud patterns, triggering a retraining cycle.

4. Automating Model Updates with MLOps

Continuous learning requires automated pipelines to ensure efficient updates without human intervention. MLOps (Machine Learning Operations) helps streamline this process.

1. Automated Data Ingestion & Preprocessing

✓ Set up automated pipelines to collect, clean, and preprocess new data.

✓ Use Apache Kafka, Airflow, or AWS Glue to handle real-time data streams.

💡 **Example**: A customer churn prediction AI updates its dataset daily using an automated ETL pipeline.

2. CI/CD for AI Models (Continuous Integration & Deployment)

✓ Automate model retraining, testing, and deployment using GitHub Actions, Jenkins, or GitLab CI/CD.

✓ Ensure that every update is versioned, tested, and rollback-ready.

💡 **Example**: A chatbot AI retrains weekly, and every new model version goes through automated performance checks before deployment.

3. Model Registry & Version Control

✓ Maintain a centralized model registry using MLflow, TensorFlow Model Garden, or Amazon SageMaker Model Registry.

✓ Track different model versions and their respective datasets.

💡 **Example**: A medical image classification AI keeps multiple approved model versions in an MLflow model registry to comply with healthcare regulations.

4. Canary Deployments & A/B Testing

✓ Deploy new model versions to a small percentage of users before full rollout.

✓ Use A/B testing to compare performance against the previous version.

💡 **Example**: A personalized shopping AI tests a new recommendation model on 10% of users before global deployment.

5. Case Study: Continuous Learning in a Real-World AI System

◆ **Scenario**: An AI-driven e-commerce recommendation system suggests products to customers based on browsing history.

◆ **Challenge**: Customer preferences change over time, making old recommendation models less effective.

◆ **Solution:**

✓ **Data Pipeline Automation**: New user interactions are collected daily.

✓ **Periodic Model Retraining**: Every week, the model is retrained with the latest data.

✓ **A/B Testing**: A subset of users receives recommendations from the new model.

✓ **Canary Deployment**: If the new model performs better, it replaces the old one across the platform.

◆ **Result**: The AI system maintains high engagement and increased sales conversions.

6. Best Practices for Continuous Learning & Model Updates

✓ **Set Up Automated Monitoring**: Use Prometheus, Grafana, or Azure Monitor to track model performance.

✓ **Use Feature Stores**: Maintain a centralized repository for reusable features (Feast, Tecton, Databricks Feature Store).

✓ **Define Clear Retraining Policies**: Avoid unnecessary retraining by setting thresholds for drift detection.

✓ **Test New Models Thoroughly**: Never replace a model without A/B testing or shadow deployment.

✓ **Incorporate Explainability**: Use SHAP, LIME, or Captum to understand how models make decisions before updating them.

Example: A healthcare AI diagnosing diseases should not be updated too frequently without ensuring clinical validation of new model versions.

Conclusion: Ensuring AI Models Stay Accurate & Relevant

Continuous learning and model updates are critical for keeping AI systems accurate, fair, and effective over time. A well-planned strategy ensures:

✅ AI models adapt to real-world changes and remain reliable.

✅ Performance stays optimized without unnecessary retraining.

✅ Business and regulatory requirements are met with compliance updates.

✅ Models stay competitive by learning from new data.

By leveraging MLOps automation, real-time monitoring, and systematic experimentation, AI teams can deploy self-improving AI systems that deliver lasting impact. 🚀

3.4 Regulatory and Compliance Considerations

Deploying AI models in real-world applications is not just about accuracy and performance—it also involves regulatory compliance, ethical considerations, and data security. With increasing global regulations around AI, data privacy, and bias mitigation, organizations must ensure their AI systems comply with legal frameworks while maintaining fairness, transparency, and accountability.

In this section, we explore key AI regulations, industry-specific compliance requirements, and best practices for ensuring responsible AI deployment.

1. Why Regulatory Compliance is Critical in AI Deployment

AI-powered systems influence hiring decisions, loan approvals, medical diagnoses, law enforcement, and more. If not properly regulated, they can lead to biased decisions, privacy violations, and legal consequences.

Risks of Non-Compliance in AI Deployment

⚖️ **Legal Penalties** – Companies may face lawsuits, fines, or bans on AI usage.

📖 **Reputation Damage** – AI bias or security breaches can lead to public distrust.

📖 **Customer & Partner Trust Issues** – Businesses may lose clients or partnerships if they fail to comply with regulations.

📖 **Security & Privacy Breaches** – Mishandling user data can result in cyberattacks and data leaks.

💡 **Example**: In 2021, a biased AI recruitment system was found to favor male candidates over female applicants, leading to legal action and reputational harm for the company.

2. Key AI Regulations and Legal Frameworks

Governments and regulatory bodies worldwide are introducing AI-specific laws to ensure responsible AI development. Below are some of the most critical global AI and data privacy regulations:

1. General Data Protection Regulation (GDPR) – Europe

🚩 **Key Focus**: Data privacy, user consent, and right to explanation.

✓ AI models must ensure transparent data processing.

✓ Users have the right to access, modify, or delete their data.

✓ Companies must provide explainability for AI-driven decisions (e.g., automated loan approvals).

💡 **Example**: A bank using AI for credit scoring must explain to customers why their loan was approved or denied.

2. AI Act – European Union (Upcoming)

🚩 **Key Focus**: Risk-based AI categorization, strict rules for high-risk AI applications.

✓ Prohibits harmful AI practices (e.g., social scoring, mass surveillance).

✓ High-risk AI (e.g., medical and financial AI) must undergo strict auditing.

💡 **Example**: A facial recognition AI used in public spaces must comply with strict transparency and fairness requirements.

3. California Consumer Privacy Act (CCPA) – USA

📜 **Key Focus**: Protecting consumer data and requiring opt-out options.

✓ Users have the right to know how AI models use their data.

✓ Companies must allow users to opt out of AI-based decision-making.

💡 **Example**: A personalized advertising AI must provide users with the option to disable AI-driven recommendations.

4. Health Insurance Portability and Accountability Act (HIPAA) – USA

📜 **Key Focus**: Protecting healthcare data used by AI systems.

✓ AI models handling medical data must ensure strong encryption and access controls.

✓ Patient data cannot be shared without explicit consent.

💡 **Example**: An AI system analyzing medical images must follow HIPAA regulations to prevent unauthorized access to sensitive patient data.

5. AI Ethics Guidelines by OECD & UNESCO

📜 **Key Focus**: Fairness, transparency, and accountability in AI.

✓ AI models must be explainable and free from harmful bias.

✓ AI decisions should be auditable and ethically aligned with human values.

💡 **Example**: A predictive policing AI should not disproportionately target specific communities.

3. Industry-Specific AI Compliance Requirements

Different industries have unique compliance needs. AI systems must be tailored to meet sector-specific regulations.

1. AI in Healthcare ⊕

✓ **Regulation**: HIPAA (USA), GDPR (Europe), FDA AI/ML guidelines.

✓ **Requirements**: Patient data privacy, bias mitigation, and clinical validation.

✓ **Best Practice**: Use federated learning to train AI on medical data without centralizing it.

💡 **Example**: A disease diagnosis AI must be clinically tested before deployment in hospitals.

2. AI in Finance 💰

✓ **Regulation**: GDPR, CCPA, Basel III (banking regulations).

✓ **Requirements**: AI-driven financial decisions must be explainable and fair.

✓ **Best Practice**: Implement AI fairness audits before deploying credit risk models.

💡 **Example**: A loan approval AI should provide clear reasons for approving or rejecting applications.

3. AI in Retail & Marketing □

✓ **Regulation**: CCPA, GDPR, FTC AI guidelines (USA).

✓ **Requirements**: User opt-in consent for AI-driven recommendations.

✓ **Best Practice**: Allow users to review and modify their AI-generated profiles.

💡 **Example**: A personalized pricing AI should not discriminate against customers based on their browsing history.

4. AI in Autonomous Vehicles 🚗

✓ **Regulation**: ISO 21448 (Safety of AI in Vehicles), NHTSA guidelines (USA).

✓ **Requirements**: AI models must pass safety validation tests before deployment.

✓ **Best Practice**: Use digital twins (virtual simulations) to train and test AI safely.

💡 **Example**: A self-driving AI system must comply with strict safety testing before commercial rollout.

4. Best Practices for AI Compliance & Ethical AI Deployment

Ensuring compliance is not just about following laws—it's about building AI systems that are ethical, unbiased, and transparent.

1. Implement AI Fairness and Bias Audits

✓ Regularly test AI models for bias in decision-making.

✓ Use tools like IBM AI Fairness 360, SHAP, and LIME for bias detection.

💡 **Example**: A hiring AI system should be audited to ensure it does not discriminate based on gender or race.

2. Ensure Explainability and Transparency

✓ AI decisions should be interpretable by humans.

✓ Use explainable AI (XAI) techniques to clarify model predictions.

💡 **Example**: A medical AI diagnosing diseases must provide clear reasons for its recommendations.

3. Secure AI Systems Against Cyber Threats

✓ Encrypt sensitive data used for AI training.

✓ Implement adversarial robustness testing to prevent AI manipulation.

💡 **Example**: A fraud detection AI must be secured against adversarial attacks that attempt to bypass fraud detection.

4. Establish AI Governance Frameworks

✓ Create internal AI ethics boards to oversee deployments.

✓ Develop AI risk assessment protocols before launching new models.

💡 **Example**: A social media AI moderating content should have a review system to flag false positives.

Conclusion: Deploying AI Responsibly

AI deployment must balance innovation, compliance, and ethics. Organizations must:

✅ Adhere to global regulations like GDPR, CCPA, and HIPAA.

✅ Mitigate bias and ensure AI models make fair decisions.

✅ Implement security measures to protect AI systems from cyber threats.

✅ Maintain transparency by making AI decisions interpretable and explainable.

By integrating compliance, fairness, and security, AI developers can build trustworthy AI systems that are not only legally compliant but also socially responsible. 🚀

4. Data Pipeline and Feature Engineering

High-quality data is the foundation of every successful AI model, and an efficient data pipeline ensures that models receive clean, structured, and relevant data in real-time. In this chapter, we explore the process of building scalable data pipelines, handling ETL (Extract, Transform, Load) operations, and integrating streaming and batch data processing for AI deployment. Additionally, we delve into feature engineering, the process of transforming raw data into meaningful features that enhance model performance. By learning techniques such as feature selection, dimensionality reduction, and automated feature engineering, you will be able to improve model accuracy, reduce computational costs, and ensure seamless AI deployment in production environments.

4.1 Designing a Scalable Data Pipeline

Data is the foundation of any AI model, and an efficient, scalable data pipeline is crucial for training, deploying, and maintaining AI models in production. A well-designed data pipeline ensures seamless data ingestion, transformation, storage, and access, allowing AI models to operate with high efficiency, accuracy, and reliability.

In this section, we explore the key components, challenges, and best practices for building a scalable and robust data pipeline for AI deployment.

1. Why Scalable Data Pipelines Are Essential for AI

AI models rely on continuous data processing to learn, adapt, and make predictions. Without a scalable data pipeline, AI systems face:

⚙ **Data Bottlenecks** – Slower processing leads to delayed model training and inference.
⚙ **Poor Model Performance** – Inconsistent or outdated data reduces AI accuracy.
⚙ **Scalability Issues** – AI applications fail to handle growing datasets efficiently.
⚙ **Compliance Risks** – Unstructured data management can lead to regulatory violations.

💡 **Example**: A fraud detection AI for banking needs real-time transaction data to detect fraud accurately. A weak data pipeline would result in delayed fraud detection, causing financial losses.

Benefits of a Scalable Data Pipeline

✓ **Handles Large Volumes of Data** – Supports big data processing without failure.

✓ **Enables Real-Time AI Applications** – Delivers low-latency data streams for AI predictions.

✓ **Ensures Data Consistency** – Keeps AI models updated with the latest data.

✓ **Improves Efficiency** – Automates data collection, transformation, and storage.

✓ **Enhances Compliance** – Ensures secure data handling for privacy laws (GDPR, HIPAA).

2. Key Components of a Scalable Data Pipeline

A modern data pipeline consists of multiple interconnected stages that process and deliver data to AI models efficiently.

1. Data Ingestion (Collection & Importing)

✓ **Batch Ingestion**: Large data chunks processed at scheduled intervals (e.g., daily sales reports).

✓ **Streaming Ingestion**: Real-time data processing from IoT sensors, web applications, and APIs.

✓ **Tools**: Apache Kafka, Apache NiFi, AWS Kinesis, Google Pub/Sub.

💡 **Example**: A recommendation engine collects real-time user interactions via Kafka streams.

2. Data Storage (Raw & Processed Data)

✓ **Data Lakes** – Store raw, unstructured data for large-scale AI processing (AWS S3, Azure Data Lake, Google Cloud Storage).

✓ **Data Warehouses** – Store structured, processed data for analytics (BigQuery, Snowflake, Redshift).

✓ **Databases** – Store real-time operational data (PostgreSQL, MongoDB, Cassandra).

💡 **Example**: A healthcare AI stores patient data in an encrypted data lake for secure access.

3. Data Transformation (Cleaning & Preprocessing)

✓ **ETL (Extract, Transform, Load):** Standardizes data for AI models.

✓ **Feature Engineering**: Extracts useful features for machine learning.

✓ **Tools**: Apache Spark, Databricks, dbt (Data Build Tool).

💡 **Example**: A financial AI cleans and structures credit history data before model training.

4. Data Validation (Quality & Integrity Checks)

✓ **Schema Validation** – Ensures data follows predefined formats.

✓ **Anomaly Detection** – Identifies outliers and corrupt data.

✓ **Tools**: Great Expectations, Deequ, TensorFlow Data Validation.

💡 **Example**: A retail AI detects missing or incorrect product pricing data before ingestion.

5. Data Access & Querying (Serving Data to AI Models)

✓ **Batch Data Access**: AI models retrieve data from stored repositories.

✓ **Real-Time Data APIs**: AI applications fetch the latest data via APIs.

✓ **Tools**: Apache Presto, Trino, Google BigQuery.

💡 **Example**: A chatbot AI accesses user conversations via a real-time database API.

3. Designing a Scalable Data Pipeline: Best Practices

Building an efficient, scalable data pipeline requires careful planning and automation.

1. Use a Modular Pipeline Architecture

✓ Decouple ingestion, storage, and processing to scale independently.

✓ Use microservices to handle different tasks (e.g., a dedicated feature store).

💡 **Example**: A self-driving car AI has separate microservices for GPS data, traffic data, and vehicle sensor data.

2. Choose the Right Data Processing Mode

✓ **Batch Processing** – Suitable for periodic model retraining.

✓ **Stream Processing** – Necessary for real-time AI applications.

💡 **Example**: A news recommendation AI streams real-time news trends to adjust recommendations dynamically.

3. Automate Data Pipeline with MLOps Tools

✓ **Continuous Integration (CI):** Automates data validation & pipeline testing.

✓ **Continuous Deployment (CD):** Automates model updates based on new data.

✓ **Tools**: MLflow, Kubeflow, Apache Airflow.

💡 **Example**: A fraud detection AI automatically retrains itself as new fraud patterns emerge.

4. Implement Data Governance and Security

✓ **Data Encryption**: Protects sensitive user data.

✓ **Access Control**: Restricts data usage based on roles.

✓ **Compliance Checks**: Ensures regulatory adherence.

✓ **Tools**: AWS IAM, Azure Purview, Google Data Catalog.

💡 **Example**: A healthcare AI encrypts patient records and restricts access to authorized personnel only.

5. Optimize for Cost & Performance

✓ **Use Auto-Scaling**: Dynamically adjust computing resources.

✓ **Leverage Serverless Data Processing**: Reduces operational costs.

✓ **Monitor Data Pipeline Performance**: Detects slowdowns and failures.

✓ **Tools**: AWS Lambda, Datadog, Prometheus.

💡 **Example**: A social media AI scales data ingestion dynamically based on peak user activity times.

4. Real-World Case Study: Scalable Data Pipeline for AI

📌 **Industry**: E-Commerce
📌 **Challenge**: The company needed real-time product recommendations for millions of users.

📌 **Solution:**

✓ Apache Kafka for streaming user click data.

✓ AWS S3 Data Lake for raw data storage.

✓ Apache Spark for batch data transformation.

✓ Redis In-Memory Database for low-latency AI recommendations.

📌 **Result:**

✓ 80% faster recommendation updates.

✓ 25% increase in user engagement.

5. Common Challenges and How to Overcome Them

Challenge	Solution
Handling Big Data	Use distributed storage (HDFS, S3, Snowflake)
Ensuring Data Quality	Automate validation with **Great Expectations**
Scalability Issues	Use **Kubernetes**-based orchestration
High Latency in AI Predictions	Use in-memory databases (Redis, Memcached)
Compliance Risks	Implement end-to-end encryption & access control

Conclusion: Building AI-Ready Data Pipelines

A scalable data pipeline is the backbone of high-performance AI models. By leveraging modular architecture, automation, real-time processing, and security best practices, businesses can ensure their AI systems operate efficiently, accurately, and at scale.

Key Takeaways:

✓ Use streaming & batch processing based on AI application needs.

✓ Automate data transformation, validation, and storage.

✓ Ensure security, compliance, and governance from the start.

✓ Optimize for cost efficiency and real-time performance.

With a robust data pipeline, AI deployments become more reliable, scalable, and adaptable to evolving data challenges. 🚀

4.2 Real-time vs. Batch Processing

AI models rely on vast amounts of data to learn, adapt, and make predictions. However, how this data is processed significantly impacts the performance, efficiency, and scalability of an AI system. The two primary approaches to data processing are batch processing and real-time processing (also known as stream processing).

Choosing the right processing method depends on the nature of the AI application, data volume, and latency requirements. In this section, we explore key differences, advantages, use cases, and best practices for implementing both approaches effectively.

1. Understanding Batch Processing

What is Batch Processing?

Batch processing involves collecting and processing data in large chunks (batches) at scheduled intervals. Instead of handling data immediately, it is accumulated over time and then processed in a single operation.

💡 **Example**: A credit card company collects all transaction data for the day and runs a fraud detection model overnight to flag suspicious activities.

How Batch Processing Works

- **Data Collection** – Data is gathered from multiple sources over time.
- **Storage** – Data is stored in a data warehouse, data lake, or database.
- **Processing** – A batch job processes the accumulated data in bulk.
- **Output** – The processed data is used for AI training, reporting, or decision-making.

Advantages of Batch Processing

✓ **Efficient for Large Data Volumes** – Ideal for handling historical data.

✓ **Cost-Effective** – Less expensive since it doesn't require continuous resource allocation.

✓ **Simple to Implement** – Easier to manage compared to real-time systems.

✓ **Ideal for Model Training** – Most AI models train on batch data rather than real-time inputs.

Challenges of Batch Processing

🔟 **Not Suitable for Time-Sensitive AI Applications** – Delayed insights can lead to missed opportunities.

🔟 **High Latency** – Data is only processed periodically, not instantly.

🔟 **Storage-Heavy** – Requires large storage infrastructure to hold raw data before processing.

Common Use Cases for Batch Processing

- **AI Model Training**: Machine learning models train on historical data in batches.
- **Business Intelligence & Analytics**: Reports and insights are generated periodically.
- **Fraud Detection (Post-Event Analysis):** Detecting fraudulent transactions in banking systems.
- **Recommendation Systems**: Periodic updates of user preferences and suggestions.

Popular Tools for Batch Processing

- **Apache Hadoop** – Distributed batch data processing.
- **Apache Spark** – Faster batch processing with distributed computing.
- **Google BigQuery** – Cloud-based batch analytics.

♦ **AWS Glue** – Serverless batch data processing.

2. Understanding Real-Time Processing

What is Real-Time Processing?

Real-time processing (stream processing) involves continuously processing data as it arrives, ensuring low-latency decision-making. Instead of waiting for data batches, AI models analyze and act on real-time streams of data.

💡 **Example**: A stock market AI system tracks and analyzes stock prices in real time to detect fluctuations and suggest trades instantly.

How Real-Time Processing Works

- **Data Ingestion** – Data is collected from live sources (sensors, APIs, IoT devices, etc.).
- **Streaming Processing** – AI models analyze data in real time.
- **Storage & Serving** – Processed data is stored and used for immediate decision-making.
- **Output & Actions** – AI takes immediate action (e.g., alerting users, updating models).

Advantages of Real-Time Processing

✓ **Low Latency** – Provides instant insights and decisions.

✓ **Ideal for Live AI Applications** – Suitable for self-driving cars, fraud detection, recommendation engines, etc.

✓ **Continuously Updated Models** – AI systems adapt dynamically to new data.

✓ **Better User Experience** – Enables real-time personalization in applications.

Challenges of Real-Time Processing

🖥 **Higher Computational Cost** – Requires powerful infrastructure to handle streaming data.

🖥 **Complex to Implement** – More challenging to maintain compared to batch systems.

🖥 **Data Consistency Issues** – Handling rapid data changes without losing accuracy is difficult.

Common Use Cases for Real-Time Processing

◆ **Fraud Detection (Instant Alerts):** Detects fraudulent transactions as they happen.

◆ **Autonomous Vehicles**: Self-driving cars analyze sensor data in real time for navigation.

◆ **Predictive Maintenance**: AI detects early signs of machine failures in industrial settings.

◆ **Live Chatbots & Voice Assistants**: AI-powered assistants process real-time user queries.

◆ **Stock Market Analysis**: AI tracks market fluctuations and executes trades instantly.

Popular Tools for Real-Time Processing

◆ **Apache Kafka** – Distributed real-time event streaming.

◆ **Apache Flink** – Real-time data processing engine.

◆ **AWS Kinesis** – Cloud-based real-time data processing.

◆ **Google Pub/Sub** – Streaming data pipeline for real-time AI applications.

3. Key Differences: Batch Processing vs. Real-Time Processing

Feature	Batch Processing	Real-Time Processing
Data Processing Mode	Periodic (batches)	Continuous (live data)
Latency	High (minutes to hours)	Low (milliseconds to seconds)
Computational Cost	Lower	Higher
Scalability	Easier to scale	More complex to scale
Use Cases	AI model training, analytics, periodic reports	Fraud detection, chatbots, stock trading, IoT applications
Example Tool	Apache Spark, Hadoop	Apache Kafka, Apache Flink

4. Choosing Between Batch and Real-Time Processing

✅ Use Batch Processing When:

✓ You need to process large amounts of historical data.

✓ Low latency is not critical (e.g., daily or weekly reports).

✓ Cost efficiency is a priority.

✓ Your AI model does not require instant updates.

💡 **Example**: A movie streaming platform updates user recommendations once a day based on watch history.

✅ Use Real-Time Processing When:

✓ Your AI system requires instant decision-making.

✓ Delayed processing could lead to missed opportunities or risks.

✓ You need dynamic model updates based on live data.

✓ The application involves IoT, finance, security, or customer interactions.

💡 **Example**: A real-time AI fraud detection system analyzes credit card transactions as they happen to block fraudulent payments.

🚀 **Hybrid Approach: Combining Batch & Real-Time Processing**

Many AI applications benefit from a combination of both approaches:

✓ Batch Processing for training AI models on historical data.

✓ Real-Time Processing for live decision-making.

💡 **Example**: A music recommendation AI uses batch processing for periodic updates of user preferences and real-time streaming for immediate song suggestions based on current listening habits.

5. Conclusion: Selecting the Right Processing Strategy for AI Deployment

Choosing between batch and real-time processing depends on:

✓ **The AI application's latency requirements** (e.g., real-time fraud detection vs. offline analytics).

✓ **Computational and cost constraints** (real-time processing requires more infrastructure).

✓ **Scalability needs** (batch processing is easier to scale, real-time requires advanced orchestration).

✓ **Data consistency** and quality requirements (real-time data can be noisy and incomplete).

Ultimately, AI-powered systems should be designed to handle both real-time and batch data effectively, ensuring scalability, efficiency, and real-time decision-making where necessary. 🚀

4.3 Feature Engineering for Production Models

Feature engineering is one of the most critical steps in building AI models, as it directly impacts model accuracy, interpretability, and efficiency. In research environments, data scientists often experiment with numerous features, but when moving AI models to production, feature engineering must be optimized, automated, and scalable. This chapter explores the best practices, challenges, and techniques for effective feature engineering in real-world AI deployments.

1. Understanding Feature Engineering in Production

What is Feature Engineering?

Feature engineering is the process of selecting, transforming, and creating input variables (features) that improve a machine learning model's performance.

In production environments, feature engineering must be:

✔ **Efficient** – Computationally optimized for real-time or batch inference.

✔ **Consistent** – Features should be generated identically during training and inference.

✔ **Scalable** – Capable of handling large volumes of incoming data.

✔ **Automated** – Integrated into machine learning pipelines with minimal manual intervention.

💡 **Example**: A fraud detection AI model may use transaction amount, transaction frequency, and device location as key features.

2. Challenges in Feature Engineering for Production

🔟 **Feature Drift** – The distribution of feature values may change over time, reducing model accuracy.

🔟 **Training-Inference Skew** – Differences in feature computation between training and production lead to inconsistencies.

🔟 **Scalability Issues** – Some complex transformations may not scale well in real-time environments.

🔟 **Latency Constraints** – Features must be computed quickly for real-time applications.

🔟 **Data Leakage** – Using future data during training leads to misleadingly high performance.

3. Types of Feature Engineering for Production AI Models

1. Feature Selection

The first step in production feature engineering is selecting only the most relevant and impactful features to reduce computational costs and improve model interpretability.

✓ **Statistical Methods**: Correlation analysis, chi-square tests.

✓ **Automated Methods**: Recursive Feature Elimination (RFE), Lasso Regression.

✓ **Domain Expertise**: Using real-world knowledge to select meaningful features.

💡 **Example**: In customer churn prediction, age, subscription length, and number of complaints might be the most relevant features.

2. Feature Transformation

Once features are selected, they must often be transformed into formats that AI models can interpret efficiently.

✓ **Scaling & Normalization** – Standardizing features (e.g., Min-Max Scaling, Z-score normalization).

✓ **Encoding Categorical Variables** – Converting text-based categories into numerical values (e.g., One-Hot Encoding, Label Encoding).

✓ **Log Transformations** – Handling skewed distributions in financial data.

💡 **Example**: Converting "High," "Medium," and "Low" risk levels into numerical values (0, 1, 2) for a credit scoring model.

3. Feature Extraction

Extracting meaningful features from raw data improves model performance.

✓ **Text Data**: Converting words into numerical features using TF-IDF, Word2Vec.

✓ **Image Data**: Using CNN-based embeddings for feature extraction.

✓ **Time-Series Data**: Extracting moving averages, seasonality, and trends.

💡 **Example**: A sentiment analysis AI converts raw customer reviews into word embeddings for better classification.

4. Feature Engineering for Real-Time AI Systems

Real-time AI applications require low-latency feature computation and retrieval.

✓ **Precomputed Features** – Storing frequently used features in a feature store for quick retrieval.

✓ **Streaming Feature Computation** – Using Apache Flink, Kafka Streams for real-time updates.

✓ **Feature Caching** – Storing features in fast-access databases like Redis.

💡 **Example**: A personalized ad recommendation system updates a user's preference profile in real-time based on recent clicks.

4. Feature Stores: Managing Features at Scale

What is a Feature Store?

A feature store is a centralized system that stores, manages, and serves features for both training and inference.

Benefits of Feature Stores:

✅ **Ensures Consistency** – Features are computed identically during training and inference.
✅ **Improves Reusability** – Engineers can reuse precomputed features across multiple models.
✅ **Enhances Real-Time AI Performance** – Enables low-latency feature retrieval.
✅ **Automates Feature Engineering** – Reduces manual feature transformation efforts.

Popular Feature Store Tools:

◆ **Feast** – Open-source feature store for ML models.
◆ **Tecton** – Enterprise-grade feature store.
◆ **Vertex AI Feature Store** – Google Cloud's feature storage solution.

💡 **Example**: A ride-hailing app uses a feature store to compute average ride duration per user and preferred payment method, ensuring real-time updates.

5. Automating Feature Engineering in MLOps Pipelines

Feature engineering must be integrated into MLOps pipelines for continuous model training and deployment.

Best Practices for Automating Feature Engineering:

✔ **Use Feature Pipelines** – Automate feature extraction using Apache Airflow, Kubeflow, or Prefect.

✔ **Leverage Feature Stores** – Store and retrieve precomputed features efficiently.

✔ **Monitor Feature Drift** – Track statistical changes in feature distributions over time.

✔ **Implement Data Validation** – Use Great Expectations or TensorFlow Data Validation to detect anomalies.

💡 **Example**: A predictive maintenance AI for manufacturing automatically updates machine failure probabilities based on sensor readings.

6. Real-World Case Study: Feature Engineering for AI Deployment

📌 **Industry**: E-Commerce
📌 **Problem**: Customer churn prediction model faced inconsistent feature computation between training and production.

📌 **Solution:**

✔ Centralized feature store to standardize feature computation.

✔ Automated feature pipelines to process real-time user behavior.

✔ Feature drift monitoring to detect changing customer behavior.

📌 **Result:**

✅ 30% improvement in churn prediction accuracy.

✅ 50% reduction in model inference time.

7. Key Takeaways & Best Practices

✔ Select only relevant features to reduce computational costs.

✔ Ensure consistency between training and production feature computation.

✔ Use real-time feature engineering techniques for low-latency applications.

✔ Leverage feature stores to manage and serve features efficiently.

✔ Monitor feature drift and retrain models to maintain accuracy.

✔ Automate feature engineering within the MLOps pipeline for scalability.

By implementing these feature engineering best practices, AI models become more robust, scalable, and production-ready for real-world deployment. 🚀

4.4 Data Storage and Management Strategies

Effective data storage and management is critical for deploying AI models in real-world applications. AI models rely on vast amounts of data, and how this data is stored, accessed, and managed significantly impacts performance, scalability, and security. This chapter explores storage architectures, data management best practices, and technologies to ensure efficient AI deployments.

1. Understanding Data Storage in AI Systems

AI data comes in various forms—structured, unstructured, real-time, and batch—requiring different storage strategies. The choice of storage solutions depends on:

✅ **Data Volume** – Small-scale vs. petabyte-scale storage.
✅ **Data Velocity** – Static datasets vs. high-speed streaming data.
✅ **Data Variety** – Structured databases vs. unstructured text, images, videos.
✅ **Access Speed** – Low-latency vs. archival storage.

💡 **Example**: A self-driving car AI system must store and process terabytes of real-time sensor data, whereas an e-commerce recommendation engine works with structured purchase history stored in databases.

2. Types of Data Storage Solutions

1. Relational Databases (SQL) – Structured Data

Relational databases store structured data in tables with predefined schemas, ensuring consistency, integrity, and ACID compliance.

✓ **Best for**: Tabular data, structured logs, user profiles.

✓ **Common Technologies**: PostgreSQL, MySQL, Microsoft SQL Server.

💡 **Example**: An AI-driven fraud detection system stores transaction details in an SQL database for pattern analysis.

2. NoSQL Databases – Unstructured & Semi-Structured Data

NoSQL databases handle dynamic, schema-less, and large-scale data such as logs, JSON files, and social media interactions.

✓ **Best for**: High-volume, unstructured, or rapidly changing data.

✓ **Common Technologies**: MongoDB (document storage), Cassandra (distributed key-value store).

💡 **Example**: A chatbot AI uses MongoDB to store user conversations dynamically.

3. Data Lakes – Big Data Storage

A data lake stores raw structured and unstructured data in a centralized repository for analysis and machine learning.

✓ **Best for**: AI model training, historical data storage, data science.

✓ **Common Technologies**: AWS S3, Google Cloud Storage, Azure Data Lake.

💡 **Example**: A healthcare AI stores X-ray images, patient records, and sensor data in a data lake for predictive analytics.

4. Data Warehouses – Business Intelligence & Analytics

Data warehouses aggregate structured data for business intelligence (BI) and analytical queries.

✓ **Best for**: High-speed querying, business intelligence, reporting.

✓ **Common Technologies**: Snowflake, Google BigQuery, Amazon Redshift.

💡 **Example**: An AI-powered marketing dashboard analyzes customer purchase trends stored in a data warehouse.

5. Object Storage – Large Files & Media

Object storage manages large, unstructured files such as videos, images, and sensor data with metadata tagging.

✓ **Best for**: Storing AI training datasets (videos, images, documents).

✓ **Common Technologies**: AWS S3, Google Cloud Storage, MinIO.

💡 **Example**: A computer vision AI model stores and retrieves millions of images in an object storage system.

6. Distributed File Systems – Scalable & Fault-Tolerant Storage

Distributed file systems store data across multiple nodes, ensuring high availability and scalability.

✓ **Best for**: Large-scale AI deployments needing redundancy.

✓ **Common Technologies**: Hadoop Distributed File System (HDFS), Ceph, Google Colossus.

💡 **Example**: A big data AI pipeline uses HDFS to process petabytes of e-commerce transaction logs.

3. Key Data Management Strategies for AI Deployment

1. Data Governance & Security

📖 **Challenges**: Unauthorized access, compliance risks (GDPR, HIPAA).
◆ **Solution**: Implement role-based access control (RBAC), encryption, and data masking.
◆ **Tools**: Apache Ranger, AWS IAM, Google DLP.

💡 **Example**: A finance AI model encrypts customer banking data before storage.

2. Data Versioning & Lineage

📖 **Challenges**: Inconsistent datasets across model versions.
◆ **Solution**: Use data versioning tools to track changes.
◆ **Tools**: DVC, LakeFS, Pachyderm.

💡 **Example**: A medical AI model stores versioned patient datasets to ensure reproducibility.

3. Real-Time Data Processing & Stream Management

📖 **Challenges**: Processing high-speed sensor data and IoT logs.
◆ **Solution**: Use event-driven architectures with stream processing tools.

- **Tools**: Apache Kafka, Apache Flink, AWS Kinesis.

💡 **Example**: A real-time AI recommendation system updates user preferences instantly based on browsing behavior.

4. Data Backup & Disaster Recovery

🔒 **Challenges**: Data loss, corruption, system failures.
- **Solution**: Implement regular backups, replication, and failover strategies.
- **Tools**: AWS Backup, Google Cloud Snapshot, PostgreSQL replication.

💡 **Example**: A fraud detection AI system uses geo-redundant storage to prevent data loss.

5. Automating Data Pipelines with MLOps

🔒 **Challenges**: Ensuring data freshness and pipeline consistency.
- **Solution**: Automate data ingestion, preprocessing, and storage with MLOps frameworks.
- **Tools**: Apache Airflow, Kubeflow, Prefect.

💡 **Example**: A news sentiment analysis AI fetches, cleans, and stores real-time news data automatically using Airflow.

4. Case Study: Scalable Data Management in AI Deployment

📌 **Industry**: Autonomous Vehicles
📌 **Challenge**: Handling terabytes of real-time sensor data per vehicle daily.

📌 **Solution:**

✓ **Data Lake**: Stores raw sensor logs.

✓ **Feature Store**: Precomputes AI model features for fast inference.

✓ **Streaming Pipeline**: Kafka + Flink for real-time data processing.

📌 **Result:**

✓ Reduced AI model inference latency by 40%.

✓ Enabled real-time decision-making for self-driving systems.

5. Best Practices for AI Data Storage & Management

✓ Choose the right storage solution based on AI model needs (real-time vs. batch).

✓ Ensure data consistency between training and production.

✓ Implement security measures to protect sensitive data.

✓ Monitor data pipelines for drift, missing values, and corruption.

✓ Use automated data pipelines to keep models updated.

✓ Leverage cloud-based solutions for scalability and cost efficiency.

By applying these data storage and management strategies, AI deployments become more efficient, scalable, and secure—ensuring high-performance AI in real-world applications. 🚀

5. Optimizing Model Performance

Deploying an AI model successfully requires more than just training it on a dataset—it must be optimized for efficiency, speed, and scalability in real-world applications. In this chapter, we explore techniques to enhance model performance, including quantization, pruning, knowledge distillation, and hardware acceleration using GPUs, TPUs, and edge devices. We also discuss latency reduction, inference optimization, and memory management, ensuring that models can handle large-scale production workloads without compromising accuracy. By implementing these optimization strategies, AI practitioners can build fast, efficient, and cost-effective models that perform seamlessly across diverse deployment environments.

5.1 Model Quantization and Compression

Deploying AI models efficiently requires balancing accuracy, speed, and resource constraints. In real-world applications, AI models often need to run on edge devices, mobile phones, embedded systems, or cloud platforms with limited computational power. Model quantization and compression techniques help reduce model size and computational requirements while maintaining performance.

This chapter explores the importance of model optimization, different quantization and compression techniques, and best practices for deploying lightweight AI models without sacrificing accuracy.

1. Why Model Quantization and Compression Matter

Large AI models consume significant memory, computation, and power, making them challenging to deploy in real-world applications.

Key Challenges in Model Deployment:

- 🔍 **High latency** – Large models take longer to process data.
- 🔍 **Memory constraints** – Some models exceed the RAM of mobile and edge devices.
- 🔍 **Power consumption** – Running large models continuously drains battery life.
- 🔍 **Bandwidth limitations** – Large models require more storage and slow down updates.

Example: A smartphone AI assistant needs an optimized speech recognition model that runs efficiently without draining battery life.

By applying quantization and compression, models can run faster, use less memory, and operate efficiently in constrained environments.

2. Model Quantization: Reducing Precision to Improve Efficiency

What is Quantization?

Quantization is the process of reducing the precision of numerical values (weights and activations) in neural networks to reduce model size and computation.

Example: Converting 32-bit floating-point (FP32) numbers to 8-bit integers (INT8) reduces memory usage by 4x while improving inference speed.

Types of Model Quantization

1. Post-Training Quantization (PTQ)

✓ Reduces model size after training.

✓ Converts weights and activations to lower precision.

✓ Works well for pre-trained models without retraining.

Example: Converting a trained ResNet-50 model from FP32 to INT8 reduces its size from 100MB to 25MB.

2. Quantization-Aware Training (QAT)

✓ Applies quantization during training, allowing the model to learn with reduced precision.

✓ Produces better accuracy than PTQ, especially for complex models.

Example: A speech-to-text AI trained with QAT retains more accuracy while running faster on mobile devices.

3. Dynamic Quantization

✅ Converts only model weights to lower precision during inference.

✅ Ideal for CPU-based deployments.

💡 **Example**: A BERT-based chatbot benefits from dynamic quantization, reducing latency while keeping accuracy.

4. Static Quantization

✅ Converts both weights and activations to lower precision.

✅ Requires calibration with sample data to determine optimal quantization levels.

✅ Best suited for edge AI and embedded systems.

💡 **Example**: A face recognition model on security cameras uses static quantization to save power while maintaining accuracy.

3. Model Compression: Reducing Size Without Losing Accuracy

1. Weight Pruning – Removing Unnecessary Connections

Pruning eliminates insignificant weights from the neural network, reducing model size and computation.

✓ **Unstructured Pruning** – Removes individual small-weight connections randomly.

✓ **Structured Pruning** – Removes entire neurons, channels, or layers.

✓ **Lottery Ticket Hypothesis** – Finds a smaller subnetwork that performs as well as the full model.

💡 **Example**: A pruned ResNet model can maintain 95% accuracy while reducing computation by 50%.

2. Knowledge Distillation – Training Smaller Models with Large Models

A smaller model (student) is trained to mimic the behavior of a larger model (teacher).

✓ The student model learns from the teacher's soft predictions, improving generalization.

✓ Great for mobile AI applications.

💡 **Example**: A tiny BERT model trained using knowledge distillation retains 90% of the original model's accuracy but runs 2x faster on mobile.

3. Low-Rank Factorization – Decomposing Weight Matrices

Factorization techniques approximate large weight matrices with smaller ones, reducing computation.

✓ Singular Value Decomposition (SVD)

✓ Matrix Factorization

✓ Tucker Decomposition

💡 **Example**: A recommendation system AI speeds up matrix multiplications by applying low-rank approximations.

4. Model Weight Sharing – Reducing Memory Usage

Weight sharing groups similar weights together to reduce redundancy.

✓ Reduces the number of unique parameters.

✓ Ideal for convolutional neural networks (CNNs).

💡 **Example**: A CNN for image classification achieves 2x compression while maintaining accuracy.

4. Tools and Frameworks for Model Quantization and Compression

1. TensorFlow Lite (TFLite)

✓ Converts TensorFlow models into lightweight versions for mobile and edge devices.

✓ Supports 8-bit quantization and pruning.

✓ Used in Android AI applications.

💡 **Example**: Google Assistant uses TFLite-optimized models for voice recognition on mobile.

2. ONNX Runtime

✓ Converts models from PyTorch, TensorFlow, and Keras into optimized versions.

✓ Supports dynamic and static quantization.

✓ Ideal for cross-platform AI deployment.

💡 **Example**: Microsoft Edge uses ONNX-quantized models for fast page loading recommendations.

3. NVIDIA TensorRT

✓ Optimizes deep learning models for GPUs.

✓ Uses precision-aware quantization for real-time AI inference.

✓ Best for high-speed AI tasks (video processing, autonomous driving).

💡 **Example**: Tesla's self-driving AI is optimized using TensorRT for real-time decision-making.

4. PyTorch FX + TorchScript

✓ Converts PyTorch models into optimized execution graphs.

✓ Supports QAT (Quantization-Aware Training).

✓ Best for AI research to production transition.

💡 **Example**: Facebook's AI models are optimized with TorchScript for efficient deployment.

5. Case Study: AI Model Optimization for Mobile Deployment

📌 **Industry**: Mobile AI – Image Recognition
📌 **Challenge**: A large ResNet-50 model (100MB) was too slow and memory-intensive for mobile apps.

📌 **Solution:**

✓ **Post-training quantization (FP32 → INT8)** – Reduced model size by 4x.

✓ **Pruning (50% of weights removed)** – Improved speed by 30%.

✓ **Knowledge distillation** – Used a smaller ResNet variant trained on the original model's predictions.

📌 **Result:**

✓ 60% reduction in inference time.

✓ 4x smaller model size.

✓ Maintained 98% accuracy of the original model.

6. Key Takeaways & Best Practices

✓ Use quantization (PTQ or QAT) to improve efficiency.

✓ Prune unnecessary connections to reduce computational cost.

✓ Apply knowledge distillation for small, high-performance models.

✓ Leverage TensorRT, TFLite, or ONNX for optimization.

✓ Test different compression techniques to balance speed and accuracy.

✓ Monitor performance after quantization to avoid accuracy degradation.

By implementing quantization and compression, AI models become lighter, faster, and ready for real-world deployment—enabling AI to run efficiently on edge devices, mobile phones, and cloud platforms. 🚀

5.2 Knowledge Distillation for Lighter Models

As AI models grow in complexity, deploying them efficiently becomes a major challenge. Knowledge Distillation (KD) is a powerful technique that allows a smaller model (student) to learn from a larger, pre-trained model (teacher) while retaining most of its performance.

This method is widely used to create lightweight AI models for mobile devices, edge computing, and cloud environments where computational resources are limited.

In this chapter, we will explore how knowledge distillation works, key techniques, practical use cases, and best practices for implementing it in real-world AI applications.

1. What is Knowledge Distillation?

Knowledge distillation is a technique where a smaller, more efficient model is trained to replicate the behavior of a larger, more complex model. Instead of training from scratch, the student model leverages the knowledge encoded in the teacher model to achieve high accuracy with fewer parameters.

Why is Knowledge Distillation Important?

🚀 **Reduces model size** – Enables deployment on mobile and edge devices.
🚀 **Increases inference speed** – Smaller models run faster with lower latency.
🚀 **Maintains accuracy** – Distilled models retain much of the teacher's performance.
🚀 **Optimizes for low-power devices** – Ideal for IoT, embedded systems, and mobile AI.

💡 **Example**: A BERT-based language model (teacher) can be distilled into TinyBERT (student), which is 10x smaller while retaining 96% of the original accuracy.

2. How Knowledge Distillation Works

Knowledge distillation transfers knowledge from the teacher model to the student model using soft targets rather than traditional hard labels.

Key Components of Knowledge Distillation

1. Soft Labels & Temperature Scaling

- Instead of using hard labels (e.g., "dog" or "cat"), the teacher provides soft labels—probability distributions over all possible classes.
- A temperature parameter (T) smooths the probabilities, helping the student learn better.

💡 **Example**: A teacher model classifies an image as:

✓ Dog – 85%

✓ Wolf – 10%

✓ Cat – 5%

The student learns not just the final label but also the relative confidence levels, improving generalization.

2. Loss Function for Distillation

The student model is trained using a combination of two loss functions:

✓ **Distillation Loss**: Compares the student's predictions with the teacher's soft labels.

✓ **Standard Classification Loss**: Ensures the student learns the actual target labels.

📌 Total Loss = (α * Classification Loss) + ((1 - α) * Distillation Loss)
📌 α is a weighting factor balancing both losses.

💡 **Example**: A student CNN model trained via knowledge distillation retains 98% of accuracy while reducing inference time by 50%.

3. Types of Knowledge Distillation

There are multiple ways to transfer knowledge from a teacher model to a student model:

1. Response-Based Distillation (Logit Distillation)

- The student model learns from the teacher's soft outputs (probabilities).
- Best for classification models like image recognition and NLP.

💡 **Example**: Distilling BERT to TinyBERT reduces model size 10x while keeping performance high.

2. Feature-Based Distillation

- Instead of learning from outputs, the student matches intermediate feature representations from the teacher.
- Used in CNN-based computer vision tasks.

💡 **Example**: YOLO object detection models use feature distillation to make smaller versions (YOLOv4-tiny).

3. Relation-Based Distillation

- The student learns relationships between multiple data points instead of just individual examples.
- Useful for tasks requiring context-awareness, like natural language processing.

💡 **Example**: Distilling GPT models for faster chatbot responses.

4. Use Cases of Knowledge Distillation

1. Optimizing NLP Models

📌 **Problem**: Large models like GPT-3 or BERT are too big for real-time applications.
📌 **Solution**: Distilling into TinyBERT, DistilBERT, or ALBERT improves speed while keeping high accuracy.

💡 **Example**: Google Assistant uses distilled NLP models for faster voice recognition on mobile devices.

2. Making Computer Vision Models Efficient

📌 **Problem**: High-resolution image models (e.g., ResNet, EfficientNet) are too slow for real-time inference.
📌 **Solution**: Distilling into MobileNet or ShuffleNet improves speed while maintaining accuracy.

💡 **Example**: Face recognition on smartphones uses distilled CNN models for instant authentication.

3. Deploying AI on Edge Devices & IoT

📌 **Problem**: Edge devices like security cameras, drones, and self-driving cars have limited processing power.
📌 **Solution**: Knowledge distillation creates lightweight models that can run on edge hardware.

💡 **Example**: Tesla Autopilot uses distilled AI models for real-time object detection.

5. Tools & Frameworks for Knowledge Distillation

1. PyTorch Distillation Libraries

✓ **torch.nn.KLDivLoss()** – Helps compute knowledge distillation loss.

✓ **DistilBERT** – A pre-trained lightweight version of BERT.

2. TensorFlow Model Optimization Toolkit

✓ **tf.keras.distillation_loss()** – Supports knowledge distillation training.

✓ Used in Google Assistant, mobile AI apps, and speech recognition.

3. Hugging Face Distillation Framework

✓ Pre-trained distilled models available for NLP tasks.

✓ Used for chatbots, text summarization, and search engines.

6. Case Study: Distilling BERT for Real-Time NLP Applications

📌 **Industry**: Conversational AI (Chatbots, Virtual Assistants)

📌 **Challenge**: BERT-based models were too large for real-time applications.

📌 **Solution:**

✓ Distilled BERT to TinyBERT (10x smaller).

✓ Maintained 96% of original accuracy.

✓ Reduced inference time from 250ms to 50ms.

📌 **Result:**

✓ Faster response time in AI chatbots.

☑ Lower compute costs in cloud deployments.

☑ Improved real-time user experience.

7. Best Practices for Knowledge Distillation

✓ **Choose the right student model** – Balance size and accuracy.

✓ **Adjust temperature scaling (T) properly** – Higher values smooth probability distribution.

✓ **Use feature-based distillation for vision tasks** – Helps retain spatial information.

✓ **Experiment with multiple loss functions** – Find the best balance between accuracy and efficiency.

✓ **Test deployment performance** – Ensure speed improvements in real-world applications.

8. Conclusion: The Future of Lightweight AI with Knowledge Distillation

As AI models continue to grow in size and complexity, knowledge distillation is becoming a critical tool for efficient deployment. It enables AI to be used on mobile devices, IoT, and real-time applications without sacrificing accuracy. By leveraging teacher-student architectures, companies can scale AI efficiently, reduce computational costs, and improve user experience.

With distilled models powering AI assistants, self-driving cars, and real-time image processing, the future of AI deployment will be faster, smarter, and more efficient than ever before. 🚀

5.3 Hardware Acceleration (GPU, TPU, FPGA)

Deploying AI models efficiently requires specialized hardware acceleration to achieve optimal speed, performance, and power efficiency. Traditional CPU-based execution often falls short for deep learning workloads, making GPUs, TPUs, and FPGAs essential for accelerating AI inference and training.

In this chapter, we explore:

✓ The differences between GPUs, TPUs, and FPGAs.

✓ How each hardware type accelerates AI workloads.

✓ Use cases, advantages, and best practices for deployment.

1. Why Hardware Acceleration Matters for AI Deployment

Key Challenges of Running AI Models on CPUs

🔲 **Slow processing speeds** – CPUs are optimized for sequential tasks, not parallel computations.

🔲 **High latency** – Large AI models require thousands of operations per inference.

🔲 **Inefficient power consumption** – Running deep learning models on CPUs drains energy rapidly.

💡 **Solution**: Specialized AI hardware (GPUs, TPUs, and FPGAs) accelerates deep learning tasks, reduces inference latency, and optimizes power consumption.

2. Graphics Processing Units (GPUs) for AI Acceleration

How GPUs Work

GPUs were originally designed for graphics rendering, but their parallel processing architecture makes them ideal for matrix multiplications and tensor operations, which are core to deep learning.

💡 **Key Features of GPUs:**

✓ **Massive parallelism** – Thousands of cores process AI tasks simultaneously.

✓ **High memory bandwidth** – Faster data movement speeds than CPUs.

✓ **Optimized for deep learning frameworks** – Compatible with TensorFlow, PyTorch, and ONNX.

Popular AI GPUs

📌 **NVIDIA A100 & H100** – Used for training large AI models.
📌 **NVIDIA RTX 4090 & 3090** – Ideal for AI inference on consumer hardware.

📌 **AMD Instinct MI250** – Competitor to NVIDIA GPUs for AI acceleration.

Best Use Cases for GPUs

✅ **Cloud-based AI training** – Google Cloud, AWS, and Microsoft Azure use GPUs for AI workloads.

✅ **Computer vision & deep learning** – Facial recognition, object detection, and medical imaging.

✅ **NLP & large language models (LLMs)** – ChatGPT, BERT, and GPT-4 rely on GPUs for fast training.

💡 **Example**: OpenAI's GPT-4 was trained on thousands of NVIDIA A100 GPUs for optimal performance.

3. Tensor Processing Units (TPUs): Google's AI Hardware

What are TPUs?

TPUs (Tensor Processing Units) are custom-designed AI chips created by Google to accelerate tensor computations for deep learning workloads.

💡 **Key Features of TPUs:**

✔ **Optimized for TensorFlow** – Designed for Google's AI framework.

✔ **Lower power consumption** – More energy-efficient than GPUs.

✔ **Faster matrix multiplications** – Handles AI tasks like speech recognition, recommendation systems, and LLMs.

Popular TPU Versions

📌 **TPU v4** – Used for training large AI models in Google Cloud.

📌 **Edge TPU** – A small TPU chip for on-device AI inference.

Best Use Cases for TPUs

✅ Training and inference of large deep learning models.

✅ AI-powered Google services (Search, Translate, Assistant).

✓ Running AI workloads in Google Cloud with high efficiency.

💡 **Example**: Google Translate's AI models run on TPUs, enabling real-time language translation with minimal latency.

4. Field-Programmable Gate Arrays (FPGAs): Customizable AI Chips

What are FPGAs?

FPGAs (Field-Programmable Gate Arrays) are reconfigurable hardware chips that can be programmed to perform AI-specific tasks efficiently. Unlike GPUs and TPUs, FPGAs can be customized for specific AI workloads.

💡 **Key Features of FPGAs:**

✓ **Highly customizable** – Can be reprogrammed for specific AI models.

✓ **Low-latency AI inference** – Faster than GPUs for some real-time applications.

✓ **Energy-efficient** – Consumes less power compared to traditional GPUs.

Popular AI-Optimized FPGAs

📌 **Xilinx Alveo U280** – Used for AI inference acceleration.
📌 **Intel Stratix 10** – Optimized for real-time AI processing.

Best Use Cases for FPGAs

✓ **Edge AI & IoT** – Running AI models in automotive, healthcare, and robotics.
✓ **Finance & trading** – Used for real-time fraud detection and high-frequency trading.
✓ **Medical AI applications** – AI-based X-ray and MRI analysis.

💡 **Example**: Microsoft Azure uses FPGAs for AI-powered cloud services like speech recognition and recommendation systems.

5. Comparing GPUs, TPUs, and FPGAs for AI Deployment

Feature	GPU (Graphics Processing Unit)	TPU (Tensor Processing Unit)	FPGA (Field-Programmable Gate Array)
Speed	Fast (optimized for deep learning)	Faster (optimized for tensor computations)	Moderate (customized for AI tasks)
Flexibility	General-purpose AI workloads	Optimized for TensorFlow & Google Cloud	Customizable for specific applications
Power Efficiency	High power consumption	More efficient than GPUs	Most energy-efficient
Customization	Predefined operations	Designed for TensorFlow	Fully customizable
Best For	Training deep learning models	Running AI in Google Cloud	Low-latency edge AI inference
Cost	Expensive	Cloud-based pricing	Custom hardware costs

💡 Key Takeaways:

✓ Use GPUs for general AI workloads (deep learning, NLP, and computer vision).

✓ Use TPUs for Google Cloud-based AI applications (training large models).

✓ Use FPGAs for customized, low-latency AI inference (IoT, finance, medical applications).

6. Case Study: Accelerating AI Model Deployment with TPUs

📌 **Industry**: Healthcare – Medical Imaging AI
📌 **Challenge**: A hospital needed to deploy a deep learning model for real-time X-ray analysis.

📌 Solution:

✓ Migrated AI inference from GPUs to Google TPUs.

✓ Reduced inference time from 300ms to 50ms per image.

✓ Cut power consumption by 40%.

📌 Result:

✓ Faster, real-time medical diagnosis.

✓ Reduced cloud infrastructure costs.

✓ Improved AI-powered healthcare efficiency.

7. Best Practices for AI Hardware Acceleration

✓ **Choose the right hardware for your workload** – GPUs for general AI, TPUs for TensorFlow models, FPGAs for specialized tasks.

✓ **Optimize AI models before deployment** – Apply quantization, pruning, and model compression.

✓ **Use cloud-based acceleration when needed** – Google Cloud TPUs, AWS Inferentia, and Azure FPGAs.

✓ **Monitor power consumption and efficiency** – Optimize for battery-powered devices in edge AI.

✓ **Test hardware compatibility with AI frameworks** – Ensure TensorFlow, PyTorch, or ONNX support.

8. Conclusion: The Future of AI Hardware Acceleration

As AI models grow more complex, hardware acceleration will be the key to efficient deployment. GPUs, TPUs, and FPGAs each offer unique advantages based on use case, power efficiency, and speed.

🚀 **Future trends include:**

✓ Smaller, more powerful AI chips for on-device processing.

✓ Better AI acceleration in cloud computing.

✓ Energy-efficient AI hardware for sustainable AI deployments.

By leveraging the right AI hardware, organizations can achieve faster, smarter, and more scalable AI solutions in real-world applications. 🚀

5.4 Balancing Accuracy and Efficiency

Deploying AI models in real-world applications requires finding the right balance between accuracy and efficiency. While highly accurate models often demand significant computational power, more efficient models may sacrifice some precision to improve speed and scalability. Striking the right balance is essential for optimizing AI performance across cloud, edge, and on-premises environments.

In this chapter, we explore:

✓ Why balancing accuracy and efficiency is critical for AI deployment.

✓ Techniques for optimizing AI models without losing too much accuracy.

✓ Real-world strategies for ensuring AI models perform effectively across various

platforms.

1. Why Balancing Accuracy and Efficiency Matters

AI models that are too large and computationally expensive can be difficult to deploy, while overly simplified models may not provide reliable predictions.

Challenges of High-Accuracy Models

🔘 **High computational cost** – Requires powerful GPUs/TPUs for training and inference.
🔘 **Slow inference time** – Latency issues make real-time applications difficult.
🔘 **Difficult to scale** – Large models may not be suitable for mobile and edge devices.

Challenges of High-Efficiency Models

🔘 **Lower accuracy** – Simplified models may lose valuable information.
🔘 **Reduced generalization** – May not perform well on unseen data.
🔘 **Limited complexity** – Some AI tasks require deep, high-parameter models.

💡 **Solution**: Implement techniques that preserve accuracy while reducing computational demands.

2. Strategies for Improving Model Efficiency Without Sacrificing Accuracy

There are multiple ways to optimize AI models for deployment while maintaining a strong balance between accuracy and efficiency.

1. Model Quantization

✓ **What it is**: Reducing the precision of numerical computations from 32-bit floating-point (FP32) to lower bit representations like FP16, INT8, or INT4.

✓ **How it helps:**

✓ Reduces model size, making it easier to deploy on mobile and edge devices.

✓ Speeds up inference by allowing hardware accelerators (GPUs, TPUs, FPGAs) to process data faster.

✓ **Trade-off**: Minor accuracy loss in some cases, but can be mitigated with fine-tuning.

💡 **Example**: Google's MobileNet model uses quantization to run efficiently on smartphones while maintaining high accuracy in image classification.

2. Model Pruning

✓ **What it is**: Removing unnecessary weights and neurons from a deep learning model.

✓ **How it helps:**

✓ Reduces the number of parameters, making the model lighter and faster.

✓ Maintains accuracy by eliminating only redundant or unimportant parts of the model.

✓ **Trade-off**: Requires careful tuning to avoid removing important information.

💡 **Example**: ResNet pruning can reduce model size by 50% while keeping classification accuracy above 95%.

3. Knowledge Distillation

✓ **What it is**: A smaller (student) model learns from a larger (teacher) model, retaining most of its performance.

✓ **How it helps**:

✅ Maintains high accuracy while significantly reducing computational cost.

✅ Ideal for deploying AI on mobile, IoT, and embedded devices.

✓ **Trade-off**: Some loss in precision, but minimal if trained correctly.

💡 **Example**: DistilBERT (student model) retains 96% of BERT's performance while being 60% smaller and 2x faster.

4. Model Compression with Low-Rank Factorization

✓ **What it is**: Breaking down large weight matrices into smaller, low-rank approximations.

✓ **How it helps**:

✅ Reduces the number of operations needed for inference.

✅ Works well for recurrent neural networks (RNNs) and transformer models.

✓ **Trade-off**: Some accuracy loss, but careful tuning can minimize impact.

💡 **Example**: Transformer models like GPT-3 use low-rank approximations to optimize performance for large-scale deployment.

5. Hardware-Aware Model Optimization

✓ **What it is**: Optimizing AI models specifically for target hardware (e.g., GPUs, TPUs, FPGAs).

✓ **How it helps**:

✅ Uses specialized hardware features to improve performance.

✅ Reduces computation bottlenecks by leveraging parallelism.

✔ **Trade-off**: Requires additional engineering effort for hardware-specific tuning.

💡 **Example**: NVIDIA TensorRT optimizes models for GPU acceleration, reducing latency in AI inference.

3. Real-World Use Cases of Balancing Accuracy and Efficiency

Case Study 1: AI in Autonomous Vehicles

📌 **Challenge**: Self-driving cars require highly accurate AI models, but low latency for real-time decision-making.

📌 **Solution:**

✔ Used pruning and quantization to optimize deep learning models.

✔ Deployed on low-power edge AI hardware like NVIDIA Jetson.

📌 **Result:**

✅ Reduced inference time by 40%, enabling faster obstacle detection.

✅ Maintained accuracy above 95% for object classification.

Case Study 2: AI-Powered Mobile Applications

📌 **Challenge**: Deploying AI-powered image recognition on smartphones requires efficient models.

📌 **Solution:**

✔ Used knowledge distillation to train a lightweight model.

✔ Optimized for Android's Neural Processing Unit (NPU).

📌 **Result:**

✅ Achieved 3x faster processing while maintaining 98% of original accuracy.

✅ Reduced model size from 300MB to 25MB, improving device compatibility.

4. Best Practices for Balancing Accuracy and Efficiency

✔ **Know your application requirements** – Determine whether accuracy or speed is more critical.

✔ **Experiment with multiple optimization techniques** – Try quantization, pruning, and knowledge distillation.

✔ **Use hardware-specific optimizations** – Deploy models efficiently based on GPU, TPU, or FPGA support.

✔ **Monitor real-world performance** – Test models on actual deployment environments, not just in development.

✔ **Continuously improve AI models** – Implement continuous learning and updates to refine accuracy.

5. Conclusion: The Future of AI Optimization

Finding the right balance between accuracy and efficiency is key to successful AI deployment. By leveraging model optimization techniques, companies can deploy AI models that are fast, scalable, and accurate enough for real-world use cases.

🚀 **Future Trends in AI Model Optimization:**

✅ Smaller, more efficient AI models for mobile and edge computing.

✅ Advanced quantization and pruning techniques to improve model performance.

✅ Better hardware integration for AI acceleration on cloud and edge devices.

By adopting the right strategies, businesses can maximize AI performance while minimizing computational costs, ensuring a seamless, scalable, and efficient AI deployment. 🚀

6. Model Packaging and Serialization

Before an AI model can be deployed, it must be packaged and serialized in a format that ensures compatibility, efficiency, and scalability across different environments. In this chapter, we explore the best practices for model packaging, including containerization with Docker and Kubernetes, and how to serialize models using ONNX, TensorFlow SavedModel, TorchScript, and Pickle. We also discuss version control, dependency management, and deployment formats to ensure smooth integration into production systems. Proper model packaging not only simplifies deployment but also enhances portability, reproducibility, and maintainability, making AI solutions more robust and adaptable across platforms.

6.1 Model Formats: TensorFlow SavedModel, ONNX, TorchScript

When deploying AI models, choosing the right model format is crucial for ensuring compatibility, efficiency, and scalability across different platforms. AI models trained in frameworks like TensorFlow and PyTorch must be saved and exported in formats optimized for deployment.

In this chapter, we explore:

✓ **TensorFlow SavedModel, ONNX, and TorchScript** – The three most common model formats.

✓ How each format works and where it is best suited.

✓ Performance, compatibility, and best practices for choosing the right format.

1. Why Model Formats Matter in AI Deployment

AI models must be converted, optimized, and exported to work seamlessly in different environments, such as:

✅ **Cloud platforms** (AWS, Google Cloud, Azure).
✅ **Edge devices** (mobile, IoT, embedded systems).
✅ **On-premises servers with specialized hardware** (GPUs, TPUs, FPGAs).

💡 The right format ensures faster inference, lower latency, and better resource utilization.

2. TensorFlow SavedModel: The Standard for TensorFlow Deployment

What is TensorFlow SavedModel?

📌 TensorFlow SavedModel is the default serialization format for TensorFlow models. It stores the model architecture, weights, computation graph, and signatures in a portable format.

💡 Why use SavedModel?

✓ Framework Compatibility: Works with TensorFlow Serving, TensorFlow Lite, and TensorFlow.js.

✓ Efficient Deployment: Optimized for cloud and on-device inference.

✓ Supports Graph Execution: Enables fast inference on GPUs and TPUs.

How to Save a Model in SavedModel Format

```
import tensorflow as tf

# Create a simple model
model = tf.keras.Sequential([
    tf.keras.layers.Dense(64, activation='relu'),
    tf.keras.layers.Dense(10, activation='softmax')
])

# Save in TensorFlow SavedModel format
model.save("saved_model")
```

This exports the model into a directory containing:

📌 **saved_model.pb** – Stores the model architecture and computation graph.

📌 **variables/** – Stores trained weights.

📌 **assets/** – Stores additional files for inference.

Where is SavedModel Used?

✅ **Cloud Deployment**: Used in Google Cloud AI Platform and TensorFlow Serving.

✅ **Mobile & Edge AI**: Converted into TensorFlow Lite (TFLite) for mobile inference.

✅ **Web Deployment**: Works with TensorFlow.js for in-browser AI applications.

✔ **Best Use Case**: If you're working in a TensorFlow-based ecosystem, SavedModel is the best choice for seamless deployment.

3. ONNX (Open Neural Network Exchange): The Universal AI Model Format

What is ONNX?

📌 ONNX (Open Neural Network Exchange) is an open-source, cross-framework model format that allows AI models to be transferred between TensorFlow, PyTorch, and other frameworks.

💡 **Why use ONNX?**

✔ **Cross-Framework Compatibility**: Works across TensorFlow, PyTorch, Keras, MXNet, and Caffe.

✔ **Optimized for Hardware Acceleration**: Supports NVIDIA TensorRT, Intel OpenVINO, and ONNX Runtime.

✔ **Faster Inference**: Optimized for low-latency and high-speed AI processing.

How to Convert a PyTorch Model to ONNX

```
import torch
import torch.onnx

# Create a simple model
model = torch.nn.Sequential(
    torch.nn.Linear(64, 128),
    torch.nn.ReLU(),
    torch.nn.Linear(128, 10)
)

# Convert to ONNX format
```

```
dummy_input = torch.randn(1, 64)  # Example input
torch.onnx.export(model, dummy_input, "model.onnx")
```

This creates model.onnx, which can be deployed on ONNX-compatible runtimes.

Where is ONNX Used?

✅ **Cloud & Edge AI**: Works with Azure Machine Learning, NVIDIA TensorRT, and Intel OpenVINO.
✅ **Cross-Platform AI Deployment**: Allows switching between TensorFlow and PyTorch without retraining.
✅ **Performance Optimization**: Used in ONNX Runtime for low-latency inference.

✔ **Best Use Case**: If you need cross-framework portability and optimized inference, ONNX is the ideal choice.

4. TorchScript: Optimizing PyTorch Models for Production

What is TorchScript?

📌 TorchScript is an intermediate representation (IR) of PyTorch models that allows them to be optimized and executed in production environments.

💡 Why use TorchScript?

✔ **Optimized for Production**: Converts PyTorch models into a format that runs efficiently on CPUs and GPUs.
✔ **Supports JIT Compilation**: Uses Just-in-Time (JIT) compilation for faster inference.
✔ **Works with C++ Deployments**: Enables low-level AI deployment in high-performance applications.

How to Convert a PyTorch Model to TorchScript

```
import torch

# Create a simple PyTorch model
class SimpleModel(torch.nn.Module):
    def __init__(self):
```

```
super(SimpleModel, self).__init__()
self.fc1 = torch.nn.Linear(64, 128)
self.fc2 = torch.nn.Linear(128, 10)

def forward(self, x):
    x = torch.relu(self.fc1(x))
    return self.fc2(x)

# Convert to TorchScript
model = SimpleModel()
scripted_model = torch.jit.script(model)
scripted_model.save("model.pt")
```

This exports the model into model.pt, which can be loaded in PyTorch production environments.

Where is TorchScript Used?

✅ **Mobile AI & Edge Devices**: Converts PyTorch models into TorchScript for Android and iOS.

✅ **C++ AI Deployments**: Used in high-performance AI systems without Python dependencies.

✅ **Optimized AI Inference**: Works with PyTorch JIT and C++ execution environments.

✔ **Best Use Case**: If you need high-performance PyTorch inference or C++ integration, TorchScript is the best choice.

5. Comparing TensorFlow SavedModel, ONNX, and TorchScript

Feature	TensorFlow SavedModel	ONNX	TorchScript
Framework Support	TensorFlow/Keras	TensorFlow, PyTorch, MXNet, Caffe	PyTorch
Portability	Works with TensorFlow tools	Works across multiple frameworks	PyTorch-specific
Optimization	Optimized for TensorFlow Serving	Supports ONNX Runtime, TensorRT	Supports PyTorch JIT, C++
Deployment Target	Cloud, Edge, Web (TensorFlow.js)	Cloud, Edge, GPUs	C++, Mobile, Edge
Best For	TensorFlow ecosystem	Cross-framework portability	High-performance PyTorch inference

💡 Key Takeaways:

✓ Use TensorFlow SavedModel if deploying within the TensorFlow ecosystem (e.g., TensorFlow Serving, Google Cloud AI).

✓ Use ONNX for cross-framework AI deployment, allowing seamless transition between TensorFlow, PyTorch, and other frameworks.

✓ Use TorchScript for optimized PyTorch model inference in high-performance applications.

6. Conclusion: Choosing the Right Model Format

Selecting the right model format is essential for ensuring smooth AI deployment across cloud, edge, and on-premises environments.

🚀 Future trends in AI model formats:

✅ Increased adoption of ONNX for universal model portability.

✅ Better hardware integration for faster inference on GPUs and TPUs.

✅ Enhanced model compression techniques for low-power AI inference.

By understanding TensorFlow SavedModel, ONNX, and TorchScript, AI practitioners can deploy AI models more efficiently and optimize performance across different platforms. 🚀

6.2 Choosing the Right Framework for Deployment

Deploying an AI model is not just about training a model; it's about ensuring scalability, efficiency, and compatibility with the target environment. The choice of the right deployment framework depends on factors such as hardware, performance requirements, platform compatibility, and ease of integration.

In this chapter, we explore:

✓ Key factors to consider when selecting a deployment framework.

✓ Comparison of popular AI deployment frameworks.

✓ Best practices for choosing the right framework for different use cases.

1. Key Factors in Choosing an AI Deployment Framework

When selecting an AI deployment framework, consider the following factors:

1️⃣ Deployment Environment

◆ **Cloud Deployment** – Requires integration with cloud services (AWS, Google Cloud, Azure).
◆ **Edge Deployment** – Needs lightweight models that run on mobile, IoT, or embedded devices.
◆ **On-Premises Deployment** – Optimized for local servers with specialized hardware (GPUs, TPUs).

2️⃣ Performance Requirements

✓ **Latency** – Real-time applications (e.g., self-driving cars, fraud detection) require low-latency inference.

✓ **Throughput** – High-volume applications (e.g., recommendation systems) require optimized batch processing.

3️⃣ Model Compatibility

✓ Some frameworks support only specific model formats (e.g., TensorFlow Serving for SavedModel, TorchServe for PyTorch models).

✓ If cross-framework compatibility is needed, ONNX Runtime is a good choice.

4️⃣ Hardware Optimization

✓ **GPU/TPU Acceleration** – Choose frameworks optimized for NVIDIA GPUs, Google TPUs, or Intel processors.

✓ **Edge Devices** – Use TensorFlow Lite, ONNX Runtime, or PyTorch Mobile for mobile and embedded AI.

2. Popular AI Deployment Frameworks and Their Use Cases

Different frameworks excel in different deployment scenarios. Below is a detailed comparison of the most popular AI deployment frameworks.

Framework	Best For	Supports	Optimized For	Example Use Cases
TensorFlow Serving	Large-scale cloud AI	TensorFlow models (SavedModel)	Cloud GPUs & TPUs	Google Cloud AI, web services
TorchServe	PyTorch model serving	PyTorch models (TorchScript)	GPUs & CPUs	AI-powered APIs, chatbots
ONNX Runtime	Cross-framework AI	TensorFlow, PyTorch, MXNet, etc.	NVIDIA TensorRT, Intel OpenVINO	Multi-framework AI deployment
TensorFlow Lite	Edge & mobile AI	TensorFlow Lite models	Mobile (Android, iOS)	AI on smartphones, IoT devices
PyTorch Mobile	PyTorch models on mobile	TorchScript models	Android, iOS	Edge AI, mobile applications
FastAPI & Flask	AI APIs & microservices	Any AI framework	Lightweight APIs	AI-powered web apps, REST APIs

3. Framework Selection Based on Deployment Needs

1️⃣ Cloud Deployment (AWS, Google Cloud, Azure)

✓ **Best Choices**: TensorFlow Serving, ONNX Runtime, TorchServe.

✓ **Why?**

✅ Supports high-performance GPU acceleration.

✅ Seamlessly integrates with cloud AI services (AWS SageMaker, Google Cloud AI).

✅ Can scale for large datasets and high user requests.

💡 **Example** Use Case: A recommendation system for an e-commerce platform deployed on AWS SageMaker using ONNX Runtime.

2️⃣ **Edge & Mobile Deployment (Smartphones, IoT, Embedded AI)**

✓ **Best Choices**: TensorFlow Lite, PyTorch Mobile, ONNX Runtime.

✓ **Why?**

✅ Optimized for low-power devices.

✅ Supports model quantization and pruning for smaller AI models.

✅ Runs on Android, iOS, and embedded systems.

💡 **Example** Use Case: A real-time image recognition app using TensorFlow Lite on Android.

3️⃣ **On-Premises AI Deployment (Local Servers, Custom Hardware)**

✓ **Best Choices**: ONNX Runtime, TensorFlow Serving, TorchServe.

✓ **Why?**

✓ Allows full control over AI models and data.

✓ Optimized for server-based AI inference.

✓ Works well with NVIDIA TensorRT, Intel OpenVINO, and AMD ROCm.

💡 **Example** Use Case: A financial fraud detection AI running on an on-premises GPU cluster using TensorFlow Serving.

4️⃣ Deploying AI as APIs and Microservices

✓ **Best Choices**: FastAPI, Flask, TensorFlow Serving, TorchServe.

✓ **Why?**

✓ Provides easy-to-use AI REST APIs.

✓ Lightweight and scalable for AI-powered web applications.

✓ Works with Docker and Kubernetes for seamless deployment.

💡 **Example Use Case**: A chatbot AI serving responses via a FastAPI-based REST API.

4. Framework Performance Comparison

Feature	TensorFlow Serving	TorchServe	ONNX Runtime	TensorFlow Lite	PyTorch Mobile
Framework Support	TensorFlow	PyTorch	Multi-framework	TensorFlow	PyTorch
Cloud Integration	☑ Excellent	☑ Good	☑ Excellent	✕ Limited	✕ Limited
Edge Deployment	✕ No	✕ No	☑ Yes	☑ Yes	☑ Yes
Performance Optimization	☑ TPUs & GPUs	☑ GPUs & CPUs	☑ TensorRT, OpenVINO	☑ Mobile & IoT	☑ Mobile & IoT
Best For	Large-scale AI APIs	PyTorch AI APIs	Cross-platform AI	AI on Mobile	AI on Mobile

💡 **Key Takeaways:**

✓ Use TensorFlow Serving for large-scale cloud deployments.

✓ ONNX Runtime is best for multi-framework portability.

✓ TensorFlow Lite and PyTorch Mobile are ideal for edge and mobile AI.

5. Best Practices for Selecting the Right Framework

✓ **Understand deployment needs** – Cloud, edge, or on-premises?

✓ **Optimize for performance** – Choose frameworks that support GPU, TPU, or specialized AI accelerators.

✓ **Consider cross-platform compatibility** – Use ONNX Runtime for flexibility.

✓ **Prioritize model size and efficiency** – Use quantization and pruning for mobile AI.

✓ **Ensure scalability** – Use frameworks that support containerization (Docker, Kubernetes) for production deployment.

6. Conclusion: Making the Right Choice

Choosing the right AI deployment framework is essential for ensuring efficiency, scalability, and real-world usability.

🚀 **Future Trends in AI Deployment Frameworks:**

✓ More optimized ONNX models for cross-framework compatibility.

✓ Better support for AI on mobile and edge devices.

✓ Improved cloud-native AI services for seamless scaling.

By carefully selecting the right framework based on performance, compatibility, and deployment environment, AI practitioners can maximize efficiency and deploy AI models successfully in real-world applications. 🚀

6.3 Model Containerization with Docker

Deploying AI models in production requires a consistent, scalable, and portable environment. Docker containerization solves this problem by packaging the AI model along with its dependencies into a lightweight, isolated container that can run on any system—cloud, on-premises, or edge.

In this chapter, we explore:

✓ What Docker containerization is and why it's essential for AI deployment.

✓ How to package an AI model in a Docker container.

✓ Best practices for containerizing AI models efficiently.

1. Why Containerization Matters in AI Deployment

AI models require specific runtime dependencies, such as:

✓ **Python libraries** (TensorFlow, PyTorch, ONNX, etc.).
✓ **Hardware drivers** (CUDA for GPU acceleration).
✓ Operating system configurations.

⚡ **Challenges in AI Deployment Without Containers:**

✗ **Dependency Conflicts** – Different versions of AI libraries can cause compatibility issues.
✗ **Inconsistent Environments** – A model trained on one system may not work properly in another.
✗ **Scalability Issues** – Difficult to deploy across multiple servers or cloud platforms.

💡 **Solution: Use Docker Containers!**

✓ **Ensures Consistency** – The AI model runs exactly the same way everywhere.

✓ **Simplifies Deployment** – Easily deploy models across cloud, edge, and on-premises servers.

✓ **Enables Scalability** – Works seamlessly with Kubernetes for large-scale AI deployment.

2. What is Docker?

📌 Docker is a tool that allows you to create lightweight, portable containers that bundle software and its dependencies into a single package.

🚀 Key Benefits for AI Deployment:

✅ **Cross-Platform Portability** – Deploy the same model on Linux, Windows, macOS, and cloud platforms.

✅ **GPU Acceleration Support** – Use NVIDIA CUDA with Docker for high-performance AI inference.

✅ **Reproducibility** – Prevents "It works on my machine" issues in AI development.

3. Building a Docker Container for an AI Model

Step 1: Install Docker

Before using Docker, ensure it's installed on your system. You can download it from Docker's official website.

To verify installation, run:

docker --version

Step 2: Create a Dockerfile for AI Deployment

A Dockerfile is a script that defines:

📌 **Base image** (e.g., Python, TensorFlow, PyTorch).

📌 **Dependencies** (AI libraries, drivers).

📌 Code execution instructions.

💡 **Example**: Dockerfile for Deploying a TensorFlow Model

```
# Use official TensorFlow image as base
FROM tensorflow/tensorflow:latest

# Set working directory
WORKDIR /app
```

```
# Copy AI model and dependencies
COPY model /app/model
COPY requirements.txt /app/

# Install dependencies
RUN pip install --no-cache-dir -r requirements.txt

# Expose API port (for serving AI model)
EXPOSE 8501

# Run the model (using TensorFlow Serving)
CMD ["tensorflow_model_server", "--rest_api_port=8501", "--model_base_path=/app/model", "--model_name=my_model"]
```

📌 **How This Works:**

✓ Uses TensorFlow Serving to deploy a trained model.

✓ Installs required Python packages from requirements.txt.

✓ Exposes port 8501 to allow API access to the AI model.

Step 3: Build the Docker Image

Run the following command in the terminal:

docker build -t ai-model .

This creates a Docker image named ai-model.

Step 4: Run the AI Model in a Container

Now, start the container:

docker run -p 8501:8501 ai-model

✓ The AI model is now running in a container and accessible via API! 🎉

4. Running AI Models with GPU Acceleration in Docker

If your AI model requires GPU acceleration, you need to use NVIDIA Docker.

Step 1: Install NVIDIA Docker

docker run --gpus all nvidia/cuda:11.0-base nvidia-smi

✓ This checks if NVIDIA Docker is installed correctly.

Step 2: Modify the Dockerfile for GPU Support

Use an image that supports CUDA:

FROM nvidia/cuda:11.0-base

Then, run the container with GPU support:

docker run --gpus all ai-model

✓ The AI model now runs faster using GPU acceleration! 🚀

5. Deploying AI Containers in the Cloud

Once you've containerized your AI model, you can deploy it on cloud services such as:

✓ AWS ECS or AWS SageMaker
✓ Google Cloud AI Platform
✓ Azure Machine Learning

Step 1: Push Your Docker Image to Docker Hub

docker tag ai-model mydockerhubusername/ai-model:v1
docker push mydockerhubusername/ai-model:v1

✓ The model is now stored in Docker Hub and can be deployed anywhere!

6. Best Practices for AI Model Containerization

✓ **Keep Images Lightweight** – Use slim versions of Python or AI frameworks to reduce size.

✅ **Use Multi-Stage Builds** – Optimize image size by removing unnecessary dependencies.

✅ **Enable GPU Support If Needed** – Use NVIDIA CUDA images for AI workloads.

✅ **Use Docker Compose for Multi-Container AI Systems** – Helps manage AI models, databases, and APIs together.

✅ **Monitor and Log Performance** – Use tools like Prometheus and Grafana for monitoring AI models in production.

7. Conclusion: Why Docker is Essential for AI Deployment

🚀 **Key Takeaways:**

✔ Docker ensures consistency, scalability, and portability for AI models.

✔ Simplifies AI deployment across cloud, edge, and on-premises environments.

✔ Supports GPU acceleration for high-performance AI inference.

💡 **Next Steps:**

Now that your AI model is containerized with Docker, the next step is to integrate it into a microservices architecture using APIs! (Covered in Chapter 10: Deploying AI with APIs and Microservices). 🚀

6.4 Ensuring Cross-Platform Compatibility

AI models need to work seamlessly across various platforms—cloud servers, edge devices, mobile phones, and on-premises infrastructure. Cross-platform compatibility ensures that a model trained on one system can be deployed and executed reliably across different hardware, operating systems, and AI frameworks.

In this chapter, we explore:

✔ Why cross-platform compatibility is essential in AI deployment.

✔ Strategies for building models that work across different platforms.

✔ Best tools and frameworks for cross-platform AI deployment.

1. Why Cross-Platform Compatibility Matters

◆ AI models are developed in different environments but must run on diverse hardware (CPUs, GPUs, TPUs, FPGAs).

◆ Companies use various cloud services (AWS, Google Cloud, Azure), requiring adaptable AI solutions.

◆ AI needs to be deployed on mobile, web, edge devices, and enterprise servers without major reconfiguration.

⚡ **Challenges Without Cross-Platform Compatibility:**

✖ **Framework Lock-in** – Models may only work with a specific AI framework (e.g., TensorFlow, PyTorch).

✖ **Hardware Constraints** – A model optimized for GPUs might not work well on CPUs or edge devices.

✖ **OS-Specific Issues** – AI models trained on Linux may have issues when deployed on Windows or macOS.

💡 **Solution**: Design AI Models with Cross-Platform Support in Mind!

2. Strategies for Cross-Platform AI Deployment

To ensure your AI model runs on any platform, follow these key strategies:

1️⃣ Use a Cross-Framework Model Format (ONNX)

The Open Neural Network Exchange (ONNX) format enables models trained in TensorFlow, PyTorch, Scikit-Learn, and others to be converted and deployed on different platforms.

✅ Benefits of ONNX:

✔ Converts models between TensorFlow, PyTorch, Keras, and MXNet.

✔ Optimized for CPUs, GPUs, and specialized AI accelerators.

✔ Works across cloud, mobile, and edge AI environments.

💡 **Example**: Converting a PyTorch Model to ONNX for Universal Compatibility

```
import torch
import torch.onnx

# Load trained PyTorch model
model = MyNeuralNetwork()
model.load_state_dict(torch.load("model.pth"))
model.eval()

# Convert to ONNX
dummy_input = torch.randn(1, 3, 224, 224)  # Example input shape
torch.onnx.export(model, dummy_input, "model.onnx")

print("Model converted to ONNX format!")
```

✓ This ONNX model can now be deployed on TensorFlow, Azure ML, or even mobile devices.

2️⃣ Choose Frameworks with Multi-Platform Support

To avoid framework lock-in, use deployment tools that support multiple platforms, such as:

Tool/Framework	Best For	Supported Platforms
ONNX Runtime	Cross-framework AI	Cloud, Edge, On-Prem
TensorFlow Lite	Mobile & Edge AI	Android, iOS, IoT
PyTorch Mobile	Mobile AI	Android, iOS
NVIDIA TensorRT	High-performance AI	GPUs, Edge, Cloud
OpenVINO	Intel CPU & Edge AI	IoT, Embedded AI
Docker Containers	AI Model Portability	Cloud, Linux, Windows

✓ **Example**: Use ONNX Runtime to deploy the same model on Azure, AWS, and Google Cloud without retraining.

3️⃣ Optimize Models for Different Hardware (CPU, GPU, TPU, FPGA)

Different deployment environments use different hardware accelerators:

✅ **Cloud AI**: High-performance GPUs & TPUs for fast inference (AWS, Google Cloud, Azure).

✅ **Edge AI**: Uses low-power CPUs, GPUs, or NPUs (e.g., NVIDIA Jetson, Intel Movidius).

✅ **Mobile AI**: Requires optimized, lightweight models (TensorFlow Lite, PyTorch Mobile).

💡 **Example**: Optimize a TensorFlow Model for Different Devices

```python
import tensorflow as tf

# Convert model for Edge TPU (Google Coral)
converter = tf.lite.TFLiteConverter.from_saved_model("model")
converter.optimizations = [tf.lite.Optimize.DEFAULT]
tflite_model = converter.convert()

# Save optimized model
with open("model.tflite", "wb") as f:
    f.write(tflite_model)

print("TensorFlow model optimized for mobile and edge deployment!")
```

✔ This converts the model into a lightweight TensorFlow Lite format for mobile and embedded AI.

4️⃣ Use Containerization for Platform Independence

🚀 Why Use Docker for AI Deployment?

✅ Runs the same AI model on any OS (Linux, Windows, macOS, Cloud).

✅ Bundles dependencies (Python libraries, CUDA drivers) into one package.

✅ Works on Cloud, Edge, and On-Prem Servers.

💡 **Example**: Running an AI Model in a Docker Container

```
docker run -p 8501:8501 my-ai-model
```

✓ The AI model runs on any system without configuration issues!

3. Testing AI Models Across Platforms

Before deploying an AI model, test it on different devices and operating systems to ensure compatibility.

✅ Steps for Cross-Platform Testing

1️⃣ Train the AI model on a standard system (e.g., Linux + GPU).

2️⃣ Convert it to a universal format (ONNX, TensorFlow Lite, TorchScript).

3️⃣ Test the model on different platforms:

- **Cloud Server** (AWS, Azure, Google Cloud)
- **Mobile Devices** (Android, iOS)
- **Edge Devices** (Raspberry Pi, NVIDIA Jetson, Intel Movidius)
- **On-Premise Servers** (Windows, Linux, macOS)

4️⃣ Run performance benchmarks to identify potential issues.

4. Best Practices for Cross-Platform AI Deployment

✅ Use ONNX to ensure framework-agnostic AI models.

✅ Optimize models for different hardware (GPUs, CPUs, TPUs, Edge AI accelerators).

✅ Use containerization (Docker, Kubernetes) for consistent deployment.

✅ Test models across multiple platforms before production deployment.

✅ Monitor performance on different devices and optimize accordingly.

5. Conclusion: Building AI Models That Work Everywhere

🚀 Key Takeaways:

✓ Cross-platform AI deployment is essential for scalability and flexibility.

✓ ONNX is the best format for deploying models on multiple AI frameworks.

✓ Optimize AI models for different hardware environments (cloud, edge, mobile).

✓ Use Docker and Kubernetes for a consistent deployment experience.

7. Deploying on Cloud Platforms

Cloud platforms provide scalable, flexible, and cost-effective solutions for deploying AI models in production. In this chapter, we explore the leading cloud AI services, including AWS SageMaker, Google Vertex AI, and Azure Machine Learning, and guide you through the process of model deployment, API integration, and serverless execution. We also cover key considerations such as scalability, security, and cost optimization when deploying AI in the cloud. Whether you're building a real-time inference system or batch processing pipelines, mastering cloud deployment ensures that your AI models are accessible, efficient, and production-ready at scale.

7.1 Overview of Cloud AI Services

Cloud computing has revolutionized the deployment of AI models, enabling businesses to scale their AI applications without the need for expensive on-premises hardware. Cloud AI services provide ready-to-use infrastructure, machine learning (ML) platforms, and AI APIs that simplify the deployment and management of AI models.

In this chapter, we explore:

✓ What Cloud AI Services are and why they matter.

✓ The key advantages of deploying AI models in the cloud.

✓ A comparison of top cloud AI providers like AWS, Google Cloud, and Azure.

✓ Best practices for selecting the right cloud service for AI deployment.

1. What Are Cloud AI Services?

Cloud AI services offer pre-built infrastructure, ML tools, and deployment environments that allow developers to:

✓ Train and deploy AI models without managing physical hardware.

✓ Scale AI workloads on-demand based on usage.

✓ Access ready-made AI APIs for computer vision, NLP, and speech recognition.

Cloud AI services eliminate the need for:

✗ Expensive GPU servers for training and inference.

✗ Manual infrastructure management for scaling AI applications.

✗ Complex software dependencies across different deployment environments.

💡 Real-World Example:

Netflix uses AWS SageMaker to train and deploy its recommendation models at scale, optimizing content suggestions for millions of users.

2. Benefits of Deploying AI Models in the Cloud

🚀 Why use cloud services for AI deployment?

✅ **Scalability** – Automatically adjust computing resources based on AI workload.
✅ **Cost Efficiency** – Pay only for the compute power you use (no upfront hardware costs).
✅ **High Performance** – Access GPUs, TPUs, and specialized AI accelerators for fast inference.
✅ **Security & Compliance** – Cloud providers offer built-in security features and regulatory compliance.
✅ **Integration with Big Data** – Seamless connection with databases, IoT devices, and enterprise software.

💡 **Example**: Self-driving car companies like Waymo use Google Cloud AI to process massive real-time sensor data and improve AI models.

3. Comparing Major Cloud AI Platforms

The three biggest cloud AI providers—AWS, Google Cloud, and Microsoft Azure—offer a range of AI services for training, deployment, and automation.

📌 Cloud AI Services Comparison Table

Feature	AWS AI	Google Cloud AI	Azure AI
Best For	Enterprise AI & Scalability	AI Research & ML Automation	Enterprise AI & Hybrid Cloud
Managed AI Services	SageMaker, Rekognition, Lex, Polly	Vertex AI, AutoML, Vision AI	Azure ML, Cognitive Services
Compute Options	EC2 (GPUs, TPUs), Lambda	Compute Engine, AI Platform	Virtual Machines, AKS
Big Data Integration	Redshift, Athena	BigQuery, Dataflow	Azure Synapse, Data Factory
Security & Compliance	IAM, KMS, HIPAA, GDPR	IAM, DLP, FedRAMP	Active Directory, SOC 2, GDPR

💡 Choosing the Right Cloud AI Provider:

✓ Use AWS AI if you need enterprise-scale AI services and automation.

✓ Use Google Cloud AI if your focus is on deep learning and AI research.

✓ Use Azure AI for enterprise AI and hybrid cloud deployments.

4. Key AI Services from AWS, Google Cloud, and Azure

Each cloud provider offers a range of AI services, from model training and deployment to ready-made AI APIs.

☐ AWS AI Services (Amazon Web Services)

✓ **Amazon SageMaker** – End-to-end machine learning platform.
✓ **AWS Lambda** – Serverless AI inference at scale.
✓ **AWS Rekognition** – Computer vision API.
✓ **AWS Lex & Polly** – NLP and text-to-speech AI.
✓ **AWS Inferentia** – Custom AI inference chip for high-speed processing.

◆ Best for: Enterprise AI solutions, large-scale cloud ML, and deep learning acceleration.

⬤ Google Cloud AI Services

✅ **Vertex AI** – Unified AI platform for training and deploying ML models.
✅ **Google AutoML** – Automated model training with minimal coding.
✅ **Google Vision AI** – Pre-built image recognition API.
✅ **Google Natural Language API** – NLP and sentiment analysis.
✅ **TPUs (Tensor Processing Units)** – Custom hardware for deep learning acceleration.

◈ **Best for**: AI research, automated ML, and high-performance deep learning applications.

☐ **Microsoft Azure AI Services**

✅ **Azure Machine Learning (Azure ML)** – Managed ML training and deployment.
✅ **Azure Cognitive Services** – Pre-built AI for vision, speech, and NLP.
✅ **Azure Bot Service** – AI chatbot development.
✅ **Azure AI Video Analyzer** – Video processing and analytics.
✅ **Azure Synapse AI** – AI-driven big data analytics.

◈ **Best for**: Enterprise AI, hybrid cloud AI deployment, and security-focused solutions.

5. Deploying an AI Model on the Cloud

Step 1: Choose a Cloud Platform

Pick AWS, Google Cloud, or Azure based on your AI model's needs.

Step 2: Upload and Train Your AI Model

Use cloud ML services like AWS SageMaker, Google Vertex AI, or Azure ML to train your model.

Step 3: Deploy AI Model as an API

Expose your trained model as a REST API for easy integration into applications.

💡 **Example**: Deploying a TensorFlow Model on Google Cloud AI

from google.cloud import aiplatform

```
# Initialize AI model deployment
aiplatform.Model.upload(
    display_name="my-ai-model",
    artifact_uri="gs://my-bucket/model/",
    serving_container_image_uri="us-docker.pkg.dev/cloud-aiplatform/prediction/tf2-cpu.2-3:latest",
)

print("AI model deployed successfully on Google Cloud AI!")
```

✓ Your AI model is now hosted on Google Cloud AI and can handle real-time inference requests.

6. Best Practices for Cloud AI Deployment

✓ Use AutoML for quick AI model development – No coding required!

✓ Optimize AI models for cloud inference – Use model quantization to reduce compute costs.

✓ Leverage cloud GPUs and TPUs – Faster AI inference at lower latency.

✓ Secure AI deployments – Use IAM roles, encryption, and API authentication.

✓ Monitor AI model performance – Use tools like AWS CloudWatch, Google AI Monitoring, or Azure AI Insights.

7. Conclusion: Why Cloud AI is the Future of Deployment

🚀 **Key Takeaways:**

✓ Cloud AI services simplify training, deploying, and scaling AI models.

✓ AWS, Google Cloud, and Azure offer powerful AI tools and APIs.

✓ Cloud AI enables cost-efficient, high-performance AI applications.

✓ Choosing the right cloud platform depends on your use case, budget, and infrastructure needs.

7.2 Deploying AI Models on AWS SageMaker

Amazon SageMaker is a fully managed service that helps data scientists and developers train, deploy, and manage machine learning models at scale. It eliminates the complexity of infrastructure management, allowing AI practitioners to focus on model development and optimization.

In this chapter, we explore:

✓ What AWS SageMaker is and why it's widely used for AI model deployment.

✓ Step-by-step guide to deploying AI models using SageMaker.

✓ Best practices for scalability, security, and cost optimization.

1. What is AWS SageMaker?

AWS SageMaker provides an end-to-end machine learning (ML) environment, including:

✅ **Data Preparation** – Tools for data cleaning and transformation.
✅ **Model Training** – Optimized training using AWS-managed GPUs and TPUs.
✅ **Model Deployment** – One-click deployment as a REST API endpoint.
✅ **MLOps & Monitoring** – Automated model updates and performance tracking.

💡 Why Use SageMaker for Deployment?

✓ **Scalability** – Deploy models that handle millions of predictions per second.

✓ **Cost Efficiency** – Pay only for the compute power used during inference.

✓ **Security & Compliance** – AWS IAM roles, VPCs, and encryption for secure AI deployments.

2. Step-by-Step Guide to Deploying an AI Model on SageMaker

Step 1: Upload Your Trained Model to S3

AWS SageMaker loads models from Amazon S3 (Simple Storage Service). First, upload your trained AI model.

◆ **Example**: Upload a trained TensorFlow model to S3

aws s3 cp my_model.tar.gz s3://my-ai-models/

✓ The model is now stored in S3, ready for deployment.

Step 2: Create a SageMaker Model

Define an AI model in SageMaker using the uploaded file.

◆ **Example**: Create a SageMaker model using Python SDK

```
import boto3

sagemaker = boto3.client('sagemaker')

response = sagemaker.create_model(
    ModelName='my-ai-model',
    PrimaryContainer={
        'Image': '763104351884.dkr.ecr.us-east-1.amazonaws.com/tensorflow-inference:2.8.0-cpu',
        'ModelDataUrl': 's3://my-ai-models/my_model.tar.gz'
    },
    ExecutionRoleArn='arn:aws:iam::123456789012:role/service-role/AmazonSageMaker-ExecutionRole'
)

print("Model created successfully:", response)
```

✓ Your AI model is registered in SageMaker.

Step 3: Deploy the Model as an Endpoint

Deploy the model as a real-time inference endpoint.

◆ **Example**: Create an endpoint configuration

```
response = sagemaker.create_endpoint_config(
    EndpointConfigName='my-endpoint-config',
```

```
    ProductionVariants=[
        {
            'VariantName': 'AllTraffic',
            'ModelName': 'my-ai-model',
            'InstanceType': 'ml.m5.large',
            'InitialInstanceCount': 1
        }
    ]
)

print("Endpoint configuration created:", response)
```

◆ **Example: Deploy the endpoint**

```
response = sagemaker.create_endpoint(
    EndpointName='my-ai-endpoint',
    EndpointConfigName='my-endpoint-config'
)

print("Endpoint deployed successfully:", response)
```

✓ Your AI model is now live and can handle inference requests.

Step 4: Test Your Deployed AI Model

Once deployed, test the model by sending a sample input to the endpoint.

◆ **Example: Send a test request using Python**

```
import json
import boto3

runtime = boto3.client('sagemaker-runtime')

response = runtime.invoke_endpoint(
    EndpointName='my-ai-endpoint',
    ContentType='application/json',
    Body=json.dumps({'input_data': [1.2, 3.4, 5.6]})
)
```

```
result = json.loads(response['Body'].read().decode())
print("AI Model Prediction:", result)
```

✓ The AI model returns real-time predictions via API calls.

3. Optimizing AI Model Deployment on SageMaker

◆ **Choosing the Right Instance Type**

✓ **CPU Instances (ml.m5.large)** – For cost-efficient AI models.
✓ **GPU Instances (ml.p2.xlarge, ml.p3.2xlarge)** – For deep learning models.
✓ **Multi-Instance Scaling** – Auto-scale based on demand.

◆ **Reducing Costs with SageMaker Serverless Inference**

✓ **Use Serverless Inference** – Only pay when requests are made.
✓ **Optimize Model Size** – Use model quantization to reduce memory usage.
✓ **Use Spot Instances** – Save up to 70% on AI training costs.

4. Monitoring and Maintaining Deployed AI Models

◆ **Enable Model Monitoring with SageMaker**

✓ Detect data drift and concept drift in real-time.

✓ Track latency, throughput, and model accuracy.

✓ Use Amazon CloudWatch for automatic alerts.

◆ **Updating AI Models with SageMaker Pipelines**

✓ Automate retraining when new data is available.

✓ Use CI/CD pipelines to deploy improved models seamlessly.

✓ Implement A/B testing to compare model versions.

5. Best Practices for Deploying AI Models on AWS SageMaker

✓ Use Amazon S3 for scalable model storage.

✓ Deploy models as REST APIs for easy integration.

✓ Optimize costs with Serverless Inference and Spot Instances.

✓ Monitor AI models for performance and drift detection.

✓ Automate model updates using SageMaker Pipelines.

6. Conclusion: Why AWS SageMaker is Ideal for AI Deployment

🚀 Key Takeaways:

✓ AWS SageMaker simplifies AI model deployment with managed infrastructure.

✓ Deployment is scalable, cost-efficient, and secure.

✓ SageMaker endpoints allow real-time AI inference via API.

✓ Automated tools like CloudWatch, Pipelines, and Monitoring ensure models stay up-to-date.

7.3 Using Google Vertex AI for Deployment

Google Vertex AI is a fully managed AI platform that enables businesses and developers to train, deploy, and scale AI models effortlessly. Unlike traditional AI workflows that require multiple services, Vertex AI unifies training, model management, deployment, and monitoring under a single framework.

What You'll Learn in This Chapter:

✓ What Google Vertex AI is and why it's useful for AI deployment.

✓ A step-by-step guide to deploying an AI model on Vertex AI.

✓ Best practices for scalability, cost optimization, and monitoring.

1. What is Google Vertex AI?

Vertex AI is a cloud-based AI platform that provides:

✅ **AutoML** – Train ML models with minimal coding.
✅ **Custom Model Deployment** – Deploy AI models as APIs for real-time inference.
✅ **MLOps Capabilities** – Automate model training, monitoring, and updates.
✅ **BigQuery ML Integration** – Seamless connection with Google's Big Data tools.

💡 **Why Use Vertex AI for Deployment?**

✔ **Simplifies AI deployment** – No manual infrastructure setup needed.

✔ **Built-in MLOps** – Automates retraining, monitoring, and versioning.

✔ **Scalable inference** – Deploy models that serve millions of predictions per second.

2. Step-by-Step Guide to Deploying an AI Model on Vertex AI

Step 1: Upload Your Model to Google Cloud Storage (GCS)

Google Vertex AI loads trained models from Cloud Storage. First, upload your model to GCS.

◆ **Example: Upload a TensorFlow model to GCS**

```
gsutil cp my_model.tar.gz gs://my-ai-models/
```

✔ The model is now stored in GCS and ready for deployment.

Step 2: Create a Model Resource in Vertex AI

Once the model is in Cloud Storage, register it in Vertex AI.

◆ **Example: Create a Vertex AI model using Python**

```
from google.cloud import aiplatform

aiplatform.init(project='my-gcp-project', location='us-central1')

model = aiplatform.Model.upload(
    display_name='my-ai-model',
```

```
    artifact_uri='gs://my-ai-models/my_model.tar.gz',
    serving_container_image_uri='us-docker.pkg.dev/vertex-ai/prediction/tf2-cpu.2-8'
)

print("Model registered successfully:", model.resource_name)
```

✓ Your AI model is registered in Vertex AI.

Step 3: Deploy the Model as an Endpoint

After registering the model, deploy it as a real-time inference endpoint.

◆ Example: Deploy the model on Vertex AI

```
endpoint = model.deploy(
    machine_type='n1-standard-4',  # Choose an appropriate instance type
    min_replica_count=1,
    max_replica_count=5,
    traffic_split={"0": 100}
)

print("Model deployed successfully:", endpoint.resource_name)
```

✓ The AI model is now live and can handle API requests.

Step 4: Test Your Deployed AI Model

Once deployed, send a sample input to the endpoint.

◆ Example: Send a test request using Python

```
import json
from google.cloud import aiplatform

endpoint = aiplatform.Endpoint(endpoint_name='projects/my-gcp-project/locations/us-central1/endpoints/123456789')

response = endpoint.predict(instances=[[1.2, 3.4, 5.6]])
print("AI Model Prediction:", response.predictions)
```

✓ Your AI model returns predictions in real time!

3. Optimizing AI Model Deployment on Vertex AI

Choosing the Right Compute Resources

✓ **CPU Instances** (n1-standard-4, e2-medium) – Best for lightweight AI models.
✓ **GPU Instances** (nvidia-tesla-t4, a100) – Ideal for deep learning models.
✓ **Autoscaling** – Configure min and max replicas for dynamic scaling.

Reducing Deployment Costs

✓ **Use Vertex AI Batch Prediction** – Cheaper than real-time inference for large datasets.
✓ **Use AutoML** – No need for expensive custom model training.
✓ **Optimize Model Size** – Apply quantization and pruning to reduce storage and latency.

4. Monitoring and Managing Deployed AI Models

Enable Model Monitoring in Vertex AI

◆ Track model drift and data inconsistencies in real time.
◆ Monitor prediction accuracy and request latency.
◆ Use Google Cloud Logging & AI Explanations for debugging.

Updating Deployed Models

◆ Use CI/CD pipelines to deploy improved models.
◆ Enable A/B testing for comparing new and old model versions.
◆ Automate retraining workflows using Vertex AI Pipelines.

5. Best Practices for Deploying AI Models on Vertex AI

✓ Use Google Cloud Storage (GCS) for efficient model storage.

✓ Leverage AutoML for rapid AI model development.

✓ Deploy models as REST APIs for seamless application integration.

✓ Optimize costs using batch inference and auto-scaling.

✓ Continuously monitor model performance with AI Explanations.

6. Conclusion: Why Use Vertex AI for AI Deployment?

🚀 **Key Takeaways:**

✓ Vertex AI simplifies AI deployment with a fully managed framework.

✓ Scalable infrastructure ensures low-latency predictions.

✓ Built-in MLOps features automate monitoring and retraining.

✓ Cost-efficient options like batch inference optimize cloud spending.

7.4 Managing AI Workloads on Microsoft Azure

Microsoft Azure AI offers a robust suite of cloud-based tools to train, deploy, and manage AI models at scale. It provides services such as Azure Machine Learning (Azure ML), AI APIs, and cognitive services, allowing developers to streamline their AI deployment and MLOps processes.

What You'll Learn in This Chapter:

✓ What Azure AI is and how it helps manage AI workloads.

✓ A step-by-step guide to deploying AI models using Azure ML.

✓ Best practices for scalability, cost-efficiency, and security in AI deployment.

1. Introduction to Microsoft Azure AI

Microsoft Azure provides a comprehensive AI ecosystem that includes:

✅ **Azure Machine Learning (Azure ML)** – A fully managed cloud-based ML platform for model training, deployment, and monitoring.
✅ **Azure Cognitive Services** – Pre-built AI models for tasks like vision, speech, and language processing.

✅ **Azure AI Infrastructure** – Supports GPU-based training, automated scaling, and high-performance computing for deep learning.

✅ **Azure MLOps** – Automates model retraining, CI/CD, and deployment pipelines.

💡 **Why Use Azure for AI Workloads?**

✔ **End-to-End AI Management** – Train, deploy, and monitor models in a single platform.

✔ **Enterprise-Grade Security** – Ensures compliance with GDPR, HIPAA, and ISO standards.

✔ **Scalability & Cost Optimization** – Supports autoscaling, serverless inference, and spot instances.

2. Step-by-Step Guide to Deploying an AI Model on Azure ML

Step 1: Upload the Model to Azure Blob Storage

Azure ML loads models from Azure Blob Storage. First, upload your trained AI model.

◆ **Example: Upload a TensorFlow model to Azure Storage**

az storage blob upload --account-name myaccount --container-name mymodels --name my_model.tar.gz --file my_model.tar.gz

✔ The model is now stored in Azure Blob Storage and ready for deployment.

Step 2: Register the Model in Azure ML

To deploy the model, first register it in Azure ML.

◆ **Example: Register a model in Azure ML using Python**

from azureml.core import Workspace, Model

ws = Workspace.from_config()
model = Model.register(workspace=ws,
*   model_name='my-ai-model',*
*   model_path='my_model.tar.gz')*

print("Model registered successfully:", model.name)

✓ The model is registered and available for deployment.

Step 3: Deploy the Model as an Azure ML Endpoint

Once registered, deploy the model as a real-time endpoint.

◆ Example: Deploy the model using Azure ML

```
from azureml.core.model import InferenceConfig
from azureml.core.webservice import AksWebservice, AciWebservice

# Define the environment for inference
inference_config = InferenceConfig(
    environment=my_env,
    entry_script="score.py"
)

# Define deployment configuration (using Azure Kubernetes Service)
deployment_config = AksWebservice.deploy_configuration(cpu_cores=2,
memory_gb=4)

# Deploy the model
service = Model.deploy(workspace=ws,
                name="my-ai-endpoint",
                models=[model],
                inference_config=inference_config,
                deployment_config=deployment_config)

service.wait_for_deployment(show_output=True)
print("Model deployed at:", service.scoring_uri)
```

✓ The AI model is now live and can handle API requests.

Step 4: Test the Deployed AI Model

Once deployed, send a sample input to the endpoint.

◆ Example: Send a test request using Python

```
import requests
import json

endpoint = "https://my-ai-endpoint.azurewebsites.net/score"

data = json.dumps({"input_data": [1.2, 3.4, 5.6]})
headers = {"Content-Type": "application/json"}

response = requests.post(endpoint, data=data, headers=headers)
print("AI Model Prediction:", response.json())
```

✓ The AI model returns real-time predictions via API calls.

3. Optimizing AI Workloads on Azure

Choosing the Right Compute Resources

✅ **CPU Instances** (Standard_DS3_v2) – Ideal for lightweight AI models.
✅ **GPU Instances** (NC6, ND40rs_v2) – Best for deep learning and computer vision.
✅ **Azure Kubernetes Service** (AKS) – Deploys models with autoscaling for large workloads.

Reducing Deployment Costs

✅ **Use Azure ML Serverless Compute** – Pay only when the model is in use.
✅ **Use Azure Spot Virtual Machines** – Save up to 90% on training costs.
✅ **Optimize Model Size** – Use quantization and pruning for faster inference.

4. Monitoring and Managing AI Workloads on Azure

Enable Model Monitoring with Azure ML

◆ Track data drift, prediction accuracy, and latency.
◆ Use Azure Monitor and Application Insights for AI observability.
◆ Configure automated alerts for model performance issues.

Automating Model Updates with Azure ML Pipelines

◆ **CI/CD for AI** – Automate model retraining and versioning.

◆ **A/B Testing** – Compare new models against existing versions.

◆ **AutoML & Hyperparameter Tuning** – Optimize model performance with minimal manual effort.

5. Best Practices for AI Deployment on Azure

✓ Use Azure Blob Storage for scalable AI model storage.

✓ Deploy models using Azure Kubernetes Service (AKS) for high availability.

✓ Optimize costs with serverless inference and Azure Spot VMs.

✓ Monitor AI models continuously using Azure ML & Application Insights.

✓ Automate model retraining with Azure ML Pipelines.

6. Conclusion: Why Use Microsoft Azure for AI Workloads?

🚀 **Key Takeaways:**

✓ Azure ML simplifies AI workload management with automated MLOps tools.

✓ Secure AI infrastructure ensures enterprise-grade compliance.

✓ Scalable inference with Azure Kubernetes Service (AKS).

✓ Cost-efficient options like serverless inference and spot VMs.

8. Deploying on Edge Devices

Edge AI enables AI models to run directly on IoT devices, mobile phones, and embedded systems, reducing latency, improving efficiency, and enhancing privacy. In this chapter, we explore techniques for deploying AI on edge devices using frameworks like TensorFlow Lite, ONNX Runtime, and NVIDIA Jetson. You'll learn about model compression, quantization, and hardware acceleration to optimize performance on resource-constrained devices. We also discuss real-world applications of edge AI in autonomous vehicles, healthcare wearables, and smart home systems. By mastering edge AI deployment, you can build low-latency, high-performance AI applications that operate seamlessly without relying on cloud connectivity.

8.1 Why Deploy AI Models on the Edge?

As artificial intelligence continues to evolve, deploying AI models on edge devices is becoming increasingly essential. Traditional cloud-based AI deployments rely on centralized servers, which can lead to latency issues, increased bandwidth costs, and privacy concerns. By shifting AI inference closer to the edge, businesses and developers can achieve faster processing, lower operational costs, and improved security.

1. What is Edge AI?

Edge AI refers to the deployment of AI models directly on edge devices such as:

✅ **Smartphones & Tablets** – AI-powered apps (e.g., facial recognition, voice assistants).
✅ **IoT Devices** – Smart cameras, drones, and industrial sensors.
✅ **Embedded Systems** – AI in medical devices, autonomous vehicles, and robotics.
✅ **On-Premise Servers & Gateways** – AI processing at local data centers.

Unlike cloud AI, which requires sending data to remote servers, Edge AI processes data locally, reducing dependency on internet connectivity and cloud infrastructure.

2. Key Benefits of Deploying AI on the Edge

✅ Reduced Latency for Real-Time Processing

Cloud-based AI models introduce network latency because data must travel to remote servers. In contrast, edge AI processes data locally, enabling real-time decision-making for applications like:

- **Autonomous vehicles** – Instant object detection and navigation.
- **Industrial automation** – Predictive maintenance and anomaly detection.
- **Smart cameras** – Real-time surveillance and facial recognition.

Example: A self-driving car using edge AI can process sensor data in milliseconds, whereas a cloud-based model would introduce significant delays.

✅ Lower Bandwidth and Cloud Costs

AI applications that rely on constant cloud communication can become expensive due to data transfer costs. By processing AI workloads locally, businesses can:

✔ Reduce cloud storage and computing costs.

✔ Minimize network congestion, improving performance.

✔ Enable AI in remote areas with limited connectivity.

Example: A smart factory using edge AI for predictive maintenance can analyze equipment data locally instead of sending terabytes of sensor data to the cloud.

✅ Enhanced Security and Privacy

Certain AI applications involve sensitive or personal data, making cloud-based processing a security risk. Edge AI helps protect user privacy by:

✔ Keeping data processing on the device, reducing exposure to cyber threats.

✔ Meeting compliance requirements (e.g., GDPR, HIPAA).

✔ Reducing the risk of data breaches associated with cloud-based storage.

Example: A hospital using edge AI for medical image analysis can keep patient data on-premise, ensuring HIPAA compliance.

✅ Offline AI Processing for Remote Areas

Cloud AI requires a stable internet connection, which isn't always available in:

- **Rural areas** – Smart agriculture and weather prediction.
- **Underground facilities** – AI-powered mining safety systems.
- **Aerospace & Marine environments** – AI in satellites and submarines.

Edge AI enables AI-powered decision-making without internet dependency, making it ideal for mission-critical applications.

Example: A drone used for wildfire detection can process images in real-time without cloud connectivity, allowing for faster emergency response.

✅ Scalability for Large-Scale AI Deployments

Deploying AI models at the edge distributes processing across multiple devices, rather than relying on centralized cloud servers. This enables:

✓ More efficient load balancing across devices.

✓ Faster response times with distributed AI inference.

✓ Cost savings on cloud infrastructure for large AI workloads.

Example: A retail chain using AI for customer behavior analysis can run edge AI models on in-store cameras instead of overloading a central cloud system.

3. Common Use Cases of Edge AI Deployment

📌 Smart Cities & Surveillance

- Traffic monitoring & intelligent streetlights.
- AI-powered security cameras for threat detection.

📌 Healthcare & Medical Devices

- AI-driven diagnostics on portable medical devices.
- Real-time ECG and MRI analysis without cloud dependence.

📌 Industrial Automation & Manufacturing

- ◆ Predictive maintenance for machinery.
- ◆ AI-driven quality inspection in production lines.

📌 Retail & Customer Analytics

- ◆ AI-powered checkout systems for faster transactions.
- ◆ Personalized shopping experiences through real-time AI.

📌 Autonomous Vehicles & Robotics

- ◆ Self-driving cars processing real-time sensor data.
- ◆ AI-powered warehouse robots optimizing logistics.

4. Challenges in Deploying AI on the Edge

✖ Hardware Constraints

Edge devices have limited processing power, memory, and storage compared to cloud-based AI servers. Solution:

✔ Use model optimization techniques like quantization & pruning.

✔ Deploy lightweight AI frameworks (e.g., TensorFlow Lite, ONNX Runtime).

✖ Power Consumption Issues

Running AI models on edge devices can drain battery life quickly. Solution:

✔ Optimize models using low-power accelerators (e.g., NVIDIA Jetson, Google Coral TPU).

✔ Implement adaptive AI inference, running models only when needed.

✖ Model Update & Maintenance

Unlike cloud AI, updating edge AI models across multiple devices is challenging. Solution:

✓ Use OTA (Over-the-Air) model updates for remote deployments.

✓ Implement federated learning for continuous AI improvements.

5. Future of AI Deployment on the Edge

Edge AI is set to revolutionize industries by bringing intelligence closer to where data is generated. Future trends include:

🔋 **5G-powered Edge AI** – Faster real-time processing with ultra-low latency.

🔋 **TinyML & Low-Power AI** – AI running on microcontrollers for IoT applications.

🔋 **Decentralized AI Processing** – AI models running across distributed edge networks.

6. Conclusion: Why Edge AI is the Future of AI Deployment

💡 **Key Takeaways:**

✓ Faster AI inference by reducing reliance on cloud computing.

✓ Lower costs by minimizing bandwidth and cloud storage expenses.

✓ Improved security & privacy by keeping data local.

✓ Offline AI capabilities for remote or unstable network environments.

✓ Scalable AI applications across industries like healthcare, manufacturing, and smart cities.

8.2 Model Optimization for Edge AI

Deploying AI models on edge devices presents unique challenges due to limited computational power, memory constraints, and energy efficiency requirements. Unlike cloud-based AI models, which can leverage powerful GPUs and large-scale data centers, edge AI models must be optimized to run efficiently on resource-constrained devices such as smartphones, IoT sensors, embedded systems, and drones.

In this chapter, we will explore key techniques for optimizing AI models to ensure fast inference, reduced power consumption, and seamless deployment on edge devices.

1. Why is Model Optimization Important for Edge AI?

AI models trained in the cloud are typically too large and computationally expensive for direct deployment on edge devices. Without optimization, these models can lead to:

$\oslash$ **Slow inference times** – Delays in real-time decision-making.
$\oslash$ **High power consumption** – Reducing battery life in mobile devices.
$\oslash$ **Large memory footprint** – Insufficient storage on IoT devices.

Optimizing AI models helps to:

✓ Reduce model size while maintaining accuracy.

✓ Lower latency for real-time inference.

✓ Minimize energy consumption to extend battery life.

✓ Improve compatibility with hardware accelerators like TPUs, GPUs, and FPGAs.

2. Techniques for Optimizing AI Models for Edge Deployment

✔ 1. Model Quantization

Model quantization reduces the precision of numerical weights in a neural network, lowering the size of the model and speeding up inference.

📌 **Types of Quantization:**

- **Post-Training Quantization (PTQ)** – Applied after training.
- **Quantization-Aware Training (QAT)** – Integrated during model training for better accuracy.

📌 **Frameworks Supporting Quantization:**

- TensorFlow Lite (TFLite)
- ONNX Runtime
- PyTorch Mobile

◆ Example: Quantizing a TensorFlow model for Edge AI

```
import tensorflow as tf

# Load trained model
model = tf.keras.models.load_model("model.h5")

# Convert to TFLite with quantization
converter = tf.lite.TFLiteConverter.from_keras_model(model)
converter.optimizations = [tf.lite.Optimize.DEFAULT]
tflite_model = converter.convert()

# Save optimized model
with open("model_quantized.tflite", "wb") as f:
    f.write(tflite_model)
```

✓ Reduces model size by up to 75% while maintaining accuracy.

✓ 2. Model Pruning

Model pruning removes unnecessary weights and neurons to make the model more efficient without significant accuracy loss.

📌 Types of Pruning:

- **Weight Pruning** – Eliminates small-weight connections in a network.
- **Structured Pruning** – Removes entire neurons or filters to compress models.

📌 Frameworks Supporting Pruning:

- TensorFlow Model Optimization Toolkit
- PyTorch TorchScript

◆ Example: Pruning a TensorFlow model

```
import tensorflow_model_optimization as tfmot

prune_low_magnitude = tfmot.sparsity.keras.prune_low_magnitude
```

```
pruned_model = prune_low_magnitude(model)

pruned_model.compile(optimizer="adam", loss="sparse_categorical_crossentropy")
pruned_model.fit(train_data, epochs=5)
```

✓ Reduces memory footprint while retaining accuracy.

✅ 3. Knowledge Distillation

Knowledge distillation compresses large AI models by training a smaller "student model" to mimic a larger "teacher model."

📌 Why Use Knowledge Distillation?

✓ Reduces model size while preserving knowledge.

✓ Improves inference speed for real-time AI.

✓ Allows deployment on low-power edge devices.

◆ Example: Training a student model from a teacher model

```
teacher_predictions = teacher_model.predict(train_data)
student_model.fit(train_data, teacher_predictions, epochs=10)
```

✓ Enables deploying complex AI models on edge devices with minimal loss in accuracy.

✅ 4. TensorFlow Lite (TFLite) and ONNX Runtime for Edge AI

TensorFlow Lite and ONNX Runtime are lightweight AI frameworks designed for deploying models on edge devices.

📌 Why Use TFLite and ONNX Runtime?

✓ Faster inference with optimized operations.

✓ Supports hardware acceleration (e.g., GPUs, TPUs).

✓ Reduces storage and memory consumption.

◆ Example: Converting a TensorFlow model to TFLite

converter = tf.lite.TFLiteConverter.from_keras_model(model)
tflite_model = converter.convert()

with open("optimized_model.tflite", "wb") as f:
  f.write(tflite_model)

✓ Ready for deployment on Android, Raspberry Pi, and microcontrollers.

✅ 5. Hardware Acceleration for Edge AI

Using specialized AI chips like GPUs, TPUs, and FPGAs improves performance.

📌 Edge AI Hardware Accelerators:

- **Google Coral TPU** – Fast AI inference for IoT devices.
- **NVIDIA Jetson Nano** – AI-powered robotics and vision applications.
- **Intel OpenVINO** – Optimized AI inference on Intel CPUs.

◆ Example: Running AI on NVIDIA Jetson Nano

python3 detect_objects.py --model optimized_model.tflite

✓ Achieves low-latency AI inference on embedded devices.

3. Best Practices for Edge AI Model Optimization

✓ Use quantization to reduce model size while maintaining accuracy.

✓ Apply pruning to remove redundant model parameters.

✓ Leverage knowledge distillation to create lightweight AI models.

✓ Choose the right AI framework (TFLite, ONNX, PyTorch Mobile).

✓ Utilize hardware accelerators (TPUs, GPUs, Edge AI chips).

✓ Optimize power consumption to extend battery life on mobile devices.

4. Conclusion: Why Model Optimization is Key for Edge AI

🚀 Key Takeaways:

✓ Optimized AI models run efficiently on edge devices with minimal power usage.

✓ Quantization, pruning, and distillation are essential for reducing model size.

✓ TensorFlow Lite & ONNX streamline AI deployment on resource-constrained devices.

✓ Hardware accelerators like Jetson Nano, Coral TPU, and OpenVINO enhance performance.

8.3 Deploying AI on Mobile (TensorFlow Lite, CoreML)

With the rapid advancement of mobile technology, deploying AI models on mobile devices has become increasingly important. Mobile devices, such as smartphones and tablets, are equipped with powerful hardware and connectivity capabilities, making them ideal for running AI applications. However, deploying AI models on mobile comes with challenges, particularly due to the constraints on processing power, memory, and battery life. Fortunately, frameworks like TensorFlow Lite and CoreML provide specialized tools and optimizations to ensure that AI models can run efficiently on mobile platforms.

In this chapter, we'll explore the best practices and techniques for deploying AI models on mobile devices using TensorFlow Lite for Android devices and CoreML for iOS devices.

1. Why Deploy AI on Mobile Devices?

The potential for AI on mobile devices is immense. By deploying AI models directly on mobile devices, applications can benefit from:

✓ **Low-latency inference** – Real-time AI processing without cloud dependency.

✓ **Offline functionality** – AI models can work without an internet connection.

✓ **Improved privacy** – Data is processed locally, reducing the need for cloud-based data storage.

✓ **Reduced cloud reliance** – Saves bandwidth and cloud processing costs.

Some common use cases for mobile AI include:

♦ **Speech recognition** – Voice assistants like Google Assistant and Siri.

♦ **Image recognition** – Object detection in real-time for apps like Snapchat and Google Lens.

♦ **Augmented Reality (AR)** – AI-driven AR experiences on mobile devices.

♦ **Health and fitness tracking** – Monitoring activities and health parameters in fitness apps.

2. TensorFlow Lite: The Solution for Android AI Deployment

TensorFlow Lite (TFLite) is a lightweight version of TensorFlow designed for mobile and embedded device deployment. It optimizes models for performance and memory efficiency without sacrificing accuracy.

✅ Why Use TensorFlow Lite for Mobile AI?

- Optimized for mobile and embedded devices, reducing model size.
- Faster inference on mobile devices, thanks to efficient operations.
- Supports hardware accelerators like Android Neural Networks API (NNAPI) and GPU.
- Compatible with Android devices, making it the go-to solution for Android AI deployment.

✅ Steps for Deploying AI Models with TensorFlow Lite

1. Convert the TensorFlow Model to TensorFlow Lite Format

The first step is to convert the trained model to the TFLite format. This conversion is necessary because TFLite models are more optimized for mobile deployment.

TensorFlow Model Conversion to TensorFlow Lite:

import tensorflow as tf

 # Load the trained model

```
model = tf.keras.models.load_model('model.h5')

# Convert to TensorFlow Lite format
converter = tf.lite.TFLiteConverter.from_keras_model(model)
converter.optimizations = [tf.lite.Optimize.DEFAULT]
tflite_model = converter.convert()

# Save the converted model
with open('model.tflite', 'wb') as f:
    f.write(tflite_model)
```

2. Integrate TensorFlow Lite Model in Android

Once the model is in the TFLite format, it can be integrated into an Android application.

Add TensorFlow Lite Dependencies to Android Project: In the build.gradle file of your Android project, include the necessary dependencies:

```
implementation 'org.tensorflow:tensorflow-lite:2.6.0'
```

Load the Model in Your Android App:

```
import org.tensorflow.lite.Interpreter;

// Load the model
Interpreter tflite = new Interpreter(loadModelFile("model.tflite"));
```

3. Use the Model for Inference

Once the model is loaded, you can use it to make predictions on input data, such as an image or sensor reading.

Example: Run inference on an image

```
float[][] output = new float[1][OUTPUT_CLASSES];
tflite.run(inputData, output);
```

This setup allows for real-time AI inference directly on an Android device without relying on an internet connection.

3. CoreML: The Solution for iOS AI Deployment

CoreML is Apple's machine learning framework for iOS, macOS, watchOS, and tvOS. It optimizes models for on-device inference, ensuring they run efficiently while consuming minimal resources. CoreML supports a variety of model formats, including TensorFlow, Keras, ONNX, and more.

✅ Why Use CoreML for Mobile AI?

- **Optimized for Apple devices** – CoreML integrates seamlessly with iOS hardware.
- **Supports accelerated inference** – Leverages Apple's A-series chips (e.g., Neural Engine) for faster processing.
- **Highly efficient** – Minimizes battery usage and storage consumption.
- **Works offline** – Enables mobile AI applications to function without network dependence.

✅ Steps for Deploying AI Models with CoreML

1. Convert the Model to CoreML Format

CoreML requires models to be in a specific format. If your model is in TensorFlow or Keras, you can use coremltools to convert it to CoreML.

Converting TensorFlow/Keras Model to CoreML:

```
import coremltools as ct
import tensorflow as tf

# Load the trained TensorFlow/Keras model
model = tf.keras.models.load_model('model.h5')

# Convert to CoreML format
coreml_model = ct.convert(model)

# Save the CoreML model
coreml_model.save('model.mlmodel')
```

2. Integrate CoreML Model in an iOS Application

Once the CoreML model is created, you can integrate it into an iOS application.

Add CoreML Framework to iOS Project:

In Xcode, add the CoreML framework to your iOS project via the Project Settings > Link Binary with Libraries.

Load and Use CoreML Model in Swift:

import CoreML

```
// Load the CoreML model
guard let model = try? VNCoreMLModel(for: YourCoreMLModel().model) else {
    fatalError("Unable to load model")
}
```

3. Use the Model for Inference

After loading the model, you can use it for inference on input data (e.g., images, text, or sensor data).

Example: Run inference on an image in iOS

```
let modelInput = try? VNCoreMLRequest(model: model, completionHandler: { (request, error) in
    // Process the output from the model
})
```

CoreML is designed to leverage Apple's hardware acceleration, making AI inference on mobile devices both fast and power-efficient.

4. Optimizing Mobile AI Models for Performance

Deploying AI models on mobile devices requires optimizing for both inference speed and battery efficiency. Here are some key strategies:

✅ Model Quantization

Both TensorFlow Lite and CoreML support model quantization, which reduces the size of the model and speeds up inference by using lower precision calculations.

✅ Use of Hardware Acceleration

Take advantage of hardware accelerators such as:

- Android Neural Networks API (NNAPI) for Android.
- Apple's Neural Engine on iPhones and iPads for iOS models.

✅ Reduce Input Size

For models like image classifiers, reduce the input image size to minimize processing time while maintaining accuracy.

✅ Efficient Data Handling

Mobile devices often have limited memory. Optimize input data handling by using batch processing and streaming data when possible to avoid overloading the device's memory.

5. Conclusion: Deploying AI Efficiently on Mobile Devices

Deploying AI models on mobile devices unlocks numerous possibilities for real-time AI applications that are both efficient and privacy-conscious. By leveraging frameworks like TensorFlow Lite and CoreML, developers can easily deploy AI models to Android and iOS devices with optimized performance and minimal resource consumption.

💡 Key Takeaways:

- TensorFlow Lite and CoreML offer optimized tools for deploying AI on Android and iOS.
- Model conversion, hardware acceleration, and quantization are key to efficient mobile AI.
- Real-time AI inference on mobile devices enables applications in speech recognition, image processing, and healthcare.

Next, we'll dive deeper into edge AI devices, where mobile meets the IoT for distributed AI deployment. 🚀

8.4 AI on IoT Devices: Raspberry Pi, NVIDIA Jetson

The integration of AI with Internet of Things (IoT) devices is revolutionizing the way we interact with and harness data from the environment. By deploying AI on IoT devices such as Raspberry Pi and NVIDIA Jetson, developers can create intelligent systems capable of performing complex tasks at the edge, reducing the need for cloud-based processing and enabling real-time decision-making.

In this chapter, we will explore how to deploy AI models on Raspberry Pi and NVIDIA Jetson, two popular IoT platforms, and the best practices for optimizing these devices for AI workloads.

1. Why Deploy AI on IoT Devices?

Deploying AI models on IoT devices brings a host of benefits:

Real-time Processing: Edge devices process data locally, enabling instantaneous decision-making. For example, a smart camera analyzing video feeds for object detection doesn't have to wait for data to be sent to the cloud and back.

Reduced Latency: Sending data to the cloud and waiting for processing can cause significant delays. By running AI models directly on IoT devices, latency is minimized, making them ideal for real-time applications.

Bandwidth Efficiency: IoT devices often operate in environments where network connectivity may be unreliable or expensive. By processing data on the device, the need to send large volumes of data to the cloud is reduced, saving both bandwidth and costs.

Improved Privacy and Security: AI running locally on IoT devices means sensitive data, such as video feeds or biometric data, never leaves the device. This enhances privacy and security by reducing exposure to external threats.

Examples of IoT devices running AI include:

- Smart cameras that perform real-time object detection.
- Smart thermostats that use AI to learn and optimize heating/cooling patterns.
- Wearable health monitors that process biometric data to provide real-time feedback.

2. Raspberry Pi for AI Deployment

The Raspberry Pi is a small, affordable computer popular in DIY and educational projects. With its GPIO pins, rich software ecosystem, and extensive community support, the Raspberry Pi has become a prime platform for deploying AI at the edge. Despite its low cost and modest specifications, the Raspberry Pi can run a wide range of AI models with the right optimizations.

✅ Why Use Raspberry Pi for AI?

- **Cost-Effective**: Raspberry Pi models are inexpensive, making them ideal for budget-conscious AI projects.
- **Small Form Factor**: Its small size allows for deployment in constrained environments.
- **GPIO Support**: Raspberry Pi provides access to physical pins, which are useful for interfacing with sensors, cameras, and other IoT devices.

✅ Steps for Deploying AI on Raspberry Pi

1. Choose a Lightweight AI Framework

The first step in deploying AI on Raspberry Pi is choosing a framework that is optimized for low-power, small-footprint environments. Some popular AI frameworks for Raspberry Pi include:

- **TensorFlow Lite**: A lightweight version of TensorFlow optimized for mobile and embedded devices.
- **OpenCV**: A powerful computer vision library that integrates well with Raspberry Pi and supports real-time image processing.

2. Set Up Your Raspberry Pi

- Install a compatible OS, typically Raspberry Pi OS (formerly Raspbian), which is optimized for Raspberry Pi hardware.
- Ensure you have sufficient RAM (at least 2GB) and storage, and connect external peripherals such as a camera module if needed.

3. Convert Your AI Model to TensorFlow Lite

AI models trained on platforms like TensorFlow or Keras need to be converted to a format that is optimized for the Raspberry Pi. Use TensorFlow Lite for this purpose.

```python
import tensorflow as tf

# Load your trained model
model = tf.keras.models.load_model('your_model.h5')

# Convert to TensorFlow Lite format
converter = tf.lite.TFLiteConverter.from_keras_model(model)
tflite_model = converter.convert()

# Save the converted model
with open('model.tflite', 'wb') as f:
    f.write(tflite_model)
```

4. Run Inference on Raspberry Pi

After converting the model, you can use TensorFlow Lite to run inference on the Raspberry Pi. To execute inference on the device:

```python
import tensorflow as tf

# Load the TFLite model
interpreter = tf.lite.Interpreter(model_path="model.tflite")
interpreter.allocate_tensors()

# Prepare the input tensor
input_details = interpreter.get_input_details()
output_details = interpreter.get_output_details()

# Run inference
interpreter.set_tensor(input_details[0]['index'], input_data)
interpreter.invoke()

# Get the result
output_data = interpreter.get_tensor(output_details[0]['index'])
```

By utilizing TensorFlow Lite, your AI model runs efficiently on the Raspberry Pi, even with limited resources.

3. NVIDIA Jetson for AI Deployment

NVIDIA's Jetson family of devices (Jetson Nano, Jetson Xavier, and Jetson TX2) provides powerful, energy-efficient AI capabilities for edge deployment. Unlike Raspberry Pi, which is suitable for lightweight AI models, NVIDIA Jetson is designed to handle more complex tasks, thanks to the integration of GPUs and CUDA cores for fast parallel computation.

✅ Why Use NVIDIA Jetson for AI?

- **Powerful GPU**: NVIDIA Jetson modules come with built-in GPUs that are optimized for deep learning and AI workloads, accelerating model inference.
- **NVIDIA CUDA**: Jetson devices can utilize CUDA for parallel processing, enhancing performance in AI applications.
- **Support for AI Libraries**: Jetson supports TensorFlow, PyTorch, and OpenCV out of the box, enabling easy deployment of AI models.
- **Versatility**: Jetson boards like the Jetson Nano are suitable for a range of applications from robotics to autonomous vehicles.

✅ Steps for Deploying AI on Jetson Devices

1. Set Up the Jetson Device

Start by flashing the Jetson device with JetPack, NVIDIA's SDK, which includes the necessary libraries and frameworks for AI development. JetPack supports various versions of TensorFlow, PyTorch, and CUDA.

2. Optimize Your AI Model

Like Raspberry Pi, models must be optimized for performance when deployed on Jetson devices. NVIDIA offers TensorRT, a high-performance deep learning inference library, to accelerate models further.

3. Run AI Models Using TensorRT

To run AI models on Jetson, we first convert models to TensorRT format for faster inference. TensorRT automatically optimizes models for the hardware and reduces execution time.

Example:

```
import tensorrt as trt
import numpy as np

# Load a trained TensorFlow model
model = load_model("your_model.h5")

# Convert the TensorFlow model to TensorRT
trt_engine = trt.create_inference_engine(model)

# Perform inference on Jetson with TensorRT
results = trt_engine.infer(input_data)
```

4. Deploy AI on Jetson for Real-Time Applications

With optimized models and the right framework (TensorFlow, PyTorch, or TensorRT), Jetson devices are capable of running real-time AI applications, such as object detection, face recognition, and autonomous navigation.

4. Best Practices for Deploying AI on IoT Devices

✅ Optimize for Low Power Consumption

Both Raspberry Pi and Jetson are low-power devices, but AI inference can be power-intensive. Use model quantization, pruning, and batching to reduce computational overhead and lower power consumption.

✅ Use Hardware Acceleration

Leverage the GPU (Jetson devices) or specialized accelerators (Raspberry Pi's NNAPI or OpenCV GPU support) to speed up inference. These accelerators provide a significant performance boost over traditional CPU-only processing.

✅ Minimize Latency

Edge AI models must be designed for low-latency, real-time inference. For example, processing images on Jetson or Raspberry Pi should be done in parallel to ensure that models don't take too long to respond.

✓ Monitor Resource Usage

Keep track of CPU, RAM, and GPU utilization to ensure the IoT device operates optimally without running out of resources. Tools like htop (Linux) or nvidia-smi (Jetson) can be used to monitor these metrics.

5. Conclusion: Harnessing AI at the Edge with IoT Devices

Deploying AI models on IoT devices like Raspberry Pi and NVIDIA Jetson allows for the creation of powerful, real-time intelligent systems that operate with minimal latency and bandwidth dependency. By leveraging the right frameworks, optimization techniques, and hardware accelerators, AI can be effectively deployed at the edge to perform tasks like image recognition, natural language processing, and sensor fusion.

🚀 Key Takeaways:

- Raspberry Pi is ideal for lightweight AI tasks and is highly customizable for DIY projects.
- NVIDIA Jetson offers high-performance AI capabilities, particularly for resource-intensive tasks.
- Optimizing for power, memory, and latency is essential when deploying AI on IoT devices.
- Use TensorFlow Lite, TensorRT, and other specialized frameworks to optimize AI models for edge devices.

The next chapter will delve into IoT AI use cases, where we will explore real-world examples of deploying AI in IoT-based applications.

9. Deploying on On-Premises Servers

For organizations that require greater control, security, and compliance, deploying AI models on on-premises servers is a powerful alternative to cloud-based solutions. In this chapter, we explore the infrastructure and tools needed for on-premises AI deployment, including Kubernetes, Docker, NVIDIA GPUs, and custom AI hardware. You'll learn how to set up scalable inference servers, manage AI workloads efficiently, and ensure high availability for mission-critical applications. We also discuss cost considerations, maintenance strategies, and best practices for optimizing performance in self-hosted environments. Mastering on-premises AI deployment allows businesses to achieve high performance, security, and operational control over their AI models.

9.1 When to Choose On-Premise Deployment

Deploying AI models on-premises refers to running them on local infrastructure, such as servers, instead of utilizing cloud services or edge devices. While cloud-based deployment has gained immense popularity due to its scalability and flexibility, there are specific scenarios where on-premise deployment may be the better choice. This approach can offer unique advantages in terms of control, security, and cost management, depending on the specific requirements of an AI project.

In this section, we will explore the circumstances under which on-premise deployment makes sense, as well as the key factors to consider when deciding between on-premise, cloud, and hybrid deployment models.

1. High Data Privacy and Security Requirements

On-premise AI deployment is particularly advantageous for organizations that handle sensitive data and require strict data privacy and security protocols. In industries such as healthcare, finance, and government, data security is paramount, and organizations may be restricted by compliance regulations such as GDPR (General Data Protection Regulation), HIPAA (Health Insurance Portability and Accountability Act), or industry-specific security standards.

By deploying AI models on-premises, organizations can ensure that all data remains within their own infrastructure, significantly reducing the risk of data breaches, unauthorized access, or leaks. This is crucial for situations where data must be kept within a controlled environment, ensuring compliance with security policies, encryption standards, and regulatory requirements.

Example: A healthcare provider that processes patient medical records may need to store sensitive health data locally to comply with HIPAA, rather than sending it to a third-party cloud service.

2. Limited or Unreliable Internet Connectivity

In remote or rural locations, or in industries where reliable internet connectivity is not guaranteed, on-premise deployment offers a dependable solution. For instance, environments like mines, oil rigs, factories, or certain military applications often face challenges in maintaining a stable and high-speed internet connection.

On-premise deployment of AI models allows businesses to perform data processing and inference locally, even in the absence of continuous internet access. This is particularly critical for real-time applications where AI models need to respond instantly, such as in automated manufacturing lines, robotics, or autonomous vehicles.

Example: An industrial plant in a remote area that uses AI-powered systems for predictive maintenance might rely on on-premise deployment to ensure continuous operation, even without robust internet access.

3. High Performance and Low Latency Requirements

For certain applications, such as real-time decision-making, low-latency processing is essential. On-premise deployment can significantly reduce the latency associated with sending data to a cloud provider and waiting for it to be processed. This is particularly important for AI models that need to operate with near-instantaneous response times.

By using local hardware, including high-performance CPUs, GPUs, and TPUs, organizations can optimize the processing power available on-premises to minimize latency. Whether it is for autonomous driving, live video surveillance analysis, or high-frequency trading, on-premise deployment provides the low-latency edge that cloud solutions may struggle to achieve.

Example: An AI-powered autonomous vehicle must process data from sensors in real-time to make decisions about its environment. The time it takes to send sensor data to the cloud and receive instructions could be too long, making on-premise deployment a far better choice.

4. Regulatory and Compliance Constraints

For industries such as financial services, healthcare, defense, and government, strict regulatory and compliance requirements often dictate where and how data can be stored and processed. Some regulations may prohibit storing data off-site or mandate that it remains within specific geographic regions.

In these situations, deploying AI on-premises ensures that organizations have full control over their data's location and usage, minimizing the risk of violating compliance standards. For example, financial institutions must ensure that they meet Sarbanes-Oxley regulations when it comes to data handling, and governments may have restrictions on outsourcing data processing.

Example: A financial institution that processes personal data of clients may be bound by strict regulations that require them to host their AI models and sensitive client data on their own servers within a specific jurisdiction to remain compliant with national laws.

5. Cost Considerations for Long-Term Use

While cloud platforms often offer pay-as-you-go pricing models, on-premise deployments may be more cost-effective in the long term for organizations with consistent and heavy AI workload requirements. Running AI models on-premises involves upfront capital expenditure for hardware, infrastructure, and setup, but the ongoing operational costs are typically lower compared to cloud-based solutions where fees can accumulate based on compute, storage, and bandwidth usage.

On-premise deployment is especially cost-effective for companies that have predictable, continuous AI workload requirements, such as those running large-scale data processing or high-frequency trading applications. Over time, owning the infrastructure can provide substantial savings and give businesses more control over their IT budgets.

Example: A large manufacturing company running AI models for predictive maintenance across a fleet of equipment may find that the costs of cloud deployment, including the storage of large volumes of data, are too high over time. Investing in on-premise servers can help reduce recurring costs in the long run.

6. Full Control Over Infrastructure and Customization

On-premise AI deployment gives organizations complete control over their infrastructure. This includes choosing the type of hardware (e.g., CPUs, GPUs, or specialized hardware), managing software versions, and customizing the environment according to specific use cases. This flexibility allows businesses to optimize the system for their unique needs, such as setting up dedicated high-performance AI clusters or integrating AI models into existing business systems.

Additionally, organizations can update or maintain their infrastructure without relying on external cloud service providers, ensuring that the deployment is always running the latest version of software and security patches. For businesses with specialized AI applications, having full control over the environment can make deployment more efficient and aligned with operational requirements.

Example: A financial institution may need to ensure that its AI models for fraud detection are running on customized hardware with specialized encryption and compliance tools, which would be difficult to achieve with cloud-based services.

7. Long-Term AI Model Ownership and Customization

On-premise deployment allows organizations to maintain ownership of their AI models, software, and hardware. For certain industries, this long-term ownership is crucial for ensuring that proprietary data and algorithms are fully protected. When deploying on cloud platforms, businesses may face concerns about vendor lock-in, where they become dependent on a specific provider's infrastructure or APIs.

On-premise solutions give companies the freedom to customize models and scale them without being subject to the limitations imposed by third-party cloud providers. This is especially valuable for industries where continuous innovation and the ability to make changes to AI models are key to staying competitive.

Example: A cutting-edge robotics company may prefer on-premise deployment to ensure that their AI-powered systems for automated manufacturing can evolve and adapt without the constraints of cloud vendor limitations.

Conclusion: Making the Right Choice

Deciding whether to deploy AI on-premises depends on multiple factors, including security, performance requirements, regulatory compliance, and cost considerations. On-premise deployment offers substantial advantages for businesses that require greater control, lower latency, data privacy, and long-term cost efficiency. However, it also comes with challenges related to upfront costs, hardware management, and scalability. By understanding these key factors, organizations can make informed decisions on the right deployment model that best suits their needs.

The next chapter will focus on how to optimize AI models for hybrid cloud and on-premise environments, providing insights into combining the benefits of both deployment models to create a flexible, scalable AI infrastructure.

9.2 Infrastructure Requirements for AI Deployment

Deploying AI models in production environments requires a robust infrastructure to handle the complex processing, storage, and computational demands of machine learning workflows. The infrastructure for AI deployment can range from on-premise servers to cloud-based environments, or even hybrid models combining both. The right infrastructure ensures that AI systems are efficient, scalable, secure, and capable of meeting the performance and reliability requirements of various use cases.

In this section, we will explore the essential infrastructure components needed for AI deployment, including hardware, software, networking, and data management requirements. By understanding these requirements, businesses can ensure they have the necessary foundation for a successful AI deployment.

1. Hardware Requirements

AI workloads, especially deep learning tasks, demand high-performance hardware that can handle intensive computations. The following hardware components are essential for effective AI deployment:

1.1 Central Processing Unit (CPU)

The CPU is the core processing unit responsible for managing the overall operations of the system. While modern CPUs are powerful and capable of running AI models, they may not be fast enough for heavy deep learning tasks that require large-scale matrix multiplications and other computationally intensive operations. However, the CPU still plays an essential role in general tasks, controlling the orchestration of AI workflows and supporting less intensive computations.

Required Specs: Multi-core CPUs with high clock speeds are generally preferable, as they can support multi-threaded tasks in AI deployment.

1.2 Graphics Processing Unit (GPU)

The GPU is one of the most crucial components for AI deployment, particularly for tasks such as deep learning, computer vision, and natural language processing (NLP). GPUs are optimized for parallel processing and can significantly speed up the training and inference of deep learning models by executing thousands of operations simultaneously.

Required Specs: GPUs like NVIDIA Tesla, A100, V100, or GTX series, or AMD Radeon are often used for their high throughput and CUDA core support in AI applications.

GPUs for Inference: Not only for training, but GPUs are also essential for real-time inference, particularly in resource-intensive applications such as autonomous vehicles, robotics, or AI in IoT devices.

1.3 Tensor Processing Unit (TPU)

A TPU is a specialized accelerator developed by Google for machine learning tasks. TPUs are designed to speed up tensor operations, which are fundamental to many machine learning algorithms, especially deep neural networks. TPUs provide faster computation speeds and energy efficiency when compared to general-purpose GPUs, making them ideal for large-scale AI deployments.

Required Specs: When selecting TPUs, consider the model type (e.g., Google Cloud TPUs, Edge TPUs) and the workload type (e.g., training vs. inference).

1.4 Field-Programmable Gate Arrays (FPGA)

An FPGA is a customizable hardware accelerator that can be programmed to optimize specific tasks within an AI model. It can be used for edge AI applications where low latency and power consumption are critical. FPGAs can be highly efficient in handling tasks like video processing, pattern recognition, and data filtering.

Required Specs: Look for FPGAs with high clock speeds, low latency, and hardware optimization capabilities for the AI workload at hand.

1.5 Storage Requirements

AI models often work with large datasets, so sufficient storage is required to store both the training data and the model itself. Depending on the application, data can range from terabytes (for large-scale data like images or videos) to petabytes (for big data use cases).

Required Specs: High-performance storage systems like solid-state drives (SSD) are preferred for faster data access speeds. For large datasets, distributed storage systems, such as Hadoop or GlusterFS, can be used.

1.6 Network Requirements

AI models, especially those deployed in large-scale environments, often need fast and reliable networking to communicate between distributed compute nodes and access remote datasets.

Required Specs: High-throughput networks (such as 10Gbps Ethernet or InfiniBand) are recommended for multi-node AI clusters. Low-latency networks are also important to ensure the speed and reliability of communications, especially in real-time applications.

2. Software Requirements

Once the physical infrastructure is in place, the right software stack is critical for effective deployment. The software stack needs to support model deployment, orchestration, scaling, and monitoring.

2.1 Operating System (OS)

AI workloads require an OS that is optimized for high-performance computing and compatibility with various AI frameworks. Linux-based operating systems are commonly used in AI deployment due to their stability, open-source nature, and support for popular machine learning libraries.

Preferred OS: Ubuntu, CentOS, and Debian are popular choices in AI deployments. For on-premise deployment, you will also need an OS that supports GPU acceleration (e.g., NVIDIA's CUDA).

2.2 Machine Learning Frameworks

The selection of machine learning frameworks is key to AI deployment. The framework should match the specific AI tasks and the hardware it will run on. Some of the most widely used frameworks for AI deployment include:

- **TensorFlow**: A flexible framework for building and deploying machine learning models, particularly useful for deep learning.
- **PyTorch**: A deep learning framework popular for research and development, with growing adoption for production deployments.
- **ONNX (Open Neural Network Exchange):** A cross-platform framework designed for model portability between different AI tools.
- **Scikit-learn**: Used for simpler models, such as decision trees and random forests.

2.3 Model Deployment Tools

To efficiently deploy, monitor, and manage AI models, specific deployment tools and platforms are often used. These tools can automate many deployment tasks, including model scaling, versioning, and integration with other applications.

- **Kubernetes**: Often used for deploying containerized AI models at scale across clusters.
- **Docker**: For containerizing AI models and ensuring consistency across different environments.
- **TensorFlow Serving**: A specialized tool for serving TensorFlow models in production environments.
- **MLflow**: An open-source platform to manage the end-to-end machine learning lifecycle, including model deployment.

3. Data Management and Pipeline Infrastructure

AI models rely on clean, well-organized, and accessible data. For large-scale AI deployments, data pipelines and storage solutions must be robust, scalable, and secure.

3.1 Data Collection and Preprocessing

AI models typically require massive amounts of data to train, which needs to be collected, preprocessed, and stored. Organizations should implement pipelines to automatically collect and preprocess data, including filtering, cleaning, and transforming raw data into a format usable by AI models.

- **Tools**: Data pipeline tools such as Apache Kafka, Apache Spark, and Apache NiFi can automate and streamline the data collection and preprocessing process.

3.2 Real-Time Data Streaming and Batch Processing

Depending on the application, AI models may require real-time data streaming for inference (e.g., autonomous vehicles or surveillance systems), or batch processing for training large datasets. A combination of both may be necessary.

- **Real-Time Streaming**: Tools like Apache Kafka or Google Cloud Pub/Sub are used to stream data in real-time.
- **Batch Processing**: Data lakes and tools like Apache Hadoop or Amazon S3 are used for batch processing and storing large datasets.

3.3 Database and Storage Solutions

Data storage needs to be carefully considered, particularly when working with large datasets for training. Data can be stored in various forms, including structured data in databases and unstructured data in object storage.

- **Data Lakes**: Used to store raw, unprocessed data for future use.
- **Relational Databases**: For structured data that requires transactional integrity.
- **NoSQL Databases**: For large-scale, semi-structured, or unstructured data.
- **Distributed Storage**: Systems like HDFS or cloud storage services like AWS S3 can store large amounts of data.

4. Scalability and Load Balancing

AI deployments often require the ability to scale rapidly in response to changing demands, especially for models that require heavy computation. The infrastructure needs to support scaling both horizontally (adding more nodes) and vertically (increasing the power of existing nodes).

4.1 Horizontal Scaling

Horizontal scaling involves adding more compute nodes to a cluster to distribute the workload. This is essential for large AI workloads such as training deep learning models on vast datasets or running high-throughput inference for millions of requests.

Tools: Kubernetes is often used for orchestrating containers and managing clusters, ensuring scalable deployments.

4.2 Vertical Scaling

Vertical scaling refers to adding more computing resources (like memory, CPU, or GPU) to an individual node to handle heavier loads. Vertical scaling is typically useful for training large models where the available compute power needs to increase for specific tasks.

5. Monitoring and Maintenance Infrastructure

Once an AI model is deployed, continuous monitoring and maintenance are essential for ensuring optimal performance. This involves tracking various aspects such as latency, model drift, and resource consumption.

5.1 Monitoring Tools

Monitoring tools like Prometheus, Grafana, or AWS CloudWatch can track system performance and alert teams to any anomalies, such as degradation in inference quality or resource exhaustion.

5.2 Model Performance Management

AI models can drift over time as they are exposed to new data. Automated model performance tracking and retraining pipelines must be established to ensure the model continues to perform accurately.

Conclusion: Building the Right Infrastructure for AI

The infrastructure required for AI deployment must support high computational workloads, fast data pipelines, robust storage solutions, and efficient scaling mechanisms. Whether deploying AI on-premises, in the cloud, or a hybrid environment, understanding these infrastructure requirements ensures that AI systems run efficiently, securely, and at scale. With the right hardware, software, and data management infrastructure in place, businesses can harness the full potential of AI models in production, enabling valuable insights and real-time decision-making.

9.3 Running AI Workloads with Kubernetes and Docker

When deploying AI models in production environments, especially at scale, efficient management of computational resources and seamless orchestration of workloads is essential. Kubernetes and Docker are two widely adopted technologies that simplify containerization and orchestration of AI workloads, providing scalability, reliability, and flexibility in managing machine learning models and their associated infrastructure.

In this section, we'll explore how Kubernetes and Docker can be utilized to deploy and manage AI workloads efficiently, ensuring smooth integration, scaling, and monitoring. Let's break down how these tools can be applied to real-world AI deployment.

1. Introduction to Kubernetes and Docker

Before diving into how these tools can be used for AI workloads, it's important to understand their fundamental concepts and roles.

1.1 Docker: Containerization Simplified

Docker is a platform for developing, shipping, and running applications inside lightweight, portable containers. Containers are isolated environments that bundle an application and all of its dependencies (such as libraries, code, and configurations), ensuring that the application runs consistently across various environments.

In AI, Docker is particularly useful for packaging machine learning models and their dependencies, ensuring that the model can be moved across different stages of the pipeline (from development to production) without any compatibility issues.

Advantages of Docker for AI:

- **Portability**: AI models can be easily transferred between development, testing, and production environments.
- **Isolation**: Different models or versions of models can run in isolated containers without interfering with each other.
- **Consistency**: Docker ensures that the AI model behaves the same, regardless of where it is deployed, minimizing "works on my machine" issues.

1.2 Kubernetes: Orchestrating Containers at Scale

Kubernetes is an open-source container orchestration platform designed to automate the deployment, scaling, and management of containerized applications. Kubernetes helps manage clusters of Docker containers, ensuring that containers are running where and when they are needed, scaling automatically, and recovering from failures.

In the context of AI, Kubernetes is used to manage the deployment of models, scaling resources dynamically, and ensuring that the infrastructure runs smoothly, even under heavy workloads.

Advantages of Kubernetes for AI:

- **Scalability**: Automatically scale AI workloads by adding or removing containers based on resource utilization.
- **High Availability**: Kubernetes ensures that AI models remain operational by automatically restarting containers or redistributing workloads in the event of failures.
- **Resource Management**: Kubernetes optimizes the use of underlying hardware resources (CPU, memory, GPU), ensuring that AI workloads receive the resources they need.
- **Distributed Training**: Kubernetes can manage distributed training processes across multiple nodes, allowing large-scale models to be trained more efficiently.

2. Using Docker to Containerize AI Models

To begin with, containerizing your AI model using Docker ensures consistency across different environments, making it easier to deploy models to any system (whether on-premise or in the cloud). Here are the steps involved in containerizing AI workloads using Docker:

2.1 Setting Up the Dockerfile

A Dockerfile is a script that contains the instructions to build a Docker image. It specifies the base image, necessary dependencies, and commands for setting up the environment required to run your AI model.

Example of a Simple Dockerfile for AI Model Deployment:

```
# Use a base image with Python and required libraries
FROM python:3.8-slim

# Set up working directory
WORKDIR /app

# Copy necessary files (model, code, etc.)
COPY . /app

# Install dependencies
RUN pip install -r requirements.txt
```

```
# Expose port for the model server
EXPOSE 5000

# Command to start the model (e.g., with Flask API or TensorFlow Serving)
CMD ["python", "model_server.py"]
```

In this example, the Dockerfile uses a Python image, installs required libraries, copies the model and its code, and sets up the environment for running the model. The container exposes port 5000 for incoming requests (such as inference requests) and runs the model server.

2.2 Building and Running the Docker Container

After defining the Dockerfile, the next step is to build the Docker image and run the container:

Build the Docker Image:

```
docker build -t ai_model:latest .
```

Run the Docker Container:

```
docker run -p 5000:5000 ai_model:latest
```

This command will run the AI model container, making it accessible on port 5000. The model is now isolated within the container, and can be tested locally, or moved to production environments without worrying about dependencies or configuration issues.

2.3 Containerizing for Inference Servers

When deploying AI models for inference, particularly in web services or APIs, Docker is an ideal solution. Using frameworks like TensorFlow Serving, TorchServe, or a custom API (like Flask or FastAPI), you can easily expose the model for predictions.

For example, with TensorFlow Serving in Docker:

```
FROM tensorflow/serving:latest

# Copy model into serving directory
```

```
COPY ./saved_model /models/ai_model

# Expose TensorFlow Serving port
EXPOSE 8501

# Run TensorFlow Serving
ENTRYPOINT ["tensorflow_model_server", "--rest_api_port=8501", "--model_name=ai_model", "--model_base_path=/models/ai_model"]
```

This Dockerfile will allow you to run TensorFlow Serving in a container, serving the model via REST APIs for real-time inference.

3. Managing AI Workloads with Kubernetes

Once the AI models are containerized using Docker, Kubernetes provides the orchestration needed to deploy, manage, and scale these containers efficiently. Kubernetes handles deployment automation, resource allocation, and high availability for your AI workloads.

3.1 Creating a Kubernetes Cluster

The first step in using Kubernetes is to create a cluster, which is a group of nodes (virtual or physical machines) that Kubernetes manages. For cloud-based deployments, you can use managed Kubernetes services like Google Kubernetes Engine (GKE), Amazon Elastic Kubernetes Service (EKS), or Azure Kubernetes Service (AKS).

For on-premise setups, you can set up a Kubernetes cluster manually or using tools like Kubeadm.

3.2 Deploying AI Models Using Kubernetes

Once your cluster is ready, you can deploy your Dockerized AI model using Kubernetes Pods. A Pod is the smallest unit of deployment in Kubernetes, which can contain one or more containers. Here's how you can deploy an AI model on Kubernetes:

Example Kubernetes Deployment YAML for AI Model:

```
apiVersion: apps/v1
kind: Deployment
metadata:
```

```yaml
  name: ai-model-deployment
spec:
 replicas: 3  # Number of replicas (Pods)
 selector:
   matchLabels:
     app: ai-model
 template:
   metadata:
     labels:
       app: ai-model
   spec:
     containers:
       - name: ai-model-container
         image: ai_model:latest
         ports:
           - containerPort: 5000
---
apiVersion: v1
kind: Service
metadata:
 name: ai-model-service
spec:
 selector:
   app: ai-model
 ports:
   - protocol: TCP
     port: 80
     targetPort: 5000
 type: LoadBalancer
```

This YAML file defines a Kubernetes Deployment, which deploys multiple replicas (for high availability) of your AI model container. It also defines a Service to expose the model for external access, routing traffic to the available Pods.

3.3 Scaling AI Workloads with Kubernetes

Kubernetes makes it easy to scale AI workloads horizontally by adding more Pods based on the load. For example, if your AI model is receiving a high volume of inference requests, Kubernetes can automatically scale the number of Pods to handle the increased traffic:

kubectl scale deployment ai-model-deployment --replicas=5

Kubernetes will automatically adjust the number of Pods running the model to meet the demand. Additionally, Kubernetes supports auto-scaling, which can scale the number of replicas based on resource usage like CPU and memory.

3.4 Monitoring and Updating AI Models in Kubernetes

Kubernetes provides robust monitoring and management tools to track the performance and health of your AI workloads. You can use Prometheus and Grafana for real-time monitoring, and kubectl to track logs and troubleshoot issues.

When you need to update your AI model, Kubernetes supports rolling updates, allowing you to update the Docker container without downtime:

kubectl set image deployment/ai-model-deployment ai-model-container=ai_model:new_version

This will initiate a rolling update, updating the containers one by one to ensure continuous availability.

4. Conclusion: Efficient AI Deployment with Kubernetes and Docker

By combining Docker and Kubernetes, AI models can be deployed at scale, with the flexibility to adapt to changing requirements. Docker simplifies the process of packaging and distributing AI models, while Kubernetes provides robust orchestration, scaling, and management of AI workloads in a distributed environment. Together, these tools enable AI developers and operators to deploy production-ready models with ease, ensuring that they are performant, scalable, and reliable in real-world applications.

9.4 High-Performance Computing for AI

As AI models become more complex and computationally intensive, particularly in areas like deep learning, High-Performance Computing (HPC) has emerged as a crucial component in deploying AI workloads at scale. HPC enables the processing of massive datasets, the training of large models, and real-time inferences, all of which are essential for modern AI applications.

In this section, we will explore the importance of HPC for AI, the technologies involved, and how HPC solutions can significantly enhance the deployment and execution of AI workloads in production environments.

1. Understanding High-Performance Computing (HPC)

High-Performance Computing refers to the use of advanced computational techniques and powerful hardware systems to perform complex calculations and process large volumes of data. HPC systems typically use clusters of powerful processors that work together to solve problems faster than a single computer could.

For AI, HPC provides the computational muscle required to train complex models, process vast amounts of data, and scale workloads across multiple machines or nodes.

1.1 Key Components of HPC Systems for AI

HPC systems designed for AI workloads generally consist of the following key components:

- **Parallel Processing**: The ability to perform multiple computations simultaneously, a critical feature for tasks like matrix multiplication and optimization, which are central to AI model training.
- **Multi-GPU/TPU Setup**: Graphics Processing Units (GPUs) and Tensor Processing Units (TPUs) are specialized hardware accelerators that significantly speed up AI computations. HPC systems leverage multi-GPU or multi-TPU setups to process large-scale AI tasks faster and more efficiently.
- **Distributed Computing**: HPC often involves the use of multiple interconnected machines or nodes, each with its own computing resources. This distributed setup allows AI tasks to be spread across different machines, reducing training times and improving efficiency.
- **High-Speed Networking**: To ensure efficient data transfer between the computing nodes, HPC systems typically include high-speed networking technologies, such as InfiniBand, which reduces latency and improves throughput.

These components work in tandem to create an environment capable of handling the intensive demands of modern AI workloads.

2. Why HPC is Essential for AI Deployment

AI applications, particularly those involving deep learning, require substantial computational power. Training large neural networks, for example, often demands tens of thousands of operations per second, especially for tasks like image recognition or natural language processing. Traditional computing setups may struggle to handle these requirements efficiently, leading to long training times or slow inference performance.

2.1 Speeding Up AI Model Training

Training deep learning models on large datasets is computationally expensive and time-consuming. Without HPC, training a model on a large dataset can take days, weeks, or even months, depending on the model size. HPC systems, equipped with powerful GPUs or TPUs, can significantly reduce training times by processing multiple tasks in parallel.

- **Example**: A convolutional neural network (CNN) for image classification can require thousands of iterations over millions of images to achieve satisfactory accuracy. Using GPUs in parallel, this process can be reduced from weeks to days, enabling faster experimentation and model improvements.

2.2 Efficient Data Processing for AI

AI models require large amounts of data for training. HPC systems are equipped with high-speed storage and computing capabilities to handle this data at scale. By enabling efficient data processing, HPC allows for the ingestion, transformation, and analysis of big data, making it possible to train models on real-world, large-scale datasets that would otherwise be infeasible on standard systems.

- **Example**: Training a recommendation system using user behavior data from millions of users requires significant storage and processing power. HPC solutions can handle the vast volume of data, efficiently preparing it for training in much less time.

2.3 Enabling Real-Time Inference

For certain AI applications, real-time or near-real-time inference is crucial. For example, autonomous vehicles rely on AI models to make decisions in real-time, processing sensor data and adapting to the environment instantly. HPC can enable the rapid execution of AI models by providing the computational resources required for high-speed inference.

- **Example**: In real-time fraud detection, the system must process and analyze a large volume of transactions as they occur. HPC systems allow the AI model to perform inference within milliseconds, ensuring that fraudulent activity is detected and addressed immediately.

3. HPC Technologies and Solutions for AI

AI deployments benefit greatly from the integration of various HPC technologies. Below, we explore some of the most commonly used solutions in AI production environments.

3.1 GPUs (Graphics Processing Units) and TPUs (Tensor Processing Units)

GPUs are the backbone of modern AI computation, particularly in deep learning, due to their ability to perform parallel calculations at high speed. GPUs can handle the massive amounts of matrix multiplications involved in training neural networks, dramatically accelerating the process compared to traditional CPUs.

- **NVIDIA GPUs**: NVIDIA's GPU architecture, with frameworks like CUDA, is widely used for training AI models. NVIDIA's A100 and V100 GPUs are particularly popular in AI workloads, offering high computational power and efficient memory handling.
- **Google TPUs**: Tensor Processing Units (TPUs) are custom-built accelerators designed by Google specifically for machine learning workloads. TPUs offer high throughput for tensor processing and can dramatically reduce training times for deep learning models.

3.2 Distributed AI Workloads

When training extremely large AI models or working with enormous datasets, the computational load can exceed the capabilities of a single machine. Distributed computing involves splitting the workload across multiple machines or nodes, each contributing processing power.

- **Distributed Training Frameworks**: Tools like Horovod, TensorFlow Distributed, and PyTorch Distributed allow AI models to be trained across multiple machines with GPUs. These frameworks handle the distribution of data and computation, ensuring efficient parallelization of training processes.

3.3 Cloud-Based HPC for AI

Many organizations are turning to cloud providers to access high-performance computing resources without investing in expensive on-premise hardware. Cloud platforms like

AWS, Google Cloud, and Microsoft Azure provide scalable HPC solutions for AI workloads, offering access to powerful GPUs, TPUs, and clusters of machines.

- **AWS EC2 P3 Instances**: AWS provides high-performance instances like the P3 series, which are equipped with NVIDIA V100 GPUs, suitable for deep learning model training and inference.
- **Google Cloud AI Platform**: Google Cloud offers AI Platform Training and Prediction, which allows users to scale their AI workloads using TPUs and GPUs on demand.
- **Azure N-Series VMs:** Microsoft Azure's N-Series virtual machines offer GPU-powered instances, optimized for training AI models and performing inference in the cloud.

3.4 High-Speed Networking and Storage

AI workloads often involve large datasets that need to be transferred quickly between compute nodes. High-speed networking, such as InfiniBand or Ethernet, is essential for minimizing latency and maximizing throughput. Additionally, AI workloads require substantial storage for datasets, checkpoints, and model parameters.

- **Example**: InfiniBand networking is commonly used in supercomputing clusters, providing low-latency, high-throughput communication between nodes, ensuring that large datasets are efficiently passed between GPUs and storage.

4. Best Practices for Integrating HPC in AI Deployment

Integrating HPC for AI workloads requires careful planning and optimization. Here are some best practices to consider when leveraging HPC in AI deployment:

4.1 Optimize Model Architecture

Although HPC can accelerate training, it's still important to design efficient models. Simplifying model architecture and reducing unnecessary parameters can help reduce computation time without sacrificing performance. Techniques like model pruning, quantization, and knowledge distillation can help achieve this.

4.2 Leverage Hybrid Computing Models

A hybrid approach that combines on-premise hardware with cloud resources can provide flexibility, allowing you to scale AI workloads on demand. You can start training on-premise and then offload heavy computational tasks to the cloud during peak demand times.

4.3 Monitor Resource Utilization

Efficient resource management is key to maximizing the value of HPC systems. Monitoring tools like Prometheus or Grafana can help track GPU utilization, memory usage, and CPU load, ensuring that resources are used optimally.

5. Conclusion: The Power of HPC in AI Deployment

High-Performance Computing plays a critical role in the successful deployment of AI models, enabling faster training times, efficient data processing, and real-time inference. With the ability to scale AI workloads across multiple nodes and leverage specialized hardware accelerators like GPUs and TPUs, HPC allows organizations to meet the increasing computational demands of modern AI applications. By integrating HPC technologies into AI workflows, businesses can stay competitive and accelerate innovation, making it an essential component of AI deployment in production environments.

10. Deploying AI with APIs and Microservices

AI models become truly useful when they can be easily integrated into applications and services. In this chapter, we explore how to deploy AI using APIs and microservices, enabling seamless communication between models and business applications. You'll learn how to build RESTful and gRPC APIs for AI inference using frameworks like FastAPI, Flask, and TensorFlow Serving. We also cover best practices for scalability, load balancing, and security in microservices-based AI architectures. By mastering API and microservices deployment, you can make AI solutions accessible, modular, and efficient across various platforms and industries.

10.1 Introduction to AI Model APIs

As artificial intelligence (AI) continues to integrate into various industries, the need for scalable and efficient methods of serving AI models in production environments has become crucial. One of the most effective ways to enable this integration is through the use of AI Model APIs (Application Programming Interfaces). APIs act as intermediaries that allow software applications to communicate with each other, and when it comes to AI, they provide an interface for interacting with machine learning models, enabling their deployment, usage, and integration with other systems.

In this chapter, we will explore the concept of AI model APIs, the benefits they offer, and how they enable organizations to deploy and scale AI solutions in production. By the end of this section, you will have a clear understanding of how AI model APIs fit into the overall deployment strategy and how to implement them effectively.

What Are AI Model APIs?

AI Model APIs are specialized interfaces that expose machine learning models to external applications. These APIs allow external systems to interact with AI models to perform tasks such as prediction (inference), training, and batch processing, without requiring the user to have direct access to the underlying code or model. They act as a bridge between the model and other software systems or applications, facilitating communication and interaction.

For example, a machine learning model trained to classify images can be wrapped into an API. Once deployed, other applications can send image data to this API, and the model will return the classification results. The simplicity and ease of access provided by APIs are crucial for enabling AI models to be used effectively across various environments.

Why Are AI Model APIs Important?

The growing adoption of AI in production systems demands efficient, scalable, and secure ways to serve machine learning models. AI Model APIs address these needs by offering several key benefits:

1. Seamless Integration

By providing a standardized interface, AI Model APIs allow different applications, platforms, and devices to interact with models without worrying about the intricacies of the underlying code. Whether it's a web application, mobile app, or IoT device, any system that can make HTTP requests can interact with the AI model API, ensuring smooth integration into existing workflows.

2. Scalability

One of the challenges of AI deployment is the ability to scale the model to handle a growing number of requests. APIs can be hosted on scalable cloud platforms or containerized environments, where requests can be distributed across multiple instances, ensuring that the system can handle increased traffic without compromising performance.

3. Flexibility and Abstraction

AI Model APIs abstract away the complexity of model architecture and deployment. Developers don't need to be concerned with how the model is trained or its internal mechanics. They only need to focus on integrating the API into their applications and making requests for predictions or other operations.

4. Security and Access Control

By wrapping models in an API, developers can control access to the model, limit the number of requests, and implement security protocols such as authentication and authorization. This adds a layer of protection around the AI model, ensuring that only authorized users or systems can interact with it.

5. Versioning and Maintenance

APIs allow for version control of machine learning models. Over time, models may need to be updated, retrained, or replaced. With an API, you can maintain backward compatibility with existing users or systems while making changes to the underlying model. The API can also handle model rollback, ensuring a smooth transition between versions.

How Do AI Model APIs Work?

AI Model APIs typically follow a client-server architecture. The client, which can be any application or service, makes an HTTP request to the server, which hosts the model. The server processes the request, performs the necessary operations on the input data (such as inference or training), and then returns the result back to the client.

The basic flow of an AI Model API is as follows:

Model Deployment: After training a machine learning model, the model is wrapped in an API. This could be done using frameworks like Flask, FastAPI, Django, or cloud services like AWS SageMaker, Google AI Platform, or Azure Machine Learning. These frameworks enable the creation of RESTful APIs that expose the model for interaction.

Request to the API: The client sends an HTTP request (e.g., a POST or GET request) to the API endpoint with input data, such as an image, text, or a structured data query.

Processing and Inference: The API receives the input, processes it, and passes the data to the machine learning model. The model then makes predictions or performs inference based on the provided data.

Response: After the model has processed the input data, it returns the output (e.g., prediction, classification, or recommendation) as a response to the client.

Integration: The client application uses the returned data to take further action or provide feedback to the user, integrating the model's capabilities into the larger system or application.

Popular Frameworks and Tools for Building AI Model APIs

There are several frameworks and tools available for building and deploying AI Model APIs. Some of the most commonly used include:

1. Flask

Flask is a lightweight Python web framework that is often used for building RESTful APIs. With Flask, you can easily create an API endpoint for serving machine learning models. It is a popular choice for rapid prototyping and smaller-scale applications.

- **Use Case**: Ideal for smaller projects or when you need a lightweight solution.
- **Example**: Wrap a pre-trained scikit-learn model into a Flask API to classify data.

2. FastAPI

FastAPI is a modern, fast, web framework for building APIs with Python 3.7+ that is based on standard Python type hints. It is known for its performance and automatic generation of documentation (Swagger UI) for the API.

- **Use Case**: Recommended for high-performance applications or APIs that need to handle high throughput.
- **Example**: Serving deep learning models with TensorFlow or PyTorch via FastAPI to achieve low-latency predictions.

3. TensorFlow Serving

TensorFlow Serving is an open-source framework specifically designed for serving TensorFlow models in production. It is highly optimized for serving models and provides built-in functionalities for batch inference, multi-model serving, and version management.

- **Use Case**: Best for TensorFlow models in large-scale production environments.
- **Example**: Deploy a pre-trained TensorFlow model for image classification through TensorFlow Serving.

4. AWS Lambda and API Gateway

AWS Lambda allows you to run machine learning models without managing servers. Combined with API Gateway, it enables the creation of serverless APIs for AI models, allowing automatic scaling based on incoming requests.

- **Use Case**: Suitable for serverless applications or when you want to scale effortlessly.
- **Example**: Deploying a model as a Lambda function and using API Gateway to expose the API.

5. Google AI Platform and Cloud Functions

Google Cloud offers managed services such as Google AI Platform and Cloud Functions that make it easy to deploy and manage AI models. With these services, you can quickly expose AI models as RESTful APIs and leverage Google's infrastructure for scaling.

- **Use Case:** Ideal for businesses already using Google Cloud or looking for managed AI model deployment solutions.
- **Example**: Deploy a model on Google AI Platform and create an API endpoint to make predictions.

AI Model APIs are an essential tool for integrating machine learning models into production environments. They offer scalability, flexibility, security, and simplified interaction between AI models and applications. By exposing AI models via APIs, businesses can unlock the full potential of their machine learning models, making them accessible to different applications, users, and devices. Whether you're working with computer vision, natural language processing, or predictive analytics, AI Model APIs provide the foundation for building powerful and scalable AI systems that can be deployed efficiently in production.

10.2 REST vs. gRPC for AI Deployment

When deploying AI models in production, one of the most important decisions is how to expose these models for use by other systems, applications, or services. Two of the most popular technologies for creating APIs that serve machine learning models are REST and gRPC. Both are widely used, but they have distinct differences that make them suited for different types of use cases. Understanding when and why to use each of these protocols is essential for ensuring efficient, scalable, and effective deployment of AI models.

In this section, we will compare REST (Representational State Transfer) and gRPC (Google Remote Procedure Call) in the context of AI deployment, discussing their differences, advantages, and use cases.

What is REST?

REST is an architectural style for designing networked applications, primarily using HTTP as the communication protocol. It is widely known for its simplicity and ease of use, making it a popular choice for web-based applications and services. RESTful APIs rely on standard HTTP methods such as GET, POST, PUT, DELETE, etc., to perform operations on resources that are represented as URLs. Data is typically transferred in JSON or XML formats.

How REST Works in AI Deployment

When deploying AI models, REST APIs provide a straightforward way to expose machine learning models. A model is often wrapped in an HTTP server (using frameworks such as Flask, FastAPI, or Django) that listens for incoming requests. The AI model performs predictions or inference based on the request and returns the results via an HTTP response.

For example, an image classification model could be deployed as a REST API where users can send an image through an HTTP POST request, and the model would return the predicted labels.

What is gRPC?

gRPC is a high-performance, open-source remote procedure call (RPC) framework developed by Google. It is designed for communication between services in distributed systems and enables efficient, low-latency communication using HTTP/2 for transport. gRPC uses Protocol Buffers (protobuf) as its serialization format, which is more compact and faster to process than JSON or XML typically used by REST.

How gRPC Works in AI Deployment

With gRPC, instead of sending and receiving data through HTTP request/response pairs as in REST, clients call methods on remote servers as though they were local methods. This approach is highly efficient and provides support for bidirectional streaming, multiplexing multiple requests over a single connection, and automatically handling retries, all of which are crucial for scalable AI deployments.

For example, a language model that performs real-time translations might use gRPC for rapid interaction, where requests and responses can be processed as streams, minimizing the latency associated with HTTP/1.1-based REST communication.

Key Differences Between REST and gRPC

Below is a comparison of REST and gRPC based on various important criteria when deploying AI models:

Criteria	REST	gRPC
Protocol	HTTP/1.1	HTTP/2
Serialization Format	JSON or XML	Protocol Buffers (protobuf)
Ease of Use	Simple and easy to implement; widely supported in various languages and frameworks.	Requires knowledge of Protocol Buffers and service definition files.
Performance	Slower compared to gRPC due to text-based JSON format and HTTP/1.1 overhead.	Faster due to compact Protocol Buffers and multiplexing capabilities in HTTP/2.
Support for Streaming	Limited support for streaming, typically handled via HTTP long-polling or WebSockets.	Native support for bidirectional streaming, useful for continuous data exchange.
Latency	Generally higher due to the overhead of text-based communication (JSON) and HTTP/1.1 protocol.	Lower latency thanks to Protocol Buffers and HTTP/2 multiplexing.
Scalability	Scales well for simple applications but can be less efficient for high-volume, low-latency services.	Better suited for highly scalable, low-latency, and high-throughput environments.
Security	Relies on HTTPS for security and encryption.	Uses HTTP/2's built-in security features, such as multiplexing, along with SSL/TLS for encryption.
API Design	Based on stateless interactions (resources exposed via URLs).	Based on service definitions, where clients call specific methods on the server.
Language Support	Excellent support across all major languages (Python, JavaScript, Java, etc.).	Support for all major languages, though requires specific libraries (e.g., gRPC libraries for Python, Go, etc.).
Tooling	Extensive tooling for documentation, testing, and monitoring.	Growing set of tools, but not as widely available as REST for general web use cases.

When to Use REST for AI Model Deployment

Despite its higher latency compared to gRPC, REST remains one of the most widely used options for exposing AI models in production. Its simplicity and widespread adoption make it an excellent choice for many AI use cases.

Advantages of Using REST for AI Deployment:

- **Widespread Compatibility**: RESTful APIs can be easily consumed by any platform that supports HTTP, making it ideal for applications that need to interact with AI models across diverse environments (e.g., web browsers, mobile apps, IoT devices).
- **Ease of Implementation**: Since REST APIs are built on top of HTTP, which is a universally supported protocol, they are simple to implement and integrate into most applications without requiring specialized knowledge of Protocol Buffers.
- **Human-readable Data Format**: The JSON format used in REST APIs is human-readable and easy to debug, making it convenient for development and testing.
- **Stateless Architecture**: REST is stateless, which simplifies API design and makes scaling easier, as each request is independent and does not rely on prior interactions.

Use Cases for REST in AI Deployment:

- **Web and Mobile Applications**: AI models that serve image classification, text recognition, and other typical AI use cases often benefit from the simplicity and accessibility of REST APIs.
- **SaaS Applications**: SaaS platforms that expose AI models for analysis, such as sentiment analysis or predictive analytics, can use REST APIs to integrate the models into customer workflows.
- **Prototyping**: For rapid prototyping of AI models, REST is a great choice due to the ease of use and quick implementation.

When to Use gRPC for AI Model Deployment

While REST is often the go-to for AI model deployment, gRPC offers several compelling advantages for certain high-performance, low-latency, or real-time use cases.

Advantages of Using gRPC for AI Deployment:

- **Performance and Efficiency**: gRPC's use of HTTP/2 and Protocol Buffers results in faster, more efficient communication, especially for high-throughput applications. The binary serialization of Protocol Buffers reduces the overhead compared to JSON, allowing more data to be transmitted in less time.
- **Low Latency**: gRPC supports bidirectional streaming and multiplexing, which makes it ideal for applications that require continuous data exchange or real-time processing with minimal latency.

- **Scalability**: Due to its efficient communication and built-in support for handling a large number of requests concurrently, gRPC is well-suited for high-volume AI applications where low-latency responses are essential.
- **Advanced Features**: gRPC supports features like retries, deadlines, and load balancing, which make it more robust in production environments where performance and reliability are critical.

Use Cases for gRPC in AI Deployment:

- **Real-time AI Applications**: Use cases such as autonomous vehicles, online fraud detection, or AI-driven recommendation systems where latency is a critical factor.
- **High-Volume, High-Performance Services**: Large-scale AI workloads, such as natural language processing (NLP) or real-time speech-to-text, that require fast processing and low-latency interactions between the client and server.
- **IoT and Edge Devices**: Systems that deploy AI models on edge devices, where fast, efficient communication between devices and the server is required.

Both REST and gRPC are excellent choices for deploying AI models, but they cater to different needs and use cases. REST is ideal for simple, widely compatible applications where ease of use and human-readable data formats are priorities. On the other hand, gRPC excels in high-performance, low-latency environments where real-time communication, scalability, and efficiency are paramount.

When deciding between REST and gRPC for your AI deployment, it's essential to evaluate the requirements of your application, such as latency sensitivity, scalability, performance, and the complexity of interactions with the AI model. By choosing the right communication protocol, you can ensure that your AI models are deployed in the most efficient and effective manner possible.

10.3 Building Microservices for AI Models

As organizations scale their AI-driven solutions, the need for more modular, maintainable, and flexible systems grows. One of the most effective architectural patterns for managing such complex systems is the microservices architecture. Microservices are small, independent services that work together to achieve a larger goal. In the context of AI, microservices allow AI models to be isolated, deployed, scaled, and updated independently, making it easier to manage and iterate on different parts of the system.

This chapter will guide you through the process of building microservices specifically for AI models, exploring the benefits, design principles, and best practices for deploying AI models in a microservices-based architecture.

What Are Microservices?

A microservice architecture is an approach to software development where an application is broken down into small, independent services, each of which performs a specific task. These services interact with each other via APIs and communicate over a network, typically using protocols like HTTP or gRPC. Each service is responsible for its own domain and data, and they are loosely coupled, meaning changes in one service don't directly affect others.

For AI model deployment, this means that different models, or even different parts of the same AI pipeline (e.g., data preprocessing, inference, post-processing), can be encapsulated within separate microservices. These microservices can be developed, deployed, scaled, and updated independently, which makes the system more flexible, scalable, and easier to maintain.

Why Build Microservices for AI Models?

Microservices offer several key advantages for deploying AI models in production environments. Some of the most notable benefits include:

1. Scalability

With microservices, each AI model or component of the model pipeline can be scaled independently. For example, if one model is receiving significantly more traffic or requires more computational power, it can be scaled without impacting other models or parts of the system. This helps optimize resource usage and ensures that your system can handle large workloads.

2. Flexibility and Maintainability

Each microservice is a self-contained unit, making it easier to update, test, and deploy AI models. This allows for more frequent iterations on individual models without disrupting the entire application. For example, if a new version of a machine learning model is ready, you can deploy it as a new microservice and update the existing deployment incrementally.

3. Modularity

AI models can be complex, with multiple components involved in the data pipeline, training, and inference. By using microservices, you can break down each stage of the process into separate services. This modularity enables better management of different parts of the pipeline, such as training services, inference services, and data processing services.

4. Technology Agnostic

In a microservice architecture, different services can be written in different languages or frameworks. For example, one microservice may be built using Python for data science tasks (such as AI model training), while another might use Go or Node.js to handle the web API interface. This flexibility allows teams to choose the best technology for each service, depending on the specific requirements of that part of the system.

5. Fault Isolation

Since each microservice operates independently, failures in one service will not affect others. If a particular AI model microservice crashes or encounters issues, it can be restarted without causing downtime in the entire system. This isolation improves the overall resilience and uptime of the deployment.

Designing AI Microservices

Building microservices for AI models requires careful design to ensure scalability, maintainability, and performance. Below are key principles and strategies for designing effective AI microservices:

1. Define Clear Boundaries for Each Service

Each microservice should have a clear responsibility. For AI, this might mean separating different models or parts of the pipeline. Some potential microservices in an AI deployment might include:

- **Preprocessing Microservice**: Handles data cleaning, transformation, and feature engineering.
- **Model Inference Microservice**: Runs the machine learning model to make predictions or classifications.

- **Post-processing Microservice**: Handles the processing of the raw model output, such as converting model predictions into a readable format or generating reports.
- **Model Training Microservice**: Periodically retrains the model on new data to ensure it remains accurate.

By defining clear boundaries between services, you can isolate the responsibilities and dependencies of each microservice, making it easier to maintain and evolve them over time.

2. Containerization with Docker

Docker is a powerful tool for containerizing microservices, ensuring they can be packaged along with their dependencies, such as model weights, libraries, and frameworks. By creating Docker containers for your AI microservices, you ensure that the models and their environments are portable and can be deployed consistently across different platforms and environments.

For example, you can create a Docker container for a Python-based model inference microservice, including all the necessary dependencies (such as TensorFlow, PyTorch, or scikit-learn). Once packaged into a container, the microservice can be deployed on any system with Docker installed, making the deployment process straightforward.

3. Use APIs for Communication

Microservices communicate with each other using APIs, often REST or gRPC. In the case of AI model microservices, you'll typically expose endpoints that allow other services to make requests and receive responses.

For instance:

- The preprocessing microservice might expose an endpoint that accepts raw data and returns a transformed version of that data ready for inference.
- The inference microservice could expose an endpoint that accepts the processed data and returns predictions or recommendations.
- The post-processing microservice might return the final formatted output, such as a report or visualization.

By using standardized APIs, you ensure that microservices can be easily integrated, updated, and scaled independently of one another.

4. Implement Version Control and Model Management

As machine learning models evolve over time, you need to implement version control for both your models and your microservices. Model versioning allows you to track and manage changes to your AI models, making it easier to roll back to earlier versions if needed.

Some strategies for versioning AI models in microservices include:

- **Model Registry**: Use a model registry to store and track versions of models. Platforms like MLflow, DVC (Data Version Control), and TensorFlow Model Management offer solutions for managing models throughout their lifecycle.
- **Microservice Versioning**: Each microservice should be versioned, allowing for backward compatibility when updating models or other components of the pipeline.

Version control ensures that you can safely deploy new models without disrupting the functionality of existing services or impacting the user experience.

Deploying AI Microservices

After designing the microservices and implementing best practices, you can deploy the services into a production environment. The deployment process typically involves:

1. Container Orchestration with Kubernetes

When deploying multiple microservices, it's important to automate the deployment, scaling, and management of containers. Kubernetes is the most popular container orchestration platform, enabling the management of containerized applications at scale. It provides features like automatic scaling, load balancing, and health checks, which are essential for managing AI microservices in production.

For example, you can deploy a set of model inference microservices across multiple Kubernetes nodes, ensuring that traffic is load-balanced and that instances are scaled up or down based on demand.

2. Continuous Integration and Continuous Deployment (CI/CD)

To ensure that updates to the AI models or microservices are deployed smoothly and reliably, you can implement CI/CD pipelines. This involves automating the process of testing, building, and deploying code changes, which is especially important for AI applications that evolve over time. Tools like Jenkins, GitLab CI/CD, or GitHub Actions can help automate the deployment process for AI microservices.

Best Practices for Building AI Microservices

- **Decouple the Model from Application Logic**: The AI model should be treated as a service that can be updated independently. Avoid coupling the model directly to the application logic to ensure flexibility and scalability.
- **Implement Robust Logging and Monitoring**: Ensure that all AI microservices include comprehensive logging and monitoring to track performance, detect issues, and debug errors.
- **Handle Model Failures Gracefully**: Since AI models can sometimes produce unexpected results or errors, ensure that microservices implement error-handling mechanisms, such as fallbacks or retries, to maintain reliability.
- **Optimize for Performance**: AI models can be resource-intensive. Ensure that your microservices are optimized for performance by caching frequently used data, optimizing model inference, and minimizing latency.

Building microservices for AI models provides a flexible, scalable, and maintainable way to deploy and manage machine learning applications in production. By breaking down AI workloads into modular microservices, organizations can develop, deploy, and scale their AI solutions independently, enabling rapid iteration and continuous improvement. With the right design principles, containerization, API integration, and deployment strategies, microservices can significantly enhance the efficiency and reliability of AI model deployments in real-world applications.

10.4 API Security and Rate Limiting

As AI models become increasingly integrated into production environments, the role of APIs in enabling communication between different services, applications, and users has never been more important. APIs act as gateways for accessing AI models, making them a critical part of AI deployment. However, with great access comes great responsibility— APIs need to be secured to protect both sensitive data and intellectual property, while also ensuring they are not overwhelmed by excessive or malicious traffic. This is where API security and rate limiting come into play.

This chapter will explore the key aspects of API security for AI models, including common threats, security best practices, and strategies for ensuring that AI-powered services are both protected and performant. We will also delve into the importance of rate limiting, a technique to prevent abuse, manage system resources, and ensure fair usage.

What Is API Security?

API security refers to the measures and protocols that are implemented to protect an API from unauthorized access, misuse, and attacks. Since APIs often serve as the primary interface for interacting with AI models and their underlying systems, they need to be secured to prevent data breaches, malicious attacks, and unintended usage. Security in the context of APIs is critical for protecting sensitive data (such as user information and model outputs), ensuring compliance with regulations (like GDPR), and maintaining the integrity and availability of the services.

Some of the most common threats to APIs include:

- **Authentication Bypassing**: Attackers trying to access the API by exploiting weak authentication mechanisms.
- **Data Interception**: The risk of data being intercepted during transmission, particularly sensitive or proprietary information.
- **Denial of Service (DoS)**: Attacks aimed at overwhelming the API with traffic to disrupt service availability.
- **Injection Attacks**: Attempts to inject malicious code into the API requests, such as SQL or XML injection.
- **Misuse of Endpoints**: Unintended use of API endpoints, resulting in overuse or exploitation.

Securing APIs is essential for maintaining the integrity and confidentiality of AI systems, especially as AI models are deployed in mission-critical applications.

Core Elements of API Security

To protect AI models and their deployment via APIs, several core security measures need to be in place. These measures focus on controlling access, ensuring data privacy, and guarding against unauthorized manipulation.

1. Authentication and Authorization

Authentication and authorization are two fundamental aspects of securing any API.

Authentication ensures that only valid users or services can access the API. The most commonly used methods for API authentication are:

- **API Keys**: A unique key assigned to each user or service, passed along with each API request.
- **OAuth**: A widely used authorization framework that allows users to grant third-party applications limited access to their data without exposing passwords.
- **JWT (JSON Web Tokens):** A token-based system where an API verifies a user's identity and grants access based on the issued token.

Authorization determines what actions authenticated users or services are allowed to perform. In a microservice architecture for AI, this might include limiting access to certain parts of the system, such as the model inference service, based on the user's role.

2. Encryption

Encryption ensures that data in transit and data at rest remain confidential and cannot be intercepted or tampered with.

- **TLS/SSL Encryption**: Use HTTPS (Hypertext Transfer Protocol Secure) for all API communication to ensure encryption of data in transit between the client and the server.
- **End-to-End Encryption**: This ensures that data is encrypted from the client to the server and prevents third parties from reading the data in between.
- **Data Encryption at Rest**: Store sensitive information (such as personal data or model weights) in encrypted databases or file systems to protect it from unauthorized access.

3. API Gateway and Firewall

An API Gateway serves as a reverse proxy between the client and the backend AI services. The API gateway is often the first line of defense, handling API requests, load balancing, and routing them to the appropriate services. It can also enforce security rules such as rate limiting, authentication, and logging.

In addition, an API firewall can detect and block potential attacks, filtering out malicious traffic and protecting the backend services from common attack vectors.

4. Input Validation and Data Sanitization

Input validation ensures that data submitted to the API is in the correct format, preventing attackers from sending harmful data that could exploit vulnerabilities. Data sanitization removes any harmful elements in the input that could result in SQL injection, cross-site scripting (XSS), or other types of attacks.

When processing input data for AI models, it's essential to validate the data format (e.g., checking for required fields or ensuring that numerical inputs fall within expected ranges) and sanitize inputs to prevent malicious code from being executed.

What Is Rate Limiting?

Rate limiting is a technique used to control the number of requests a user or service can make to an API within a given period. This is essential for managing traffic and ensuring that the API remains available and performant, especially during periods of high demand. Without rate limiting, an API can become overwhelmed by too many requests, which could lead to slow response times, service degradation, or even complete service failure.

Rate limiting also serves as a deterrent against malicious attacks, such as Denial of Service (DoS) or Distributed Denial of Service (DDoS) attacks, where attackers flood the API with large numbers of requests to overload the system.

There are different strategies for rate limiting, such as:

- **Fixed Window Rate Limiting**: This approach limits the number of requests within a fixed time window, such as allowing 100 requests per minute. Once the window expires, the count is reset.
- **Sliding Window Rate Limiting**: A more flexible version of fixed window limiting, where the time window "slides" forward. For example, if a user makes a request every 10 seconds, the window moves forward with each request.
- **Token Bucket**: This strategy allows bursts of requests while maintaining a steady flow over time. The API is given a "bucket" of tokens, and each request consumes a token. Tokens are added back over time, allowing for bursts of requests when necessary.
- Implementing Rate Limiting for AI APIs

AI models can be resource-intensive, especially for high-complexity tasks such as image classification or language generation. To ensure that resources are used efficiently and to avoid overwhelming the system, rate limiting can be used for both external users and internal services.

- **External Users**: For APIs exposed to the public or to clients, you can apply rate limiting to ensure fair usage, prevent abuse, and protect your infrastructure. For example, you might limit the number of requests a user can make to an AI model API to 100 requests per hour.
- **Internal Services**: Rate limiting is also useful when different microservices in a distributed system need to interact. For instance, a service that processes data for model inference might be rate-limited to prevent it from overloading the system and slowing down other tasks.

To configure rate limiting, an API Gateway or a reverse proxy like NGINX or Kong can be used. These tools provide built-in support for rate limiting, allowing you to define policies based on IP address, user account, or other request attributes.

Best Practices for API Security and Rate Limiting

To ensure that your AI model APIs are secure and performant, consider the following best practices:

- **Use Secure Authentication Methods**: Implement strong authentication mechanisms such as OAuth2 and JWT tokens to verify the identity of users and services.
- **Implement Role-Based Access Control**: Limit access to different API endpoints based on the user's role, ensuring that only authorized users can access sensitive or critical functions.
- **Encrypt Sensitive Data**: Ensure that all sensitive data is encrypted in transit and at rest to protect it from unauthorized access.
- Validate Inputs: Always validate input data to prevent injection attacks and ensure data integrity.
- **Apply Rate Limiting Strategically**: Use rate limiting to prevent abuse, protect system resources, and ensure fair usage. Define appropriate limits based on the expected traffic and model requirements.
- **Monitor API Usage**: Regularly monitor API usage to detect unusual traffic patterns that may indicate a security breach or excessive load.
- **Use API Management Tools**: Leverage API management platforms (such as AWS API Gateway or Azure API Management) to enforce security policies, handle rate limiting, and monitor API traffic.

API security and rate limiting are essential components of a robust AI deployment strategy. Securing AI APIs helps protect sensitive data, intellectual property, and system resources, while rate limiting ensures that services remain performant and resilient under heavy traffic. By implementing authentication, encryption, and rate limiting techniques, organizations can safeguard their AI-powered applications, ensuring reliable service delivery while preventing abuse and maintaining system integrity.

11. MLOps: Automating AI Deployment

Deploying AI models is not a one-time task—it requires continuous integration, monitoring, and optimization to ensure long-term success. MLOps (Machine Learning Operations) automates and streamlines the AI deployment pipeline, making it more scalable, reproducible, and maintainable. In this chapter, we explore the key components of MLOps, including CI/CD pipelines, model versioning, automated retraining, and monitoring using tools like Kubeflow, MLflow, and Airflow. We also discuss best practices for collaboration between data scientists, engineers, and DevOps teams. By implementing MLOps, organizations can achieve efficient, reliable, and scalable AI deployments with minimal manual intervention.

11.1 What is MLOps and Why It Matters

As the use of machine learning (ML) continues to grow in real-world applications, the need for efficient and reliable deployment, management, and monitoring of ML models has become more critical. This is where MLOps—short for Machine Learning Operations—comes into play. MLOps is a set of practices, tools, and cultural changes that bridge the gap between the development and deployment of machine learning models, enabling the continuous integration, delivery, and monitoring of machine learning systems in production.

MLOps combines the principles of DevOps (Development and Operations) with the specific challenges of machine learning, including data handling, model training, versioning, and monitoring. It aims to streamline and automate the process of taking machine learning models from the experimental phase in development to production environments where they can be used in real-world applications. By introducing automation, monitoring, and collaborative workflows, MLOps helps organizations maximize the value derived from machine learning by improving scalability, efficiency, and reproducibility.

In this chapter, we will explore what MLOps is, why it matters for the successful deployment of AI models, and the benefits it brings to teams, organizations, and machine learning projects.

The Evolution of MLOps

In the early days of machine learning, models were developed, trained, and tested in isolated environments, often by data scientists working alone. However, as machine learning models started to be applied to more complex, real-world problems, the need for more scalable, reproducible, and efficient processes became apparent. Deploying a model from development to production involved multiple steps and handoffs between teams, often resulting in delays, inefficiencies, and difficulties in managing the lifecycle of a model.

Traditional software development models—such as the waterfall or agile methods—were not enough to address the unique challenges of machine learning systems. These challenges include the need for:

- **Data Collection and Preparation**: Unlike traditional software, ML models require vast amounts of data for training and testing, and ensuring high-quality data pipelines is crucial for success.
- **Model Training and Tuning**: Machine learning models need to be continuously trained and fine-tuned on updated data, requiring coordination across teams and systems.
- **Model Versioning**: Managing different versions of models to track improvements or ensure rollback in case of failure can become complex in the absence of structured processes.
- **Continuous Monitoring**: Once deployed, models need to be monitored to ensure they continue to perform as expected and adapt to changes in data distribution over time.

To address these challenges, MLOps emerged as a way to unify the development, deployment, and monitoring of ML models with the same rigor that DevOps has brought to traditional software engineering.

What Does MLOps Involve?

MLOps integrates various stages of the machine learning lifecycle, which includes:

Model Development:

- In the initial phase, machine learning models are designed and trained using historical data. During this stage, data scientists experiment with different algorithms, parameters, and features to achieve the best possible results.
- MLOps ensures that the code, datasets, and model configurations used in development are well-documented, versioned, and reproducible. This is often

accomplished through tools such as Git for version control and Docker for containerization.

Model Deployment:

- Once the model is trained and validated, it must be deployed into a production environment. MLOps emphasizes the importance of automating this deployment process to reduce errors, speed up the time to market, and allow teams to deploy models frequently.
- Deployment in MLOps typically uses containerization (e.g., with Docker) and orchestration tools (e.g., Kubernetes) to scale deployments and handle rolling updates or model rollbacks without downtime.

Monitoring and Maintenance:

- After deployment, it is critical to monitor how the model is performing in the real world, including tracking model drift (when the model's predictions start to degrade due to changes in the input data).
- MLOps tools provide monitoring capabilities that allow teams to track important metrics such as accuracy, latency, and throughput, and send alerts when models need retraining or updating.

Model Retraining:

In dynamic environments, models may need to be retrained periodically to maintain their accuracy as new data becomes available. MLOps supports automated retraining pipelines, which help in scheduling and managing model retraining workflows based on predefined criteria (such as data drift or model performance thresholds).

Collaboration and Automation:

MLOps also facilitates collaboration between different teams involved in the model's lifecycle, including data engineers, data scientists, IT operations, and business stakeholders. By automating various tasks (like data preprocessing, model training, and deployment), MLOps reduces the manual effort and friction between teams, increasing the efficiency of the entire workflow.

Why MLOps Matters for AI Deployment

The importance of MLOps cannot be overstated in the context of AI deployment. Several reasons explain why MLOps is essential for the smooth and successful operation of machine learning models in production.

1. Accelerates Time-to-Market

MLOps enables continuous integration and continuous deployment (CI/CD) for machine learning models. With automated pipelines for training, testing, and deploying models, organizations can shorten the development cycles and get models into production faster. This results in quicker delivery of new features, improvements, or models that drive business value.

2. Enhances Model Reliability and Consistency

Deploying machine learning models without a structured operational workflow often leads to inconsistencies across different environments. MLOps ensures that models deployed in production environments are reliable and consistent, as all dependencies (such as libraries, datasets, and training code) are versioned, tested, and deployed in a controlled manner.

3. Facilitates Scalability

In many AI applications, models must be scaled to handle large amounts of data or support millions of users. MLOps practices allow organizations to scale their models and infrastructure as needed. By leveraging cloud platforms and container orchestration systems like Kubernetes, models can be efficiently scaled without disrupting ongoing operations.

4. Reduces Operational Risk

When models are deployed in production, there is always the risk that they might not perform as expected due to issues like model drift or unexpected data patterns. MLOps introduces robust monitoring tools and automated alerting systems that allow teams to track model performance, detect anomalies, and act quickly to correct any issues before they impact users.

5. Improves Collaboration Across Teams

MLOps establishes clear roles and responsibilities for each team involved in the machine learning lifecycle, creating a collaborative environment where data scientists, engineers, and operations teams work closely together. By automating workflows and facilitating the sharing of best practices, MLOps enhances communication and coordination among teams, ensuring a more efficient process for deploying and maintaining AI models.

6. Ensures Compliance and Governance

As AI models are increasingly used in regulated industries (such as healthcare, finance, and law), ensuring that AI deployments comply with legal and ethical standards is essential. MLOps incorporates versioning, auditing, and documentation practices that help organizations meet regulatory requirements and maintain transparent processes for model governance.

MLOps is an essential practice for organizations seeking to deploy machine learning models in production at scale. By combining the best practices from DevOps with the unique challenges of machine learning, MLOps provides a structured, automated approach to model deployment, monitoring, and maintenance. With MLOps, organizations can accelerate the time-to-market for AI-powered solutions, improve model performance, enhance collaboration among teams, and ensure that their AI systems remain operational, scalable, and compliant with regulations. As AI continues to transform industries, MLOps will play a key role in the seamless integration and success of machine learning models in real-world applications.

11.2 CI/CD Pipelines for AI Models

Continuous Integration and Continuous Deployment (CI/CD) are foundational practices in modern software engineering that have significantly improved the efficiency, quality, and speed of software development and operations. CI/CD pipelines, which automate the building, testing, and deployment of code, have become essential components of successful software engineering workflows. However, when it comes to AI models, the traditional CI/CD processes need to be adapted due to the unique characteristics of machine learning (ML) workflows, such as the need for data pipelines, model training, hyperparameter tuning, and model evaluation.

In this chapter, we will explore how CI/CD pipelines for AI models work, the challenges they address, and how they can be tailored to the specific needs of machine learning systems. By implementing CI/CD pipelines, teams can accelerate the development lifecycle of AI models, improve collaboration between data scientists and engineers, and ensure high-quality model deployment in production.

What Is CI/CD for AI Models?

In traditional software development, Continuous Integration (CI) and Continuous Deployment (CD) focus on automating the integration of code changes, running tests, and deploying the application into a production environment. For AI models, CI/CD is extended to include automated processes for training, validating, versioning, and deploying machine learning models.

Continuous Integration (CI) for AI models involves the frequent merging of changes to the model training code, data, and associated pipelines. This ensures that all team members are working with the most up-to-date version of the model and that changes are validated through automated tests and checks.

Continuous Deployment (CD) involves automatically deploying new versions of the model into production as soon as they pass the necessary tests. This can include deploying the model to an API endpoint, a cloud platform, or edge devices.

Key Components of CI/CD Pipelines for AI Models

To effectively implement CI/CD for AI, several key components and practices need to be integrated into the pipeline to address the specific requirements of machine learning workflows. These include versioning, data management, automated testing, and model deployment.

1. Version Control

In traditional software development, version control systems like Git are used to track changes in the source code. For AI models, version control also extends to training data, model configurations, and the models themselves.

- **Model Versioning**: Each trained model should be versioned and stored in a repository, allowing teams to track changes, compare models, and roll back to previous versions if necessary. Tools like MLflow or DVC (Data Version Control) are commonly used to version machine learning models and datasets.
- **Data Versioning**: Machine learning models rely heavily on data, and changes in the data can impact the model's performance. Data versioning tools like DVC, LakeFS, or Delta Lake allow teams to track changes in training datasets and ensure that the model is trained on the correct version of the data.

2. Automated Model Training and Validation

In traditional CI pipelines, code is built and tested in an automated fashion. Similarly, CI for AI involves automating the process of training and validating machine learning models.

- **Automated Model Training**: Once a code change or new dataset is pushed to the repository, the CI pipeline can automatically trigger model training using the latest data and model configurations. Popular platforms like KubeFlow or TensorFlow Extended (TFX) help orchestrate model training workflows.
- **Model Validation and Evaluation**: Automated validation involves evaluating the model on a validation set and ensuring that its performance meets predefined metrics (e.g., accuracy, precision, recall). If the model's performance degrades, the pipeline can trigger an alert or halt the deployment process.

3. Automated Testing

While unit tests are common in traditional software, testing in the context of machine learning models involves validating several aspects of the model, such as:

- **Unit Tests for Preprocessing**: Ensuring that data transformation functions (e.g., feature engineering, data cleaning) work as expected.
- **Model Performance Testing**: Verifying that the model meets certain performance criteria based on the evaluation metrics (such as accuracy or AUC) on a held-out validation set. If the performance drops below an acceptable threshold, the pipeline can reject the model.
- **Regression Testing**: Verifying that changes in the model or data don't introduce new errors, such as performance degradation. Regression tests track the model's performance on a set of known test cases to ensure that its predictions are consistent over time.

4. Model Deployment

Once a model is validated and approved through the CI pipeline, it needs to be deployed into a production environment. This is where Continuous Deployment (CD) comes into play.

- **Model Deployment Pipelines**: After a model passes validation, the deployment process can be automated through tools like Kubernetes, AWS SageMaker, or Azure ML. Deployment involves sending the model to an endpoint (e.g., an API or cloud service) where it can start processing real-world data and providing predictions.

- **Rolling Updates and Rollbacks**: CI/CD pipelines should support rolling updates, where new versions of the model are deployed gradually to avoid downtime or performance issues. If a model fails or its performance degrades after deployment, the pipeline should also support rolling back to a previous version of the model seamlessly.

5. Model Monitoring and Logging

Once the model is deployed, it is crucial to continuously monitor its performance in production. This includes tracking metrics such as latency, throughput, and accuracy to ensure that the model continues to perform as expected.

- **Model Drift Detection**: Over time, the data the model is exposed to may change, leading to model drift (i.e., a decline in performance). A robust CI/CD pipeline will automatically monitor for changes in input data distribution or model performance and alert the team to retrain the model when necessary.
- **Logging and Audit Trails**: Logging all changes made to models, datasets, and deployments is essential for ensuring transparency and traceability. Tools like Prometheus for monitoring and ELK Stack (Elasticsearch, Logstash, and Kibana) for logging can help with tracking model performance and troubleshooting.

Best Practices for Implementing CI/CD Pipelines for AI Models

Automate End-to-End Workflows: CI/CD pipelines for AI should automate the entire machine learning workflow, from data collection and preprocessing to model training, validation, and deployment. Automation reduces manual errors and accelerates the process of bringing models to production.

Use Modular and Reusable Components: To maintain flexibility and reduce duplication, divide the pipeline into reusable components for training, testing, and deployment. For example, you could have separate modules for data preprocessing, model training, and performance evaluation.

Ensure Model and Data Versioning: As machine learning models are highly dependent on the data they are trained on, it's crucial to implement versioning for both the models and the datasets. This ensures that the correct version of the data is used for training and allows teams to easily track and reproduce results.

Implement Robust Testing: Machine learning models require specialized testing strategies, including performance tests, regression tests, and model validation. These tests should be automated as part of the pipeline to ensure that the model meets performance criteria and doesn't degrade in quality over time.

Monitor Models in Production: After deployment, it's essential to monitor models continuously to track performance, detect model drift, and trigger retraining when necessary. Automation of monitoring ensures that performance issues are identified early and resolved quickly.

Enable Rollbacks: CI/CD pipelines for AI should have rollback capabilities in place to revert to a previous model version if the new model causes issues in production. This minimizes the impact of failed deployments.

Iterate and Improve: The pipeline should be flexible and iterative. As new models, tools, and best practices emerge, the CI/CD pipeline should evolve to accommodate these changes and improve efficiency.

CI/CD pipelines for AI models represent a key innovation in the way machine learning workflows are managed and deployed. By automating the training, validation, deployment, and monitoring processes, MLOps teams can achieve faster, more reliable model deployments, minimize risks, and maintain continuous model performance over time. As machine learning becomes an increasingly integral part of business operations, the implementation of effective CI/CD pipelines will be essential for ensuring that AI models are deployed at scale and deliver sustained value to organizations.

11.3 Automated Model Retraining and Deployment

As machine learning models are deployed in production environments, their performance can degrade over time due to various factors such as changes in data distributions, evolving user behavior, or environmental shifts. This phenomenon, known as model drift, requires continuous monitoring and updates to keep the models accurate and relevant. Automated model retraining and deployment are key components of Machine Learning Operations (MLOps) that help organizations maintain the accuracy of their AI models and ensure their long-term success in production.

In this chapter, we will explore the concept of automated model retraining and deployment, why it is crucial for AI model maintenance, and how to effectively implement it in a robust CI/CD pipeline.

What is Automated Model Retraining and Deployment?

Automated model retraining refers to the process of automatically updating machine learning models when they experience performance degradation or when new data becomes available. Retraining ensures that the model can adapt to the latest trends or patterns in the data, keeping it accurate and relevant for real-world use.

Automated model deployment, on the other hand, ensures that once a new version of the model has been trained, it is automatically deployed into the production environment without manual intervention. This includes all the steps necessary to move the retrained model from a staging or testing environment to production, making it ready for real-time predictions.

The combination of automated retraining and deployment enables organizations to maintain high-performing models in a scalable and efficient manner. This is particularly important in dynamic environments where the data that drives the model's predictions can change frequently, such as in e-commerce, financial markets, healthcare, and IoT applications.

Why Automated Retraining and Deployment Matter

Model Drift Management:

- Model drift occurs when a model's performance begins to degrade because the underlying data changes over time. For example, in an e-commerce recommendation system, shifts in user preferences may result in outdated recommendations. Retraining the model with new data helps to mitigate drift and maintain the model's relevance.
- Automating this process reduces the need for manual intervention, ensuring that models are retrained as soon as performance begins to dip.

Data Evolution:

- Data in many real-world applications changes over time. New data points may become available, or the distribution of features may change (known as data distribution shift or covariate shift). Regularly retraining models on updated data helps to capture new patterns and prevent overfitting to outdated training data.
- Automation ensures that models are continuously exposed to the most up-to-date data without requiring human effort, which is crucial for dynamic environments.

Faster Time-to-Market:

- Automated retraining and deployment allow organizations to iterate quickly, deploying new versions of the model without delay. This speeds up the process of integrating improvements into production and minimizes the time required to bring newly trained models online.
- Teams can continuously deploy improvements without waiting for manual approval processes, leading to faster time-to-market for AI-driven solutions.

Reduced Human Error:

The manual retraining and deployment process is prone to errors. Automated pipelines eliminate human mistakes by ensuring that models are retrained and deployed using consistent, predefined workflows. Automation reduces the risk of inconsistencies, such as deploying the wrong version of a model or overlooking the need for retraining.

Scalability and Efficiency:

Automation enhances scalability by allowing retraining and deployment to occur without manual intervention, enabling organizations to manage large-scale machine learning systems efficiently.

Automation also helps teams to scale operations and handle multiple models or multiple instances of the same model deployed across various environments without increasing operational costs or workloads.

Key Components of Automated Model Retraining and Deployment

To implement automated retraining and deployment effectively, there are several components and practices to consider:

1. Data Monitoring and Quality Checks

Before a model is retrained, the incoming data must be constantly monitored to detect any significant changes or anomalies that could affect model performance. Data quality checks can include:

- **Anomaly Detection**: Monitoring the data for sudden shifts in distribution or unexpected spikes in certain feature values.
- **Data Drift Detection**: Using statistical tests, such as Kolmogorov-Smirnov test or Chi-Square test, to track changes in feature distributions over time.

- **Missing Data**: Checking for missing or corrupted data and ensuring that it is handled appropriately before retraining.

These checks ensure that the model is retrained based on quality data, avoiding issues that may arise from poor or inconsistent input.

2. Triggering Retraining Events

Automated retraining must be triggered based on predefined events or conditions. These can include:

- **Performance Monitoring**: Tracking key performance indicators (KPIs), such as model accuracy, precision, recall, or loss on a test set. When performance falls below a threshold, retraining is automatically triggered.
- **Scheduled Retraining**: For some use cases, models may be retrained periodically (e.g., weekly or monthly) to ensure they remain up to date with the latest data trends, regardless of performance.
- **Data Update**: If new data becomes available, the pipeline can trigger a retraining process to incorporate the latest information.

The system should automatically trigger retraining based on one or more of these conditions to ensure that the model is updated as needed.

3. Training Pipelines

Once the retraining process is triggered, an automated training pipeline must be set up to handle the entire process, including:

- **Data Preprocessing**: Cleaning, normalizing, and transforming data before it is fed into the model.
- **Model Training**: The pipeline should automatically train the model using the latest data and evaluate it on a validation set to ensure its performance meets predefined metrics.
- **Hyperparameter Tuning**: This can be automated using techniques like grid search or random search to find the best set of hyperparameters for the model.
- **Model Evaluation**: After training, the model should be evaluated using a separate test set to validate that the retrained model improves upon the previous one.

Tools like Kubeflow, TensorFlow Extended (TFX), or MLflow can be used to automate the training pipeline and manage the entire workflow from data ingestion to model training and evaluation.

4. Model Versioning

Versioning is crucial in ensuring traceability and reproducibility when deploying AI models. Model versioning tracks changes to the model, including updates in training data, code, and hyperparameters. This allows teams to:

- Keep track of which model version is deployed in production.
- Compare performance across different versions.
- Roll back to previous models in case the new version causes issues.

Tools like DVC (Data Version Control) or MLflow allow teams to version models and their associated metadata.

5. Model Deployment Pipeline

Once the model is retrained and validated, it needs to be deployed into production. The deployment process should be automated to:

- **Package the Model**: Once the model is trained, it should be serialized (e.g., using Pickle, ONNX, or TensorFlow SavedModel) and stored in a version-controlled artifact repository.
- **Deploy the Model**: The deployment pipeline ensures that the model is automatically deployed to the production environment (cloud, on-premises, or edge devices). This can involve containerizing the model using Docker and deploying it using Kubernetes or cloud-specific services like AWS SageMaker or Azure ML.
- **Rolling Updates and Rollbacks**: Automated deployment pipelines should support rolling updates, ensuring minimal downtime during deployment. In the event that the retrained model fails in production, the pipeline should also support rollback to a previous stable version.

6. Continuous Monitoring and Retraining Triggers

Once the model is deployed, it should be continuously monitored for performance degradation. Tools like Prometheus, Grafana, or Seldon allow teams to track model predictions, latency, and error rates. If the model's performance drops below a certain threshold, the pipeline will automatically trigger retraining.

Best Practices for Automated Model Retraining and Deployment

- **Start Small and Iterate**: Begin with a small-scale implementation of automated retraining and deployment for a single model, then gradually expand the pipeline to include more models and environments.
- **Set Clear Retraining Criteria**: Define clear performance metrics and conditions for triggering retraining, and ensure that these criteria align with business goals and model accuracy.
- **Ensure Data Quality**: Focus on the quality of the data being fed into the retraining pipeline. Use robust data monitoring and validation techniques to ensure that the model is trained on relevant, accurate, and up-to-date data.
- **Version Control for Everything**: Version not only the models but also the data, code, and hyperparameters. This ensures that every aspect of the model's evolution is traceable and reproducible.
- **Monitor Continuously**: Implement continuous monitoring to detect performance issues, model drift, and changes in data. Automated monitoring should alert teams to any significant shifts in model behavior.

Automated model retraining and deployment are crucial components of a successful MLOps strategy. By automating these processes, organizations can ensure that their models remain accurate, scalable, and aligned with real-world conditions. The combination of retraining, model versioning, and automated deployment helps teams maintain the high performance of AI models over time, reduces human intervention, and accelerates the delivery of AI-driven insights. Ultimately, this automation empowers businesses to continuously improve their AI models while minimizing operational overhead.

11.4 Managing AI Model Repositories

In the world of AI and machine learning (ML), managing models is just as important as building them. As AI models become more complex and are deployed across multiple environments, keeping track of different versions, experiments, and configurations becomes a critical task. This is where AI model repositories come into play. An AI model repository is a centralized storage system designed to store, organize, and manage the lifecycle of AI models, from development to production. Proper management of these repositories ensures that teams can efficiently access, update, and deploy models without unnecessary overhead.

In this section, we will delve into the importance of AI model repositories, best practices for managing them, and the tools that help streamline the process. Whether your organization is dealing with a handful of models or managing a large portfolio, a well-organized repository can dramatically improve the scalability, reproducibility, and maintainability of AI models.

What is an AI Model Repository?

An AI model repository is a system or platform used to store and manage machine learning models and their associated metadata, including training data, hyperparameters, version histories, and performance metrics. The repository allows data scientists, machine learning engineers, and other stakeholders to organize and track models throughout their lifecycle—from initial development to deployment and continuous updates.

These repositories are essential for ensuring that models are properly versioned, retrained, and updated while also enabling easy access and reproducibility of experiments. A well-maintained repository not only improves collaboration among teams but also enhances the transparency and governance of AI projects.

Why Managing AI Model Repositories is Important

Version Control and Traceability:

Just like in software development, AI models undergo frequent updates, modifications, and experiments. Keeping track of which model version is deployed, which experiments have been run, and what changes have been made is crucial for maintaining consistency and reproducibility.

An effective model repository facilitates model versioning, enabling teams to quickly switch between different versions and compare their performance over time. This traceability is crucial for debugging, auditing, and improving model performance.
Collaboration Across Teams:

Large AI projects often involve multiple teams working in parallel, from data scientists to deployment engineers. A centralized model repository allows teams to easily share models, datasets, and experiment results, reducing friction and enabling better collaboration.

Repositories often come with features such as metadata tracking, access control, and annotations, making it easier to share context and insights about a particular model's design or performance.

Reproducibility of Experiments:

Reproducibility is a cornerstone of any scientific endeavor, and it is no different in machine learning. Ensuring that experiments can be recreated with the exact same results is vital for validating research and model development.

Model repositories store metadata about the training environment, hyperparameters, code versions, and training data, making it possible to reproduce an experiment with precision. This ensures that AI models can be audited and verified, which is particularly important for industries that require regulatory compliance.

Efficient Model Deployment:

Models in the repository are often organized by environments or deployment stages, such as development, staging, or production. Having a well-organized repository allows for smooth transitions of models from one stage to another, reducing deployment errors and ensuring that only validated models are pushed to production.

By using a version-controlled system, teams can ensure that the right model is deployed in the right environment without needing to manually verify each one.

Tracking Performance and Improvements:

AI models undergo continuous improvement, whether through retraining on new data, hyperparameter tuning, or updates to the underlying architecture. Keeping track of these iterations is essential to measure their impact on model performance.

A repository stores performance metrics, such as accuracy, precision, recall, and F1 score, for each model version, allowing teams to monitor improvements over time. This data-driven approach helps teams identify which changes are contributing to performance improvements and which may be detrimental.

Best Practices for Managing AI Model Repositories

To effectively manage AI model repositories, organizations should follow several best practices to ensure smooth operation, scalability, and effective collaboration:

1. Version Control for Models

Just as software code relies on version control systems like Git, machine learning models require a robust version control system for managing updates and iterations. Key practices include:

- **Assigning Unique Version Numbers**: Each model version should have a unique identifier (e.g., v1.0, v1.1, v2.0), which makes it easier to track changes, compare performance, and manage releases.
- **Storing Metadata**: Along with model weights and artifacts, store metadata such as hyperparameters, training configurations, evaluation metrics, and training datasets. This ensures that models can be fully reproduced and retrained in the future.
- **Branching and Experimentation**: Use branches or separate directories for experiments, allowing for A/B testing or testing new ideas without affecting the mainline version. This practice makes it easier to evaluate multiple approaches and roll back if necessary.

2. Standardizing Model Formats

Standardizing the model format helps ensure compatibility between different environments and systems, making it easier to deploy models across a variety of platforms.

- Use common formats like ONNX, TensorFlow SavedModel, PyTorch TorchScript, or Hugging Face Model Hub to ensure models can be easily integrated into production pipelines.
- A standardized format allows for easy migration between frameworks, ensuring cross-platform compatibility and reducing the overhead of format conversion.

3. Centralized Metadata Management

AI models often come with a wealth of metadata, including code, training scripts, configuration files, performance metrics, and more. Managing this metadata in a consistent and structured manner is essential.

- **Automated Logging**: Use automated tools to log key information about each model, such as training data, experiment results, model architecture, hyperparameters, and performance metrics. Tools like MLflow, DVC (Data Version Control), and Weights & Biases can be integrated into the pipeline to automatically track these details.
- **Metadata Tags**: Tag models with useful metadata like model type (e.g., classification, regression), dataset, use case, and performance thresholds, making it easier for team members to search and identify the right model for a particular use case.

4. Organizing Models by Stage

It's essential to organize models in the repository according to their deployment stages, ensuring that models are easily accessible and can be moved seamlessly from development to production. Common stages include:

- **Development**: Models in this stage are still being trained and validated. They may not be ready for production yet, but they are under active development and iteration.
- **Staging**: Once models have passed initial validation, they are moved to staging to be tested in a production-like environment. This stage helps simulate real-world conditions and test performance before going live.
- **Production**: These models are deployed and actively serving real-time predictions. Only well-tested models should be moved to production.
- **Archived**: Older models that are no longer in active use but may need to be referenced or retrained in the future.

5. Access Control and Security

AI models often contain sensitive data or proprietary algorithms, so access control is a crucial part of managing model repositories. Key practices include:

- **Role-Based Access Control (RBAC):** Implement RBAC to limit access to model repositories based on team roles. For example, only senior data scientists or engineers may have permission to deploy models to production.
- **Audit Trails**: Maintain detailed logs of who accessed or modified the models, providing an audit trail for compliance and security purposes.
- **Encryption**: Ensure models are stored securely using encryption, especially if they contain confidential information or proprietary intellectual property.

Tools for Managing AI Model Repositories

Several tools and platforms are available to help teams manage their AI model repositories:

MLflow:

MLflow is an open-source platform that allows teams to manage the entire machine learning lifecycle, including experimentation, reproducibility, and deployment. It provides model versioning, experiment tracking, and integration with various deployment tools.

DVC (Data Version Control):

DVC is a tool designed for versioning machine learning models and datasets. It integrates with Git and supports large files, enabling version control for datasets and models.

Weights & Biases:

Weights & Biases is a popular tool for tracking machine learning experiments, managing datasets, and visualizing model performance. It includes features for model versioning, hyperparameter optimization, and real-time monitoring.

TensorFlow Model Hub:

The TensorFlow Model Hub is a repository of pre-trained models that can be easily shared, downloaded, and reused. It provides a centralized platform for managing models in the TensorFlow ecosystem.

Hugging Face Model Hub:

Hugging Face Model Hub provides a repository for pre-trained NLP models, allowing teams to share, discover, and version models within the Hugging Face ecosystem.

Managing AI model repositories is an essential practice for ensuring that machine learning models remain reproducible, traceable, and scalable. A well-maintained repository improves collaboration, reduces errors, and enhances the efficiency of model deployment. By following best practices such as version control, metadata management, standardized formats, and implementing strong access control, organizations can streamline the management of AI models throughout their lifecycle. Whether using tools like MLflow, DVC, or TensorFlow Model Hub, a well-structured repository plays a pivotal role in keeping AI projects on track and ensuring their long-term success.

12. Monitoring and Maintaining AI Models

Deploying an AI model is just the beginning—ensuring long-term accuracy, reliability, and efficiency requires continuous monitoring and maintenance. In this chapter, we explore strategies for tracking model performance, detecting model drift, and implementing automated retraining using tools like Prometheus, Grafana, and MLflow. We also discuss error handling, logging, and real-time monitoring to maintain model integrity in production. By proactively addressing performance degradation, data shifts, and system failures, you can ensure that your AI models remain robust, scalable, and aligned with evolving business needs.

12.1 Identifying Model Drift and Degradation

As AI models are deployed in production, they face changing environments that can lead to a gradual decline in performance. This decline in model accuracy or reliability over time is known as model drift or model degradation. It's essential to identify and mitigate these issues to ensure that AI models continue to provide accurate, reliable results. In this section, we will explore the concept of model drift, how it occurs, the different types of drift, and the methods used to detect and address it.

What is Model Drift?

Model drift refers to the change in a model's performance over time due to shifts in the data distribution. It occurs when the model, trained on historical data, is exposed to new data in production that differs from the training set. As a result, the model's predictions become less accurate, leading to a degradation of its performance.

Model drift is a natural phenomenon in real-world systems where data is constantly evolving. Whether due to changes in user behavior, market trends, seasonal variations, or external factors, the data that the model encounters in production can often be different from the data used to train the model. This discrepancy can cause the model to make poor predictions, which can affect business outcomes, customer experiences, and operational efficiency.

Types of Model Drift

Model drift can be categorized into several types, each with its own characteristics and causes. Understanding these types of drift helps in identifying the root causes and applying the correct mitigation strategies.

1. Concept Drift

Concept drift occurs when the underlying relationships between the input features and the target variable change over time. In other words, the patterns that the model learned during training no longer hold true as the data evolves. Concept drift can result from external changes such as:

- Changes in consumer behavior
- Shifts in economic conditions
- Alterations in regulations or market dynamics

For example, an AI model used to predict credit risk may experience concept drift when the economic environment changes (e.g., during a recession), causing the financial behavior of borrowers to differ from previous patterns. The model may struggle to make accurate predictions because the relationships it learned are no longer valid.

2. Data Drift (Covariate Drift)

Data drift, also known as covariate drift, happens when the input data distribution changes over time while the relationship between input and output remains stable. In this case, the model's inputs—such as features or variables—change in distribution, but the target variable remains unchanged.

For instance, a model used to predict sales based on various input features, such as pricing, demographics, and website traffic, may encounter data drift when consumer behavior changes due to new trends or product offerings. If certain features (e.g., customer demographics) start to shift in the population, the model may not perform as effectively, even though the underlying relationship (sales prediction) remains consistent.

3. Label Drift (Target Drift)

Label drift, also known as target drift, occurs when the distribution of the target variable changes over time. This type of drift is less common but can still have a significant impact, particularly when the target variable is influenced by external factors that are not accounted for in the model.

For example, in a model predicting customer churn for a subscription service, label drift could occur if the number of customers canceling their subscriptions increases due to external events, such as a competitor offering a more attractive promotion. If the distribution of the target variable (churn) changes, the model may fail to accurately predict which customers are likely to churn.

4. Label Shift

Label shift is a form of drift where the distribution of the target labels (output classes) changes, but the distribution of the features remains relatively stable. This can occur when there is an imbalance in the target classes over time, which can lead to performance degradation.

For instance, a classification model trained on predicting whether a transaction is fraudulent might experience label shift if fraud becomes more or less common in the dataset over time. If the model was trained on a specific ratio of fraudulent to non-fraudulent transactions and the ratio shifts, the model's predictions may become biased toward the dominant class, resulting in decreased accuracy.

Causes of Model Drift

Model drift can be caused by a variety of factors, often related to changes in the underlying system, environment, or data collection methods. The primary causes of model drift include:

Changes in Data Distribution:

As mentioned earlier, shifts in the data distribution, whether due to changing consumer preferences, market conditions, or other external factors, can lead to drift. These changes are often difficult to predict and can affect the model's performance.

Seasonal Variations:

Many models are sensitive to time-related patterns. For example, a retail sales prediction model may perform well during the holiday season but struggle during the off-season. Seasonality introduces variations in data, causing drift when the model is exposed to new seasonal trends.

Behavioral Changes:

Changes in user or customer behavior can also contribute to model drift. For instance, a recommendation system may suffer from drift as user preferences evolve over time, or a fraud detection model may face challenges as fraudulent behavior adapts to bypass detection.

External Factors:

External events, such as changes in government policy, economic conditions, technological advancements, or natural disasters, can all affect data patterns and lead to model drift. These factors can be difficult to anticipate and mitigate proactively.

Feature Engineering and Data Collection Changes:

Sometimes, drift can occur due to changes in how data is collected, preprocessed, or represented. If the data pipeline is modified, or new features are introduced or removed, it can lead to discrepancies between the training and production environments, causing degradation in model performance.

Detecting Model Drift

Detecting model drift early is crucial to maintaining high performance and ensuring that the AI model continues to generate accurate predictions. Several techniques can be used to identify drift, including:

1. Monitoring Model Performance Over Time

One of the simplest ways to detect drift is by monitoring model performance continuously. By regularly measuring key performance indicators (KPIs) such as accuracy, precision, recall, F1 score, or area under the curve (AUC), teams can identify any sudden drops or trends indicating a decrease in the model's ability to perform.

Implementation:

- Establish baseline performance metrics during deployment.
- Continuously track and compare real-time performance to the baseline.
- Set thresholds for acceptable performance deviation, so you are alerted if the model is underperforming.

2. Data Distribution Comparison

Data drift can be detected by comparing the distribution of input data between the training and current production datasets. If there is a noticeable difference in feature distributions, data drift may be occurring.

Implementation:

- Use statistical tests, such as the Kolmogorov-Smirnov test or Jensen-Shannon divergence, to compare the distributions of features in the training and production data.
- Visualize the data distributions using histograms, box plots, or other techniques to detect significant shifts.

3. Drift Detection Algorithms

Several advanced algorithms and tools can automatically detect model drift. Examples include:

- **Drift Detection Method (DDM):** This algorithm monitors performance metrics and triggers a drift alert when there's a significant decline in model performance.
- **Early Drift Detection Method (EDDM):** EDDM improves upon DDM by focusing on detecting gradual drifts, which are harder to detect in real-time.
- **Population Stability Index (PSI):** PSI measures how much the distribution of features or labels has changed over time, helping to detect when a model's assumptions about the data are no longer valid.

4. Retraining and A/B Testing

Frequent retraining of models on new data helps mitigate drift. Additionally, A/B testing with different versions of models can identify which model is better adapted to new data patterns.

Implementation:

- Retrain models periodically on new data to keep them up to date and reduce drift.
- Use A/B testing or shadow deployment to test updated models against the existing ones and compare their performance.

Mitigating Model Drift

Once model drift has been identified, there are several strategies to mitigate its impact:

Continuous Monitoring and Retraining:

Periodically retrain models with updated data to ensure they stay relevant and accurate. This can be done on a scheduled basis or as new data arrives (e.g., via incremental learning).

Adaptive Learning:

Implement adaptive learning techniques that allow the model to update itself dynamically as new data flows in. This enables the model to adjust to data changes in real-time.

Model Ensembles:

Use ensemble models (i.e., a combination of multiple models) to reduce the impact of drift by averaging the predictions from different models. This can help stabilize performance, even when individual models are affected by drift.

Feature Monitoring:

Regularly monitor key features to detect early signs of data drift. If significant changes in feature distributions are identified, consider retraining the model or applying feature engineering adjustments.

Identifying and mitigating model drift is a crucial aspect of managing AI models in production. Drift can significantly affect the accuracy and performance of a model, leading to poor decision-making and adverse business outcomes. By understanding the different types of drift, monitoring model performance, and using advanced techniques like drift detection algorithms and continuous retraining, organizations can ensure their models remain robust and effective in the face of changing data environments. Implementing strategies to detect and address drift in real-time will help maintain the quality and reliability of AI models, ultimately ensuring their long-term success in production environments.

12.2 Logging and Observability for AI Models

Logging and observability are critical components of maintaining and improving the performance of AI models in production. In traditional software applications, logging and observability help developers monitor system performance, troubleshoot issues, and ensure smooth operations. Similarly, for AI models, these practices enable teams to track model behavior, identify anomalies, and gain deep insights into how models perform in real-world environments. This is especially important as AI models can behave unpredictably, and without proper monitoring, model drift, errors, and degraded performance can go unnoticed, leading to significant business consequences.

In this section, we will explore the importance of logging and observability in AI model deployment, the best practices for implementing them, and the tools and techniques used to gather valuable insights into model performance.

What is Logging and Observability?

Before diving into how logging and observability work in the context of AI models, let's define these terms in more detail:

Logging refers to the process of capturing and storing specific events, actions, or messages related to the execution of AI models. Logs contain detailed information about model predictions, input features, errors, and performance metrics, among other things. These logs provide a historical record of how the model is operating, making it easier to diagnose issues or audit the model's decision-making process.

Observability, on the other hand, is the practice of collecting and analyzing data to understand and monitor the internal state of a system (in this case, AI models) based on the outputs it generates. In the context of AI models, observability goes beyond simple logging—it includes comprehensive monitoring, metrics collection, visualization, and tracing. It helps teams to proactively identify issues before they affect end users.

In short, logging helps you capture the data you need, while observability enables you to turn that data into actionable insights.

Why Logging and Observability Matter for AI Models

AI models are complex systems that often operate in dynamic environments. Unlike traditional software applications, which are deterministic and follow a predictable flow of execution, AI models are influenced by data, features, and external factors that can vary in unpredictable ways. Logging and observability help mitigate the challenges posed by these unpredictable behaviors by allowing you to track and analyze the performance and decision-making of your AI models over time.

Here are several reasons why logging and observability are essential for AI models:

1. Tracking Model Performance

AI models require continuous monitoring to ensure they perform well and remain aligned with business goals. Without tracking performance metrics, it's difficult to detect when a model starts underperforming or when issues like model drift occur. Logging and observability tools allow you to measure key performance indicators (KPIs), such as accuracy, precision, recall, and F1 score, on an ongoing basis. Monitoring these metrics helps you maintain the reliability of your model and intervene when performance degradation is detected.

2. Detecting Anomalies and Errors

AI models can encounter various anomalies or errors during runtime, such as incorrect predictions, misclassifications, or outlier data points that the model struggles to handle. Without proper logging, it becomes challenging to identify and diagnose these issues. Logging provides detailed records of inputs, predictions, and any errors that arise, making it easier to identify when something goes wrong.

3. Understanding Model Behavior

AI models, especially deep learning models, are often seen as "black boxes." This means that it can be difficult to explain why a model made a specific decision or prediction. Observability tools provide valuable insights into the internal workings of the model, such as feature importance, decision pathways, and model outputs. This transparency helps data scientists and engineers understand the model's decision-making process and allows them to spot potential biases, inefficiencies, or other issues.

4. Enhancing Accountability and Auditing

In many industries, especially healthcare, finance, and legal sectors, there is a strong need for auditability and accountability in AI models. Being able to track exactly how a model arrived at a specific decision can be crucial for compliance and transparency. Logging provides an audit trail that records the decisions made by AI models and the data they were based on. This trail ensures that the model can be inspected or explained if needed, helping organizations maintain regulatory compliance.

5. Enabling Continuous Improvement

AI models are not static entities. As new data becomes available and business requirements evolve, models need to be retrained, fine-tuned, or replaced. Logging and observability play a crucial role in the continuous improvement of models by providing feedback on model performance and areas for enhancement. By analyzing logs and observed patterns, teams can identify gaps, make informed decisions about model updates, and improve accuracy over time.

Best Practices for Logging and Observability in AI Models

To fully leverage the power of logging and observability, AI teams should follow best practices to ensure that their monitoring efforts are effective, scalable, and meaningful. Below are some key best practices:

1. Capture Detailed Logs for Every Prediction

For effective logging, it's essential to record all relevant details about each prediction made by the AI model. This should include:

- **Input data**: The features or data points used as input for the model.
- **Prediction**: The output generated by the model (e.g., classification, regression result).
- **Model version**: The specific version of the model that made the prediction (important when multiple versions are deployed).
- **Timestamps**: Time and date of each prediction for chronological tracking.
- **Error messages**: Any issues or errors that occurred during the prediction process.
- **Performance metrics**: Metrics such as confidence scores, probability distributions, or uncertainty estimates.

Capturing this level of detail enables teams to debug issues quickly, track the evolution of predictions, and gain insights into how the model is responding to real-world data.

2. Log Model Inputs, Outputs, and Errors

In addition to tracking performance metrics, it's crucial to log both inputs and outputs. These logs should be structured in a way that makes them easy to analyze and query. It's important to capture any errors or exceptions that may occur during the inference process so they can be investigated and addressed promptly.

3. Use Distributed Tracing for Monitoring Model Inference

In production systems where models are part of a larger pipeline or microservice architecture, distributed tracing helps track how requests flow through the system and how different components interact. Using distributed tracing tools like OpenTelemetry or Jaeger allows teams to monitor the performance of their AI models in real time, detect bottlenecks, and improve system efficiency.

4. Integrate with Centralized Logging Systems

As AI models are often deployed in large, distributed systems, it's essential to consolidate logs from multiple sources into a centralized logging system. Tools like ELK Stack (Elasticsearch, Logstash, and Kibana) or Splunk can be used to aggregate and store logs, making them easier to analyze and search through. Centralized logging systems allow teams to have a unified view of model performance across different stages of deployment and across different environments (e.g., development, staging, production).

5. Implement Real-Time Monitoring Dashboards

To provide real-time insights into model performance and health, set up monitoring dashboards that visualize key metrics and logs. Tools like Grafana, Prometheus, and Datadog can help visualize performance metrics such as model accuracy, latency, and error rates in real time. These dashboards enable stakeholders to quickly spot anomalies or performance degradation and take appropriate action.

6. Set Alerts for Anomalous Behavior

Automated alerts can help detect issues early, reducing the time between problem detection and resolution. Set up threshold-based alerts for performance metrics such as accuracy, response time, or error rates. If these metrics exceed predefined thresholds, an alert is triggered, enabling your team to investigate and take corrective actions promptly.

7. Monitor Data Quality and Drift

Apart from monitoring model performance, it's essential to track the quality and consistency of the data fed into the model. Monitoring data drift and feature distribution over time ensures that the model is not exposed to dramatically different data that could lead to performance degradation. Tools like Evidently AI and WhyLabs specialize in model and data monitoring, allowing teams to track data drift and spot emerging trends.

Tools for AI Model Logging and Observability

A variety of tools and platforms are available to assist in logging and observability efforts. Some of the most commonly used tools include:

- **TensorBoard**: Primarily for TensorFlow models, TensorBoard provides a suite of visualizations that track various aspects of model training and inference, including metrics, histograms, and distributions.
- **MLflow**: A comprehensive platform for managing the machine learning lifecycle, MLflow enables logging of experiments, models, and metrics, making it easier to track and monitor performance.
- **Prometheus**: An open-source monitoring and alerting toolkit, Prometheus can collect and store metrics from various sources, including AI models, and allows you to set up custom alerts based on thresholds.
- **Datadog**: A cloud-based monitoring platform that provides infrastructure and application performance monitoring, as well as AI-specific insights, including model performance and health.
- **Seldon**: A machine learning deployment platform that integrates with existing logging and observability systems to provide model monitoring, performance tracking, and drift detection.

Logging and observability are fundamental practices for maintaining and improving AI models in production. By capturing detailed logs, monitoring performance, detecting anomalies, and providing real-time insights, organizations can ensure that their AI models are running smoothly and continue to provide value over time. Implementing these practices effectively enables teams to identify issues early, optimize model performance, and ensure long-term success in deploying AI models.

12.3 Performance Monitoring with A/B Testing

A/B testing is a widely used method for comparing two or more variants of a model, feature, or strategy to determine which one performs best under real-world conditions. In the context of AI model deployment, performance monitoring with A/B testing is an essential practice that helps data scientists, engineers, and business teams assess how well a newly deployed model performs relative to an existing model or alternative versions.

A/B testing provides a controlled environment to experiment with different models or algorithms, helping organizations make data-driven decisions when choosing the best-performing model for production. This technique not only allows you to measure the effectiveness of AI models but also ensures that the new models meet business objectives, user expectations, and regulatory requirements.

In this section, we will delve into how A/B testing can be used for performance monitoring in AI deployment, including best practices, common pitfalls, and real-world applications of A/B testing in AI systems.

What is A/B Testing?

A/B testing, also known as split testing, involves comparing two or more versions (or "variants") of a system, model, or feature to determine which one achieves the desired outcome. In AI model deployment, A/B testing typically involves deploying two or more models in parallel (often referred to as the control and treatment models) and measuring their performance across specific key performance indicators (KPIs).

The process involves randomly assigning incoming requests or user interactions to one of the models, collecting results, and analyzing the performance to decide which model is superior. A/B testing is particularly useful for evaluating the impact of different AI models, hyperparameters, and algorithms under real-world conditions.

For example, an organization may be deciding between two machine learning models for a recommendation system. One model could be the current version (control), while the other is an updated version (treatment). A/B testing allows the organization to evaluate both models' real-time performance based on metrics like accuracy, user engagement, revenue impact, or click-through rates.

Why A/B Testing is Essential for AI Model Performance Monitoring

AI models are frequently deployed in dynamic environments where factors like user behavior, data quality, and external conditions can change over time. Performance monitoring through A/B testing is essential for ensuring that AI models continue to deliver value in the face of these changes. Here's why A/B testing is crucial:

1. Comparing Multiple Models or Versions

One of the primary benefits of A/B testing is that it enables teams to compare the performance of multiple models or versions in a controlled manner. This helps data scientists and engineers determine whether a new model outperforms an existing one or if alternative algorithms are more suited to the task at hand.

2. Minimizing Risk of Model Deployment

When deploying new models, there is always a risk that the new model may not perform as expected or may lead to unintended consequences. A/B testing allows organizations to mitigate this risk by running both the old and new models in parallel, allowing teams to ensure the new model doesn't negatively impact the user experience or business outcomes.

3. Evaluating Business Impact

AI models are deployed to achieve specific business goals, whether it's improving conversion rates, increasing user engagement, or reducing churn. A/B testing helps organizations assess not only the technical performance of a model but also its direct impact on business metrics. This ensures that the model meets business objectives before a full-scale rollout.

4. Data-Driven Decision Making

A/B testing empowers teams to make informed, data-driven decisions. Instead of relying on intuition or assumptions, the testing process provides concrete evidence of which model or feature works best. This is especially important for AI models that are often viewed as "black boxes"—A/B testing helps demystify the results and allows stakeholders to make decisions with confidence.

5. Continuous Improvement and Optimization

AI models are rarely perfect from the start. A/B testing allows organizations to iterate and refine models continuously. By testing multiple variants over time and collecting performance data, teams can make informed adjustments to models, algorithms, and features to maximize long-term success.

How A/B Testing Works in AI Model Deployment

Implementing A/B testing in AI model deployment involves several steps. Here is a high-level overview of how the process works:

1. Define the Objective and Metrics

Before running an A/B test, it's critical to define the objectives of the experiment and the KPIs you want to measure. These objectives can vary depending on the use case. For example:

- **Accuracy**: How well does the model predict outcomes?
- **Precision/Recall/F1-Score**: Evaluation of classification models.
- **Engagement Metrics**: For recommendation systems, tracking user interactions, click-through rates, or conversions.
- **Latency**: How quickly does the model respond to requests or predictions?
- **Revenue Impact**: Measuring the effect of a recommendation model on customer purchases.

Selecting the right performance metrics is essential to ensure that the results of the A/B test align with the business goals and provide a clear picture of which model is performing better.

2. Design the Test and Select Variants

Once the objective and metrics are defined, the next step is to design the test. This typically involves:

- **Control Group**: This is the existing or baseline model that will be compared against new models. It represents the current state of the AI system.
- **Treatment Group(s):** These are the new model(s) or alternative versions that will be tested. You can test multiple variants to compare their performance.
- **Sample Size**: A/B testing requires enough traffic or interactions to ensure that results are statistically significant. A sample size that is too small may lead to unreliable conclusions.

Each incoming request or interaction will be randomly assigned to one of the models (control or treatment) based on predefined conditions.

3. Implement the Test and Collect Data

Once the models and test parameters are set, it's time to deploy the models in production. During this phase, requests from users or interactions with the system are routed to either the control or treatment models, and the data is logged for analysis. Both models will operate simultaneously in a "live" setting, and the performance of each model will be measured against the selected KPIs.

Real-time data collection is essential to ensure that the A/B test provides valuable insights. For AI models, the data collected during the test will often include input features, predictions, model latency, and any other relevant metrics.

4. Analyze Results

After running the test for an appropriate period, the next step is to analyze the data. The analysis should focus on comparing the performance of the control and treatment models. Statistical tests (e.g., t-tests, confidence intervals) can be used to determine if the differences between the models are significant or due to random chance.

Some key aspects to consider during analysis:

- **Statistical Significance**: Ensure that the observed differences in performance are statistically significant and not due to random fluctuations.
- **A/B Test Duration**: The test should be run long enough to account for any variability in user behavior and model performance.
- **Segmentation**: Depending on the business case, it may be valuable to segment users based on demographics, behavior, or other factors to ensure that the results apply to all relevant groups.

5. Make Data-Driven Decisions

Based on the results of the A/B test, you can make informed decisions about the model deployment:

- If the treatment model outperforms the control model, it can be rolled out to all users.
- If the control model outperforms the treatment model, the new model may need further adjustments or refinements before being deployed.
- If the performance difference is negligible, other factors (e.g., resource consumption, scalability) may be considered when deciding which model to deploy.

Best Practices for A/B Testing AI Models

To ensure that A/B testing is effective and yields accurate results, follow these best practices:

- **Ensure Randomization**: Randomly assign users or interactions to the control and treatment models to eliminate bias.
- **Test Incremental Changes**: For more meaningful results, test small changes to your model (e.g., tweaking hyperparameters or changing data preprocessing) rather than major overhauls.
- **Monitor for Biases**: Be mindful of potential biases that may skew the results, such as demographic biases or biases in the training data.
- **Allow Sufficient Test Duration**: Ensure the A/B test runs long enough to collect a statistically significant amount of data and capture variations in user behavior.
- **Use a Large Enough Sample Size**: A/B testing requires sufficient data to make reliable conclusions, so ensure that the sample size is large enough to detect differences.
- **Control External Factors**: Try to minimize external factors (e.g., marketing campaigns, seasonal trends) that might impact model performance during the test.

Real-World Applications of A/B Testing in AI Deployment

A/B testing is widely used in industries where AI models influence user-facing products or business operations. Some common use cases include:

- **E-commerce**: Testing different recommendation algorithms or personalized content delivery systems to see which boosts conversion rates or sales.
- **Advertising**: Comparing different bidding algorithms or ad placement strategies to determine which one generates the highest click-through rates.
- **Healthcare**: Evaluating the performance of AI models for predicting patient outcomes or diagnosing diseases, while ensuring that the model meets clinical standards and improves patient care.
- **Finance**: Comparing different fraud detection models to see which one minimizes false positives and accurately identifies fraudulent transactions.

A/B testing is an indispensable tool for performance monitoring in AI model deployment. By allowing organizations to test different models and strategies under real-world conditions, A/B testing provides valuable insights into which AI models will best meet business needs and user expectations. Through well-designed and carefully executed A/B tests, teams can ensure their models are optimized for real-time performance, improve decision-making, and continually enhance their AI systems to achieve long-term success.

12.4 Retraining Models Based on Real-World Data

In the ever-evolving world of AI, one of the most critical aspects of maintaining a successful deployment is ensuring that your models remain relevant and accurate over time. A model that performs well during development or testing may not always continue to deliver optimal results when exposed to real-world data. This discrepancy can arise due to a variety of factors, such as shifts in data patterns, evolving user behavior, or new trends that weren't accounted for during the initial training phase.

Retraining models based on real-world data is a crucial process that ensures the continued effectiveness of AI models in production. This process involves updating and fine-tuning the model with fresh data or feedback to adapt to changes in the underlying data distribution, user behavior, or business objectives. By doing so, organizations can improve the accuracy, robustness, and relevance of their AI models, ensuring that they provide maximum value over time.

This section will explore the importance of retraining models, when and how it should be done, the methods used, and best practices for managing the retraining process in a live AI deployment.

Why Retraining Models is Essential

AI models often rely on historical data to make predictions or decisions, but real-world conditions can change rapidly. Retraining models helps address several key challenges:

1. Handling Model Drift

Model drift, also known as concept drift, occurs when the underlying patterns or relationships in the data change over time. For example, a machine learning model trained on historical customer behavior may not perform as well if consumer preferences or purchasing habits shift due to seasonal trends, economic changes, or external events. Retraining helps to recalibrate the model and adapt to these evolving data trends, ensuring the model remains accurate and useful.

2. Incorporating New Data

Real-world environments generate new data continuously. For example, a recommendation system for an e-commerce site might need retraining as new products are added to the catalog, or a predictive maintenance model for industrial equipment requires updates based on newly collected sensor data. Retraining models with the latest data ensures they stay current and incorporate the most up-to-date information available, which enhances their decision-making capabilities.

3. Improving Model Performance

As a model is exposed to more real-world data, it may uncover patterns or nuances that weren't initially apparent. Retraining allows the model to learn from new examples, improving its generalization ability and boosting its predictive accuracy. Over time, as more diverse data is added to the training set, models can become more robust and adaptable to a wider range of inputs.

4. Addressing Biases in Data

Biases in training data can lead to skewed predictions and unfair outcomes. If the model's training data is not representative of all relevant subgroups or scenarios, it may perform poorly for certain users or populations. Retraining with a more diverse and representative dataset helps to mitigate these biases and ensures that the model performs fairly and inclusively across all segments.

When to Retrain an AI Model

Deciding when to retrain an AI model is crucial to maintaining its performance in production. While there is no one-size-fits-all answer, there are a few key indicators and events that signal the need for retraining:

1. Performance Degradation

If a model begins to show signs of performance degradation over time, it may be an indication that it needs retraining. This can be detected through regular monitoring of performance metrics such as accuracy, precision, recall, or F1-score. A sudden drop in performance suggests that the model is no longer capturing the current patterns in the data effectively, necessitating an update.

2. Changes in Data Distribution

If there are significant shifts in the data distribution—such as seasonality, market changes, or demographic changes—retraining is necessary to ensure the model can adapt. These shifts can be detected through statistical tests, such as comparing the distribution of features in the new data with those used during initial training.

3. Introduction of New Data or Features

Whenever new features, variables, or data sources are introduced into the system, the model may require retraining to incorporate these changes. For example, if a new product category is added to a recommendation system, retraining the model ensures that it can make relevant suggestions for the new products.

4. User Feedback or Error Analysis

User feedback is invaluable for identifying areas where a model might be making incorrect predictions or producing unsatisfactory results. Collecting this feedback and analyzing errors can reveal shortcomings in the model that require retraining. Additionally, if there are consistent patterns in user dissatisfaction or inaccurate predictions, these can inform the retraining process to improve the model's accuracy.

5. Model Drift Detection

Model drift occurs when the underlying data patterns or relationships that the model relies on start to change over time. There are multiple ways to detect drift, such as tracking model performance on test data over time, monitoring predictions against actual outcomes, or using specialized algorithms designed to detect concept drift. If drift is detected, retraining is needed to realign the model with the new data patterns.

Methods for Retraining AI Models

Retraining models involves several methods, each suited for different scenarios. Here are some common strategies:

1. Full Retraining

Full retraining involves training a model from scratch using the most current data available. While this method can be resource-intensive, it ensures that the model is fully updated with the latest information. Full retraining is typically used when there is a significant shift in data patterns or when the model architecture needs to be adjusted.

2. Incremental Learning

Incremental learning, or online learning, is a method where the model is updated progressively with new data, without retraining from scratch. This approach is more efficient in terms of computational resources and can be applied when the model needs to adapt to new data in real-time. It is particularly useful in environments where data is continuously streaming, such as in financial systems or sensor networks.

3. Fine-Tuning

Fine-tuning is a type of transfer learning in which a pre-trained model is further trained on a smaller dataset with updated information. Fine-tuning adjusts the weights of the model slightly, rather than retraining it completely. This is a cost-effective method that can be used when new data is available, but the overall structure of the model remains relevant.

4. Active Learning

Active learning involves selecting the most informative examples from a pool of unlabeled data and using them to retrain the model. This method reduces the amount of data needed for retraining by focusing on areas where the model is uncertain or where errors are most likely to occur. Active learning can be combined with human-in-the-loop approaches to ensure high-quality model updates.

Best Practices for Retraining AI Models

To ensure that the retraining process is successful and efficient, consider the following best practices:

1. Automate the Retraining Pipeline

Automating the retraining process ensures that the model is updated regularly without manual intervention. Tools such as MLOps platforms, CI/CD pipelines, and model management systems can help automate the collection of new data, retraining, and deployment, ensuring that the process is seamless and timely.

2. Use Version Control

Maintaining version control for models is essential to track changes and roll back to previous versions if necessary. Tools like Git, DVC (Data Version Control), and MLflow enable you to keep track of both the model code and the data used for training, ensuring that you can maintain a record of different model iterations.

3. Monitor Retraining Impact

After retraining a model, it is important to monitor its performance closely to ensure that the update has led to improvements. Continuous monitoring allows you to identify any unintended consequences of the retraining process, such as new types of errors or biases.

4. Test New Models in a Staging Environment

Before deploying a retrained model into production, it should be tested in a staging environment that simulates real-world conditions. This helps to ensure that the retrained model performs as expected and that no critical issues arise during deployment.

5. Incrementally Update the Model

Rather than retraining a model with a large batch of new data all at once, consider retraining incrementally with small batches of fresh data. This reduces the risk of overfitting to new data and ensures that the model remains stable while being updated.

Challenges in Retraining AI Models

While retraining is necessary for keeping AI models relevant, there are several challenges associated with the process:

- **Data Quality**: Retraining models is only useful if the data used for training is of high quality. Poor-quality data can introduce noise and degrade model performance.
- **Computational Resources**: Retraining models, especially large models, requires significant computational resources. This can be a challenge for organizations with limited infrastructure or budget.
- **Model Stability**: Retraining can introduce instability in the model, leading to unexpected outcomes or a decline in performance. Careful validation and testing are necessary to prevent this.
- **Monitoring Retraining Outcomes**: Continuously monitoring the results of retraining is essential to detect whether the new model is truly better than its predecessor.

Retraining AI models based on real-world data is a crucial practice for ensuring that AI systems remain relevant, accurate, and valuable over time. By addressing challenges like model drift, incorporating new data, and adapting to changing user behavior, organizations can maintain high-performing AI models in production. Implementing a robust retraining pipeline, supported by best practices such as automation, monitoring, and version control, is key to achieving long-term success in AI deployments.

13. Security, Privacy, and Ethical Considerations

As AI models are deployed in real-world applications, ensuring security, privacy, and ethical integrity becomes a top priority. In this chapter, we explore best practices for securing AI models, protecting against adversarial attacks, data breaches, and model inversion threats. We also discuss privacy-preserving AI techniques, such as federated learning, differential privacy, and secure multi-party computation, to safeguard user data. Additionally, we address ethical challenges like bias in AI models, transparency, and regulatory compliance (GDPR, CCPA, etc.). By implementing strong security and ethical frameworks, organizations can deploy AI responsibly while maintaining trust, fairness, and compliance in their AI systems.

13.1 AI Model Security: Protecting Against Attacks

As AI technologies continue to evolve, their deployment in real-world applications becomes more widespread, making AI models valuable targets for various types of security attacks. With the increasing reliance on AI systems in critical sectors such as healthcare, finance, autonomous vehicles, and cybersecurity, ensuring the security of AI models has become a top priority. The integrity of these models is crucial not only to maintain their accuracy and reliability but also to safeguard sensitive data, protect intellectual property, and prevent malicious exploitation. This section explores the different types of attacks that AI models are vulnerable to, the potential risks they pose, and the strategies for protecting AI systems from these threats.

Types of Attacks on AI Models

AI models, like any other software system, are susceptible to a range of security threats. These attacks can compromise their functionality, lead to inaccurate predictions, or allow malicious actors to gain unauthorized access to data or control over the system. Here are some common types of attacks on AI models:

1. Adversarial Attacks

Adversarial attacks are one of the most well-known and dangerous types of threats in AI security. In this form of attack, small, carefully crafted perturbations are added to the input data to mislead the AI model into making incorrect predictions or classifications. These changes are often imperceptible to humans, but they can significantly degrade the model's performance. For example, an adversarial attack on an image classification model could involve altering a few pixels of an image to trick the model into misclassifying it while leaving the image visually unchanged.

These attacks highlight the vulnerabilities of AI models to inputs that are not part of the training data distribution, which can be exploited by attackers with malicious intent. Adversarial attacks can be a serious concern, particularly in applications such as autonomous vehicles, where slight changes to sensor inputs can result in disastrous consequences.

2. Model Inversion Attacks

Model inversion attacks occur when an attacker is able to reverse-engineer sensitive information about the training data used to build an AI model. By querying the model and observing its outputs, the attacker can infer private details about the data, such as the characteristics of individuals or proprietary data used in training. For example, an attacker may be able to determine personal information, like medical records, from a model that was trained on sensitive datasets, even if the data itself was never directly exposed.

In industries like healthcare or finance, where confidentiality and privacy are critical, model inversion attacks pose significant threats to the security and ethical use of AI.

3. Data Poisoning Attacks

Data poisoning attacks involve manipulating the training data used to build an AI model in order to introduce biases or cause the model to make incorrect predictions. In this type of attack, malicious actors inject misleading or harmful data into the training set, which then influences the model's learning process and causes it to produce faulty or biased predictions in production.

For example, an attacker could manipulate data in a way that causes a machine learning model for fraud detection to overlook certain types of fraudulent transactions. Data poisoning can be particularly problematic in environments where the model learns continuously from new data inputs, making it difficult to detect or mitigate the attack in real-time.

4. Model Stealing Attacks

Model stealing attacks occur when an attacker attempts to replicate or "steal" a trained AI model. By querying a model repeatedly and analyzing its responses, the attacker can approximate the original model's behavior and create a similar model without needing access to the original training data or algorithms. This type of attack is especially concerning for organizations that rely on proprietary machine learning models, as it could result in the theft of intellectual property or a competitive advantage.

Model stealing attacks can also lead to security vulnerabilities if the stolen model is used for malicious purposes, such as to evade security systems or bypass authentication mechanisms.

5. Evasion Attacks

Evasion attacks are a type of attack where the adversary manipulates the input data in a way that allows it to bypass detection or classification by the AI model. For instance, an attacker might feed a malicious input that is designed to evade a spam detection system or a security model by altering the features of the data in a way that the model no longer recognizes it as malicious.

These attacks are particularly relevant in the context of intrusion detection systems, antivirus software, and fraud detection, where attackers try to deceive the model into failing to identify harmful inputs or activities.

Impact of AI Model Security Attacks

The potential impact of attacks on AI models extends beyond mere performance degradation. They can have far-reaching consequences for both organizations and individuals. Below are some of the most significant risks associated with security breaches in AI systems:

1. Loss of Trust

When AI models are compromised, the first casualty is often user trust. If an attacker can manipulate or deceive an AI model, it can lead to a loss of confidence in the model's ability to deliver accurate or reliable results. For example, in a healthcare setting, if a diagnostic AI model is manipulated, patients may lose confidence in the system's ability to make accurate medical decisions, leading to severe consequences for both the healthcare provider and the individuals relying on the model.

2. Financial Losses

In financial sectors, attacks on AI models can lead to substantial financial losses. For example, an attacker might manipulate a fraud detection model to allow fraudulent transactions to go undetected. In cases of financial fraud or cybercrime, the resulting monetary damages can be significant.

3. Compromised Personal or Sensitive Information

AI models used in industries such as healthcare, finance, and security often process sensitive personal information. A successful attack could expose private data, including medical records, personal identification details, or financial information, putting individuals at risk of identity theft, discrimination, or other malicious activities.

4. Reputational Damage

Organizations that fall victim to AI model security attacks risk damage to their reputation. If a breach occurs, especially in high-profile industries like healthcare or autonomous vehicles, the public and regulatory bodies may view the organization as negligent in protecting its AI systems, leading to loss of business, legal consequences, and public backlash.

Strategies for Protecting AI Models from Attacks

Given the significant risks posed by AI model security attacks, organizations must take proactive steps to protect their models. Here are some key strategies for safeguarding AI systems:

1. Adversarial Training

Adversarial training is one of the most effective ways to defend against adversarial attacks. It involves training the model on adversarial examples—inputs that have been intentionally modified to confuse the model. By exposing the model to these perturbations during training, the model learns to be more robust to similar attacks in the real world. Adversarial training can help reduce the model's susceptibility to adversarial manipulations.

2. Differential Privacy

Differential privacy is a technique that helps protect the privacy of individuals in datasets used for training AI models. By introducing noise into the data during the training process, differential privacy ensures that the model cannot memorize or extract information about individual data points, making it more difficult for attackers to launch model inversion attacks.

3. Model Encryption

Model encryption can help protect the integrity and confidentiality of AI models. By encrypting models before deploying them, organizations can ensure that the model's structure and parameters are shielded from unauthorized access. This is particularly important for cloud-based AI deployments, where the model may be exposed to external threats.

4. Robust Data Validation

Ensuring the integrity and quality of the training data is essential for preventing data poisoning attacks. Implementing robust data validation and monitoring processes can help detect and filter out any malicious data that might be introduced into the system. This can be done by implementing anomaly detection techniques that identify unusual patterns or errors in the data.

5. Secure Model Deployment and API Management

Securing the deployment environment is another critical aspect of AI model security. Organizations should implement strict access control policies and authentication mechanisms to ensure that only authorized users or systems can interact with the model. Additionally, APIs should be protected using rate limiting, encryption, and security protocols to prevent unauthorized queries or model stealing attempts.

6. Regular Audits and Monitoring

Ongoing monitoring of AI models is essential for detecting unusual behavior, potential attacks, and model drift. Regular audits of model performance, input data, and system outputs can help identify signs of security breaches early, enabling a swift response to mitigate potential threats.

AI model security is a critical aspect of deploying AI systems in production environments. From adversarial attacks to model inversion and data poisoning, the risks posed to AI models are varied and complex. However, by understanding the potential threats and implementing robust security measures, organizations can protect their AI systems from exploitation and maintain their integrity, performance, and trustworthiness. Through strategies such as adversarial training, differential privacy, encryption, and regular monitoring, businesses can ensure that their AI models remain secure and resilient against evolving threats in the dynamic world of AI.

13.2 Data Privacy Laws and AI Compliance

As AI technologies are increasingly integrated into industries worldwide, they come with the significant responsibility of handling vast amounts of data, including personal and sensitive information. With this responsibility comes a need for robust compliance with data privacy laws and regulations. Data privacy laws are designed to protect individuals' rights to privacy and safeguard their personal information from misuse. Non-compliance with these regulations can lead to legal consequences, financial penalties, and damage to an organization's reputation. This section explores the critical role of data privacy laws in AI deployment and how organizations can ensure compliance while utilizing AI technologies.

Key Data Privacy Laws Impacting AI

In recent years, governments around the world have introduced and updated data privacy laws to address concerns about data security and individuals' privacy. These laws often set specific guidelines for the collection, processing, storage, and sharing of personal data. AI systems, particularly those that process large-scale data, need to be designed and deployed in compliance with these regulations to avoid potential risks. Below are some of the most important data privacy laws and their implications for AI:

1. General Data Protection Regulation (GDPR) – European Union

The General Data Protection Regulation (GDPR), which came into effect in May 2018, is one of the most comprehensive and stringent data privacy laws globally. It governs the processing and protection of personal data within the European Union (EU) and applies to any organization that processes data about EU citizens, regardless of the organization's location.

The GDPR establishes several key principles for organizations, such as:

- **Data Minimization**: Organizations should only collect and retain data necessary for the specific purpose for which it was collected.
- **Data Subject Rights**: Individuals have the right to access, correct, and delete their data. They also have the right to withdraw consent for processing their data at any time.
- **Transparency**: Organizations must inform users about the type of data being collected, its purpose, and how it will be used.

- **Automated Decision-Making and Profiling**: The GDPR requires that individuals not be subject to decisions based solely on automated processing, including profiling, that significantly affects them. AI systems that rely heavily on automated decision-making may be restricted unless certain safeguards are in place, such as offering the individual the right to contest or appeal automated decisions.

For AI models, this means that organizations must ensure that personal data is handled in a transparent, secure, and compliant manner throughout the entire AI lifecycle, from data collection and processing to deployment.

2. California Consumer Privacy Act (CCPA) – United States

The California Consumer Privacy Act (CCPA) is a data privacy law that came into effect in January 2020 and applies to businesses operating in California that collect personal data. The CCPA gives California residents the right to access, delete, and opt out of the sale of their personal information. Some key provisions of the CCPA include:

- **Right to Know**: Consumers have the right to request information about the data collected about them and how it is used.
- **Right to Delete**: Consumers can request that businesses delete their personal data, with certain exceptions.
- **Right to Opt-Out**: Consumers can opt out of having their data sold to third parties.

The CCPA has significant implications for AI systems because it requires businesses to maintain transparency about how data is used and shared, especially if AI models leverage personal data for analysis, predictions, or profiling. AI systems must be designed to respect users' data privacy rights and give them the ability to exercise their rights under the CCPA.

3. Health Insurance Portability and Accountability Act (HIPAA) – United States

The Health Insurance Portability and Accountability Act (HIPAA) is a U.S. law that regulates the use and disclosure of protected health information (PHI) by healthcare providers, insurers, and other entities in the healthcare industry. For AI models deployed in healthcare applications, HIPAA compliance is crucial, as it governs the confidentiality and security of patient data.

HIPAA mandates strict protocols around the collection, storage, and transmission of health data, including:

- **Data Security**: Healthcare organizations must implement robust security measures to protect PHI from unauthorized access or breaches.
- **Data Minimization**: AI models in healthcare should minimize the use of sensitive data and only process the information necessary to achieve the intended purpose.

Organizations utilizing AI in healthcare must ensure their models and systems comply with HIPAA's data security and privacy provisions, particularly when handling sensitive medical information.

4. Personal Data Protection Act (PDPA) – Singapore

The Personal Data Protection Act (PDPA) is Singapore's main law governing the collection, use, and disclosure of personal data. It sets out a comprehensive framework for managing personal data and establishes rules for businesses to follow when handling such data.

Key principles of the PDPA include:

- **Consent**: Organizations must obtain consent from individuals before collecting their personal data.
- **Purpose Limitation**: Data must only be used for the purposes for which it was collected.
- **Access and Correction**: Individuals have the right to access and request corrections to their personal data.

Organizations deploying AI models in Singapore must ensure that they obtain explicit consent for collecting data, minimize data usage, and comply with all data protection principles set out by the PDPA.

AI Compliance and Ethical Considerations

Ensuring compliance with data privacy laws is just one aspect of deploying AI systems responsibly. Ethical considerations play a significant role in the deployment of AI, particularly when it comes to ensuring that AI systems are not discriminatory, biased, or harmful to individuals or communities. Some important ethical considerations include:

1. Data Bias and Fairness

AI models can unintentionally reinforce or exacerbate biases present in the training data. If the data used to train an AI system is biased (e.g., based on gender, race, or socioeconomic status), the model may produce biased results, leading to discrimination in decision-making. Compliance with data privacy laws requires that data used in AI models be accurate, representative, and free from unfair bias.

Organizations must ensure that their AI models are fair and transparent, particularly in areas such as hiring, lending, and law enforcement, where biased decisions could have significant consequences for individuals.

2. Transparency and Accountability

Transparency is a key principle of data privacy laws like GDPR. Organizations should be transparent about how they collect, store, and process personal data, particularly when AI models are involved. Additionally, organizations must be accountable for the decisions made by AI systems. This includes ensuring that models are interpretable, allowing stakeholders to understand how decisions are made and identifying any potential issues that may arise.

3. Protecting Data Subject Rights

As discussed in the GDPR, data subjects (individuals whose data is being processed) have certain rights, such as the right to access, correct, delete, and object to the processing of their data. AI systems must be designed to respect these rights, including offering individuals the ability to challenge or opt out of decisions made by automated systems, ensuring compliance with regulations like the GDPR's automated decision-making provisions.

4. Consent Management

Obtaining and managing consent is a fundamental requirement of most data privacy laws, and this is particularly challenging when dealing with AI models that continuously process large volumes of personal data. Ensuring that individuals are properly informed about how their data will be used by AI systems and that they have the ability to withdraw consent is crucial for maintaining compliance.

Strategies for Ensuring AI Compliance with Data Privacy Laws

To ensure AI compliance with data privacy laws, organizations should implement the following strategies:

1. Data Protection by Design and by Default

Adopt a "data protection by design and by default" approach, which means incorporating data privacy and security measures into the AI model development process from the outset. This can include implementing privacy-preserving techniques, such as anonymization and encryption, and ensuring that the data collected is strictly necessary for the AI system's operation.

2. Regular Audits and Monitoring

Conduct regular audits and monitoring of AI models to ensure compliance with data privacy laws. This includes reviewing data access logs, checking for potential violations of privacy rights, and evaluating how AI models are processing and using data.

3. Employee Training and Awareness

Provide ongoing training to employees involved in AI development and deployment on the importance of data privacy and legal compliance. Employees should be familiar with relevant data privacy laws and ethical guidelines to avoid any inadvertent violations during the AI development lifecycle.

4. Collaborating with Legal and Compliance Teams

AI developers should work closely with legal and compliance teams to stay updated on changes in data privacy laws and regulations. This collaboration ensures that AI systems are aligned with the latest legal frameworks and best practices.

As AI continues to revolutionize industries and redefine how businesses operate, it is essential for organizations to remain vigilant about data privacy and ensure compliance with the growing body of data privacy laws. From the GDPR to the CCPA and beyond, compliance is a critical aspect of deploying AI systems responsibly. By understanding the legal requirements, adopting ethical AI practices, and implementing robust privacy protection measures, organizations can harness the power of AI while safeguarding individuals' rights and building trust with users. As the regulatory landscape continues to evolve, ongoing attention to data privacy and AI compliance will remain essential for the success and longevity of AI systems in the real world.

13.3 Addressing AI Bias and Ethical Risks

As artificial intelligence (AI) systems continue to permeate various industries and impact real-world decision-making, it becomes increasingly critical to address ethical concerns and biases that may arise in the design, deployment, and use of these models. AI is often seen as a neutral, objective tool, but the reality is that AI models can perpetuate or even exacerbate existing biases, leading to harmful consequences for individuals and communities. Ethical considerations in AI deployment are not only about ensuring fairness, transparency, and accountability but also about minimizing and mitigating bias in AI systems.

This section explores the root causes of AI bias, the ethical risks associated with deploying biased models, and practical strategies for addressing and mitigating these risks. It emphasizes the need for organizations to implement responsible AI practices to prevent discrimination and ensure that AI systems operate in an equitable and fair manner.

Understanding AI Bias

AI bias refers to systematic errors in AI models that result from biased data or biased algorithms. These biases can manifest in various ways, including racial, gender, economic, or geographical disparities. AI systems learn from historical data, and if the data reflects existing societal biases, the AI system may replicate and even amplify these biases.

Some key sources of bias in AI systems include:

1. Bias in Data

AI models are only as good as the data used to train them. If training data reflects historical or societal biases, the model is likely to learn and perpetuate these biases. For example:

- **Gender Bias**: An AI model trained on hiring data that disproportionately favors male candidates may continue to favor men when recommending job applicants.
- **Racial Bias**: Facial recognition systems trained on datasets lacking racial diversity may perform poorly for people with darker skin tones, leading to misidentifications or discriminatory outcomes.

2. Algorithmic Bias

Even when data is balanced and diverse, the algorithms used to build AI models may introduce bias. These biases can arise due to the choices made during the model design and training process. For example, the weighting of certain features in a predictive model may inadvertently favor one demographic over another.

3. Historical and Societal Bias

Many AI systems are trained on historical data that reflects pre-existing societal inequalities. These disparities can reinforce and perpetuate discrimination if the system is not designed to identify and correct for such biases.

4. Sample Bias

Sample bias occurs when the dataset used to train the AI model is not representative of the target population or real-world conditions. For instance, training an AI model with data from one demographic group but applying it to a broader population can lead to inaccurate or biased outcomes.

Ethical Risks of AI Bias

The ethical risks of AI bias are significant and can have far-reaching consequences for individuals and society. Bias in AI models can lead to discrimination, exclusion, and unfair treatment of certain groups, especially in sensitive domains such as healthcare, hiring, criminal justice, and finance.

1. Discrimination and Inequality

When AI systems are biased, they can discriminate against specific groups, leading to unfair treatment and outcomes. For instance, AI models used in hiring might inadvertently favor one gender or ethnic group, while models used in lending might provide biased credit scores based on socioeconomic factors, reinforcing economic disparities. This can result in:

- **Exclusion from Opportunities**: Groups that are systematically disadvantaged, such as women, racial minorities, or lower-income individuals, may face unjust barriers to access, employment, or education.
- **Perpetuating Historical Inequalities**: AI bias can perpetuate longstanding societal inequalities by reinforcing existing stereotypes and prejudices.

2. Lack of Trust and Accountability

Bias in AI models erodes trust in AI systems. When people perceive AI as being biased or unfair, they may be less likely to adopt or rely on these technologies. This can be particularly damaging for organizations that depend on AI to provide decisions in high-stakes areas, such as law enforcement or healthcare. Furthermore, if the decision-making process of an AI system is opaque, individuals may not understand why certain outcomes are produced or how they can contest or appeal those decisions. Lack of transparency and accountability in AI systems can further deepen public mistrust.

3. Unintended Harm and Ethical Dilemmas

AI systems that make decisions with biased data can inadvertently cause harm. For example, in healthcare, AI systems used for diagnosis and treatment recommendations might provide different recommendations based on gender or race, leading to poorer outcomes for certain groups. In criminal justice, biased algorithms could result in unfair sentencing or risk assessments, disproportionately affecting marginalized populations. Such harms raise significant ethical concerns about the role of AI in decision-making and the moral responsibility of organizations deploying these systems.

Addressing AI Bias and Ethical Risks

Addressing AI bias and ethical risks requires a comprehensive approach that spans the AI development lifecycle, from data collection and model training to deployment and ongoing monitoring. Below are several key strategies to mitigate bias and ensure that AI systems are fair, ethical, and transparent:

1. Diverse and Representative Data

One of the most effective ways to address AI bias is by ensuring that the training data is diverse, representative, and inclusive of all groups that the AI system will impact. This involves:

- **Balancing Datasets**: When training AI models, ensure that the dataset includes adequate representation from different demographic groups, including various races, genders, socioeconomic statuses, and geographic regions.
- **Data Augmentation**: In cases where it is difficult to obtain diverse data, techniques like data augmentation or synthetic data generation can help balance underrepresented groups.
- **Ensuring Data Quality**: Ensure that the data used for training is of high quality, accurate, and free from errors that could contribute to biases.

2. Fairness-Aware Algorithms

Bias can often be mitigated through the careful design and implementation of fairness-aware algorithms. This involves:

- **Bias Detection Tools**: Implementing tools and techniques that help identify bias in datasets and model outputs, such as fairness metrics, disparity analysis, and auditing frameworks.
- **Fairness Constraints**: Incorporating fairness constraints into the optimization process of machine learning models to ensure that they do not favor one group over another. These constraints can be adjusted to minimize bias while maintaining model accuracy.
- **Model Explainability**: Using explainable AI techniques to make the decision-making process of AI models transparent. Understanding how and why a model makes certain decisions allows for better identification and rectification of biased outcomes.

3. Ethical Frameworks and Governance

Organizations deploying AI models must establish strong ethical frameworks and governance structures to guide the responsible development and use of AI. This includes:

- **Ethical Guidelines**: Developing and adhering to a set of ethical guidelines that prioritize fairness, transparency, accountability, and respect for human rights. These guidelines should be integrated into every stage of the AI lifecycle, from design and development to deployment and monitoring.
- **Ethics Committees and Oversight**: Creating multidisciplinary ethics committees that include experts in AI, law, social science, and ethics. These committees should provide guidance on the ethical implications of AI models and monitor their real-world impact.
- **Continuous Monitoring**: Conducting regular audits of AI systems post-deployment to ensure that they remain fair and unbiased as they interact with real-world data and scenarios.

4. Accountability and Transparency

Organizations must be held accountable for the decisions made by their AI systems. This requires:

- **Transparent Development Process**: Providing full transparency about how AI models are developed, including the data used, the algorithms employed, and the decision-making processes that govern them.
- **Model Documentation**: Maintaining detailed documentation for AI models, including an explanation of how they work, their limitations, and potential sources of bias.
- **Right to Contest**: Offering individuals the ability to challenge or appeal decisions made by AI systems, especially in high-stakes applications such as credit scoring, hiring, and criminal justice.

5. Ethical AI Training for Developers

Ensuring that AI developers and practitioners are equipped with the knowledge and skills to recognize and mitigate bias is essential. This involves:

- **Training in Ethics**: Providing AI developers with training on ethical issues, including data privacy, fairness, transparency, and accountability.
- **Bias Mitigation Techniques**: Teaching AI practitioners how to implement bias mitigation techniques throughout the AI lifecycle, from data collection to model deployment.

AI bias and ethical risks are significant challenges that organizations must address in the deployment of AI systems. By understanding the sources of bias and the ethical implications of AI, organizations can take proactive steps to ensure that their models are fair, transparent, and accountable. Through the use of diverse data, fairness-aware algorithms, strong ethical frameworks, and continuous monitoring, organizations can minimize the risk of bias and build AI systems that operate responsibly and equitably. As AI continues to shape industries and society, addressing these ethical risks is crucial to ensuring that AI benefits all people, regardless of their background or identity.

13.4 Explainability and Transparency in AI

As artificial intelligence (AI) systems become increasingly integral to decision-making processes across various industries, one of the key challenges that has emerged is ensuring that these systems operate in a transparent, understandable, and accountable manner. While AI, particularly machine learning (ML) and deep learning models, can provide powerful insights and make highly accurate predictions, the complex nature of many AI models often makes it difficult for users to understand how these decisions are made. This lack of transparency and explainability can lead to trust issues, especially when AI is deployed in high-stakes domains such as healthcare, finance, criminal justice, and autonomous vehicles.

This section delves into the importance of explainability and transparency in AI, explores the challenges that come with making AI models interpretable, and provides strategies for improving transparency without sacrificing performance.

The Importance of Explainability and Transparency

Explainability and transparency in AI are crucial for building trust and ensuring that AI systems operate ethically and responsibly. The more transparent and understandable an AI system is, the easier it is for stakeholders to trust the outcomes it produces. There are several reasons why explainability and transparency matter:

1. Trust and Adoption

For AI systems to be widely adopted, especially in sectors like healthcare, finance, and law, stakeholders—including users, customers, and regulators—must trust the system. If an AI system's decision-making process is a "black box," users are likely to feel uneasy about relying on it, particularly if the outcomes have significant personal, legal, or financial consequences. Providing clear explanations of how AI models arrive at decisions enhances trust and encourages adoption.

2. Accountability and Responsibility

In cases where AI systems make errors or produce biased results, transparency is crucial for accountability. Users need to understand how and why an AI model made a specific decision so that errors can be traced back to their sources. If the model is opaque, identifying and rectifying mistakes becomes nearly impossible, and accountability becomes blurred. Explainability helps organizations take responsibility for AI's decisions, allowing them to make adjustments, take corrective actions, and ensure fairness.

3. Ethical Considerations

In many domains, particularly in areas affecting vulnerable groups (such as healthcare or criminal justice), decisions made by AI systems must adhere to ethical principles, including fairness, non-discrimination, and respect for human rights. If an AI system's behavior cannot be explained or understood, it becomes difficult to assess whether it is adhering to ethical guidelines or perpetuating biases. Making AI systems explainable ensures that ethical standards are met and can be independently verified.

4. Legal and Regulatory Compliance

As AI systems become more pervasive, regulatory bodies are increasingly focusing on ensuring that AI technologies meet specific standards, including fairness and transparency. For instance, the European Union's General Data Protection Regulation (GDPR) includes a provision known as the "right to explanation," which states that individuals should be able to understand and contest decisions made by automated systems that significantly affect them. In addition, regulations such as the U.S. Fair Lending Act require that AI models used in lending decisions be interpretable to avoid discriminatory practices. Organizations must ensure that their AI models can provide transparent and understandable explanations of their decisions to comply with such regulations.

Challenges to Explainability and Transparency

While explainability and transparency are important, achieving them in AI models, particularly complex ones like deep learning, is no easy feat. Several challenges hinder efforts to make AI systems interpretable:

1. Complexity of Models

Many AI models, particularly deep learning algorithms such as neural networks, are highly complex and involve millions (or even billions) of parameters. These models learn from vast datasets and adjust their parameters based on intricate patterns that are often difficult for humans to comprehend. For instance, a deep neural network might make predictions based on non-linear interactions between variables that do not have an intuitive, human-understandable explanation. This complexity makes it difficult to pinpoint exactly why a model made a particular decision.

2. Trade-off Between Performance and Interpretability

In some cases, there is a trade-off between model performance and explainability. Highly interpretable models, such as decision trees or linear regression, are easier to understand but may not capture the full complexity of the underlying data, leading to lower performance. On the other hand, complex models like deep neural networks may achieve superior performance but are much harder to explain. This creates a dilemma for organizations seeking to balance the need for transparency with the desire for high-performing models.

3. Lack of Standardized Methods

There is no universally accepted framework or method for explaining AI models. Different types of models require different approaches to interpretability, and some models (like deep learning) have more established techniques for explaining their decisions than others. This lack of standardization makes it difficult for organizations to know how best to explain the decision-making process of their AI systems and create consistent approaches across various types of models.

4. Computational Costs

Explaining complex models, particularly deep learning models, often requires additional computational resources. Techniques like "local explainability," which attempt to explain individual predictions made by a model, may require multiple passes through the model and significant computational overhead. For real-time systems or large-scale AI applications, the cost of implementing these explainability techniques can be prohibitive.

Techniques for Achieving Explainability and Transparency

While there are significant challenges to achieving explainability, various techniques and approaches can help improve the transparency of AI systems. These techniques vary depending on the type of model, its complexity, and the level of explanation required.

1. Model-Agnostic Methods

Model-agnostic methods can be applied to any type of AI model to help explain its behavior, regardless of its underlying architecture. Some popular model-agnostic techniques include:

- **LIME (Local Interpretable Model-agnostic Explanations):** LIME is a method that approximates complex models with simpler, interpretable models (such as decision trees) locally around the prediction of interest. By perturbing input data and observing changes in predictions, LIME can provide an explanation of how the model makes decisions for individual instances.
- **SHAP (Shapley Additive Explanations):** SHAP values are based on game theory and provide a way to measure the contribution of each feature to a model's prediction. By computing Shapley values, SHAP can help break down a complex model's prediction and give insight into which features were most influential.

2. Interpretable Models

In some cases, choosing interpretable models from the outset can be an effective strategy. These models, such as decision trees, logistic regression, and linear regression, are easier to understand because they explicitly show how features contribute to the final prediction. Though they may not capture the full complexity of the data, these models can often provide sufficient explainability for certain tasks and industries, especially when decisions need to be transparent and explainable to users.

3. Feature Importance Analysis

Feature importance techniques help to identify which input features are most responsible for the predictions made by an AI model. Common methods for computing feature importance include:

- **Permutation Importance**: This method involves shuffling the values of each feature and measuring the impact on model performance. Features that significantly affect model accuracy are considered important.
- **Partial Dependence Plots (PDPs):** PDPs visualize the relationship between a feature and the predicted outcome, holding other features constant. This can help users understand the effect of a particular feature on the model's predictions.

4. Attention Mechanisms in Deep Learning

For deep learning models, particularly those used in natural language processing (NLP) and computer vision, attention mechanisms can help improve explainability. Attention mechanisms highlight which parts of the input data the model is focusing on when making a prediction. For example, in NLP tasks, attention maps can show which words in a sentence are most relevant to the model's prediction. In image classification, attention maps can highlight areas of an image that the model considers when making its decision.

5. Counterfactual Explanations

Counterfactual explanations provide a way to understand the decisions made by AI models by showing what would have happened if the input data had been slightly different. For example, in a loan approval system, a counterfactual explanation might show how changing a person's income or credit score would have affected their approval outcome. This helps users understand the decision-making process by comparing actual results with hypothetical scenarios.

Explainability and transparency are essential components of responsible AI deployment. By making AI systems more understandable and accessible to users, organizations can build trust, ensure accountability, and avoid unintended harm. Although achieving explainability in complex models presents challenges, techniques such as model-agnostic methods, feature importance analysis, and attention mechanisms provide ways to gain insight into AI decision-making. As AI continues to impact society in profound ways, prioritizing transparency and explainability will be crucial to ensuring that these systems are used ethically, fairly, and responsibly.

14. Case Studies of AI Deployment in Industry

Real-world AI deployment comes with unique challenges and insights that vary across industries. In this chapter, we explore practical case studies of AI implementation in sectors such as healthcare, finance, retail, manufacturing, and autonomous systems. You'll learn how companies have successfully deployed AI models for medical diagnostics, fraud detection, personalized recommendations, predictive maintenance, and self-driving technology. Each case study highlights deployment strategies, technical challenges, business impact, and lessons learned, providing valuable insights for anyone looking to implement AI in production. By analyzing these real-world examples, you'll gain a practical understanding of AI deployment at scale and how to navigate common hurdles.

14.1 AI Deployment in Healthcare

Artificial Intelligence (AI) is rapidly transforming the healthcare industry, enabling improvements in patient care, diagnosis accuracy, operational efficiency, and drug discovery. AI deployment in healthcare brings new possibilities for revolutionizing how medical professionals diagnose diseases, treat patients, manage healthcare data, and streamline administrative processes. However, its successful deployment also faces unique challenges, including ethical considerations, regulatory requirements, data privacy, and the integration with existing healthcare infrastructure. This section explores how AI is deployed in healthcare, its various applications, the challenges involved, and the impact it has on the healthcare ecosystem.

AI Applications in Healthcare

AI deployment in healthcare can be broadly categorized into several key areas:

1. Diagnostic Support and Imaging

One of the most prominent applications of AI in healthcare is diagnostic support, particularly in medical imaging. AI models, especially those leveraging deep learning algorithms, have shown exceptional capabilities in interpreting medical images such as X-rays, MRIs, and CT scans. These models can detect anomalies such as tumors, fractures, and other signs of diseases with accuracy comparable to or even exceeding that of experienced radiologists.

For example, AI-powered tools like IBM's Watson Health and Google Health's AI models have been developed to analyze medical images and assist doctors in making quicker and more accurate diagnoses. The advantage of using AI in imaging lies in its ability to process vast amounts of data quickly, providing healthcare professionals with real-time support and reducing the risk of human error.

2. Predictive Analytics and Personalized Medicine

AI models, particularly those based on machine learning, have the potential to predict disease outbreaks, forecast individual health risks, and optimize treatment plans. By analyzing patient data—such as medical history, lifestyle factors, and genetic information—AI systems can provide personalized treatment recommendations that are tailored to an individual's unique needs.

Predictive analytics can also be used for early detection of chronic conditions like diabetes, heart disease, and cancer. By leveraging vast datasets, AI models can identify at-risk patients before the onset of symptoms, enabling preventive measures and reducing healthcare costs over the long term.

In personalized medicine, AI algorithms are increasingly used to identify which treatments will work best for patients based on their genetic makeup, thereby improving treatment efficacy and minimizing side effects. Companies like Tempus and Foundation Medicine are already integrating AI in precision oncology, helping doctors make data-driven decisions when prescribing cancer treatments.

3. Natural Language Processing (NLP) for Medical Records

Another impactful AI application in healthcare is Natural Language Processing (NLP), which allows AI models to process and extract meaningful insights from unstructured data, such as medical records, doctor's notes, and research papers. Healthcare providers generate vast amounts of unstructured textual data, and AI-powered NLP systems can streamline this data, enabling better decision-making and more efficient workflow management.

For example, NLP can assist in extracting relevant patient information from electronic health records (EHRs) to improve clinical decision-making, alert clinicians to potential risks, and automate routine administrative tasks like coding and billing.

4. Drug Discovery and Development

AI has proven to be a valuable asset in the pharmaceutical industry, where it accelerates the drug discovery and development process. Traditionally, discovering new drugs requires extensive testing and trial phases that take years to complete and cost billions of dollars. AI is changing this paradigm by simulating and predicting how molecules will interact within the body, allowing researchers to identify promising compounds much faster.

For instance, AI algorithms like those developed by BenevolentAI and Insilico Medicine analyze massive datasets of biological information, research papers, and chemical structures to predict the efficacy of potential drugs. By shortening the drug development timeline and reducing costs, AI is poised to revolutionize how new treatments are brought to market, offering hope for faster cures to diseases such as Alzheimer's, cancer, and rare genetic disorders.

5. Virtual Health Assistants and Chatbots

Virtual health assistants powered by AI have the potential to greatly enhance patient engagement and provide support outside of traditional clinical settings. These AI-driven tools can assist with answering patient queries, scheduling appointments, sending reminders for medications, and offering general health advice.

AI-powered chatbots like Ada Health and Babylon Health are already being deployed to provide virtual consultations. These systems use machine learning to understand patient symptoms, ask relevant questions, and offer potential diagnoses or recommendations. They help reduce the burden on healthcare providers by offering patients immediate, accessible care, particularly for routine inquiries or in underserved areas where access to doctors may be limited.

Challenges of AI Deployment in Healthcare

While AI holds great promise for transforming healthcare, its deployment in this sector is not without challenges. Healthcare systems are often complex, with a variety of stakeholders, regulations, and legacy infrastructure. Some of the key challenges include:

1. Data Privacy and Security

Healthcare data is some of the most sensitive information that exists, and protecting it from breaches is crucial. In many countries, strict regulations such as the Health Insurance Portability and Accountability Act (HIPAA) in the U.S. and the General Data

Protection Regulation (GDPR) in the European Union govern how healthcare data is handled.

AI deployment in healthcare often requires access to vast amounts of patient data for training models, raising concerns about data privacy and security. AI systems must ensure that sensitive data is protected, and proper consent is obtained from patients before their data is used. Moreover, AI algorithms need to be transparent about how data is processed and ensure that models are trained without biases that could lead to discriminatory outcomes.

2. Model Interpretability and Trust

As discussed earlier, AI models can sometimes be seen as "black boxes," meaning that their decision-making processes are not always transparent or easily understood by healthcare professionals. In healthcare, where lives are at stake, it is essential that clinicians trust the recommendations made by AI systems. Without clear explanations for how decisions are made, doctors may be hesitant to fully rely on AI-driven insights.

Efforts to improve explainability and transparency in AI models, such as through techniques like LIME and SHAP, are crucial for building trust and enabling healthcare providers to confidently use AI systems in clinical settings.

3. Regulatory Approval and Standardization

The healthcare industry is heavily regulated, and any AI tool used for medical purposes must undergo rigorous testing, validation, and approval by regulatory bodies such as the U.S. Food and Drug Administration (FDA) or the European Medicines Agency (EMA). These regulatory agencies are still adapting to the rapid advancement of AI in healthcare, and the approval process for AI-driven tools is often slow and complex.

Furthermore, there is a lack of universal standards for AI in healthcare. Different AI solutions may work in vastly different ways, and without clear standards, interoperability between systems can be problematic. Developing standardized frameworks for AI deployment in healthcare will be essential for ensuring the safe and effective integration of these technologies.

4. Integration with Existing Healthcare Systems

AI tools need to be integrated into existing healthcare infrastructure, which can often be fragmented and outdated. Electronic health records (EHR) systems, for example, are not always designed to accommodate the advanced capabilities of modern AI models. Ensuring that AI systems work seamlessly with existing software and platforms is critical for successful deployment.

Healthcare organizations must also train their staff to effectively use AI tools, which may involve significant changes in workflow. Adoption can be slow if healthcare professionals are not properly educated on how AI can support their work, leading to resistance in the transition to AI-powered practices.

Impact of AI on Healthcare

Despite the challenges, the impact of AI in healthcare is profound and growing. AI-driven tools are improving diagnostic accuracy, reducing costs, enhancing patient outcomes, and enabling personalized treatments. As AI continues to evolve and become more integrated into healthcare, it holds the potential to revolutionize how care is delivered, making healthcare more efficient, accessible, and patient-centric.

In the future, we may see AI being deployed not only for clinical decision support but also for routine check-ups, continuous monitoring of chronic diseases, and improving public health initiatives. By enabling healthcare providers to make data-driven, evidence-based decisions, AI can help to bridge gaps in care, particularly in underserved regions and populations.

AI deployment in healthcare presents exciting possibilities for improving the quality of care, accelerating medical research, and enhancing patient engagement. However, it also brings significant challenges, particularly around data privacy, regulatory approval, and model interpretability. For AI to reach its full potential in healthcare, developers, healthcare providers, and policymakers must work together to address these challenges while ensuring that AI is deployed responsibly, ethically, and in a way that benefits all stakeholders.

14.2 AI in Finance and Fraud Detection

The financial sector has long been a frontrunner in adopting cutting-edge technologies to improve services, enhance customer experiences, and ensure the security of transactions. Artificial Intelligence (AI) is one of the most transformative technologies in the finance industry today, playing a crucial role in everything from automating trading to providing personalized financial services. Among its most vital applications is in the area of fraud detection, where AI has proven to be indispensable in identifying fraudulent activities and securing financial transactions. In this section, we'll explore how AI is deployed in finance, its role in fraud detection, and the challenges and benefits it brings to the industry.

AI Applications in Finance

AI has become embedded in various facets of the finance industry, including credit scoring, algorithmic trading, customer service, and risk management. Here are some key areas where AI is revolutionizing finance:

1. Algorithmic Trading

Algorithmic trading refers to the use of computer algorithms to automatically execute financial transactions based on predetermined criteria. These algorithms can process vast amounts of market data, identifying trends, making predictions, and executing trades at speeds far beyond human capabilities. AI, particularly machine learning, can analyze complex market data patterns and adapt to changing conditions in real-time, helping traders make faster and more informed decisions.

AI models used in algorithmic trading are able to detect market inefficiencies, optimize strategies, and minimize risks. Hedge funds and financial institutions are increasingly relying on AI-based systems to enhance their trading strategies, improving returns and mitigating risks in the highly volatile financial markets.

2. Credit Scoring and Risk Assessment

Credit scoring is an essential process in finance, used by lenders to assess the creditworthiness of individuals and businesses. Traditional credit scoring models rely on static, historical data such as credit history, income, and outstanding debts. However, AI is taking credit scoring to a new level by incorporating a broader range of dynamic data sources, including spending habits, social media activity, and even online behavior.

Machine learning algorithms are capable of processing and analyzing these diverse datasets, identifying patterns that humans may miss. This enables lenders to make more accurate and reliable credit assessments, leading to better decision-making and reducing the risk of defaults. Additionally, AI can provide real-time credit scores, allowing for faster loan approvals and more personalized financial products for consumers.

3. Personalized Financial Services

In recent years, AI has been used to provide personalized financial advice to clients. Through natural language processing (NLP) and machine learning, AI systems are able to analyze individual customer profiles, financial goals, risk tolerance, and spending habits to offer tailored recommendations.

Robo-advisors, powered by AI, have emerged as a cost-effective alternative to traditional financial advisors. These AI-driven platforms help individuals manage their investments, offering advice based on data-driven insights rather than relying on human advisors. AI is also being used to personalize banking services, providing customers with proactive notifications and advice based on their financial behaviors, such as alerting them to upcoming bill payments, or suggesting savings and investment strategies based on their financial goals.

Fraud Detection in Finance: The Role of AI

Fraud detection is one of the most significant applications of AI in the finance sector. Fraudulent activities, such as credit card fraud, identity theft, money laundering, and insider trading, pose a severe threat to financial institutions and their customers. Traditional fraud detection systems rely on rule-based models that look for predefined patterns of fraudulent activity. However, these systems are often limited by their inability to adapt to new and evolving fraud tactics.

AI, particularly machine learning, has revolutionized fraud detection by enabling financial institutions to detect and prevent fraud more effectively, efficiently, and in real-time. Here's how AI is transforming fraud detection:

1. Anomaly Detection

Anomaly detection is a key technique used in AI-based fraud detection systems. Machine learning algorithms, particularly unsupervised learning models, can identify unusual patterns or behaviors in transaction data. By analyzing historical data and understanding what constitutes "normal" behavior for a particular customer or transaction, AI systems can detect deviations from these patterns, which may indicate fraudulent activity.

For example, if a customer's credit card is used for a large transaction in a foreign country within a short time frame after being used domestically, AI can flag this as an anomaly and alert the customer or financial institution. Unlike rule-based systems, AI models can learn to recognize new forms of fraud that may not be explicitly defined in the rules, making them more adaptive and effective.

2. Real-Time Fraud Prevention

AI systems can work in real-time, analyzing transactions as they occur and flagging suspicious activities immediately. This is particularly important in sectors like e-commerce and online banking, where rapid response times are critical in minimizing financial losses.

Real-time AI fraud detection systems continuously analyze multiple factors, including transaction amount, location, frequency, and device used, to detect any irregularities. In the case of a fraudulent transaction, AI can automatically block the transaction, freeze accounts, or request additional verification steps, significantly reducing the chances of fraudulent activities slipping through unnoticed.

3. Machine Learning for Fraud Pattern Recognition

Machine learning algorithms excel at identifying patterns in large datasets. In the context of fraud detection, AI systems are trained on historical transaction data to recognize patterns associated with fraud. Over time, these algorithms improve their ability to spot subtle signs of fraud, even when the fraudsters are using novel methods or disguising their activities.

For instance, AI systems can detect phishing attempts by analyzing patterns in emails, websites, or phone calls. They can identify fraudulent behavior in financial markets, such as insider trading or market manipulation, by tracking patterns in market data and identifying suspicious activity that deviates from normal trading patterns.

4. Preventing Money Laundering

Money laundering is a serious issue in the financial sector, where illegally obtained funds are made to look legitimate through a series of complex transactions. AI is increasingly being used to combat money laundering by analyzing transaction data for signs of suspicious activity, such as large, rapid, or unusual transfers of money across different jurisdictions.

AI-powered systems can track and analyze vast amounts of financial transactions in real-time to identify money laundering patterns. By using machine learning to understand typical behavior, AI can flag suspicious activities, such as structuring (breaking down large sums into smaller transactions) and layering (moving money through different accounts), alerting financial institutions and authorities for further investigation.

Benefits of AI in Finance and Fraud Detection

The integration of AI into finance, particularly in fraud detection, brings numerous benefits:

1. Improved Accuracy and Efficiency

AI systems can process vast amounts of financial data much faster and more accurately than humans. This allows for the detection of fraudulent transactions and behaviors in real time, preventing financial losses and safeguarding customer accounts.

2. Reduced False Positives

Traditional fraud detection systems often result in high rates of false positives—when legitimate transactions are flagged as fraudulent. This can inconvenience customers and result in costly manual interventions. AI models, particularly those using machine learning, can reduce false positives by becoming more accurate over time, learning to differentiate between legitimate transactions and fraudulent ones.

3. Scalability

AI-based fraud detection systems can scale effortlessly to accommodate growing volumes of data, making them ideal for large financial institutions. As transaction volumes increase, AI can continue to analyze data in real time, ensuring that fraud detection capabilities remain robust even as businesses grow.

4. Proactive Fraud Prevention

By identifying and preventing fraud early, AI systems help financial institutions avoid the significant costs associated with fraud, including chargebacks, reputational damage, and regulatory fines. Additionally, AI can help build trust with customers, as they know their financial data is being constantly monitored for potential threats.

Challenges in AI Deployment for Fraud Detection

While AI brings significant benefits to fraud detection in finance, there are challenges that need to be addressed:

1. Data Privacy Concerns

AI systems require access to vast amounts of sensitive customer data to detect fraud effectively. This raises concerns about data privacy and security, particularly given the regulatory requirements surrounding customer data. Financial institutions must ensure that AI systems comply with data privacy laws, such as GDPR and CCPA, and that customer data is handled securely.

2. Bias in AI Models

AI models, if not carefully trained, can inherit biases from the data they are trained on. This can lead to biased fraud detection outcomes, where certain demographic groups may be unfairly targeted or certain fraud patterns are overlooked. It's important to ensure that AI systems are trained on diverse datasets and that they are continuously monitored and adjusted to mitigate bias.

3. Evolving Fraud Tactics

As AI systems become more adept at detecting fraud, fraudsters are also evolving their tactics to bypass detection. It is an ongoing challenge for AI systems to keep up with new and emerging fraud techniques. Regular updates and retraining of AI models are necessary to maintain the effectiveness of fraud detection systems.

AI is playing a pivotal role in transforming the finance industry, particularly in the areas of fraud detection and prevention. By harnessing the power of machine learning, financial institutions can detect and prevent fraud in real-time, safeguard customer accounts, and ensure secure financial transactions. While there are challenges to overcome, particularly around data privacy, model bias, and evolving fraud tactics, the benefits of AI in finance are undeniable. As technology continues to advance, AI will undoubtedly play an increasingly central role in securing the financial industry and building trust with customers.

14.3 AI for E-Commerce and Personalization

The world of e-commerce has experienced an extraordinary transformation over the past decade, largely driven by advancements in technology. One of the most significant contributors to this transformation is Artificial Intelligence (AI), which is now at the core of many e-commerce platforms. From personalized shopping experiences to automated customer service, AI has become a key player in shaping the future of online retail.

In this section, we'll explore how AI is deployed in e-commerce, with a focus on its role in personalization—one of the most important areas where AI is making a profound impact. We'll discuss how AI helps e-commerce businesses understand their customers, create customized experiences, and enhance customer satisfaction, all while driving higher sales and improving operational efficiency.

AI Applications in E-Commerce

E-commerce platforms are increasingly leveraging AI to gain a competitive edge and deliver more intuitive and effective shopping experiences. Here are some key AI applications in e-commerce:

1. Personalized Product Recommendations

Personalization is a cornerstone of modern e-commerce strategies, and AI plays a central role in delivering customized product recommendations to customers. Using machine learning algorithms, AI can analyze customers' browsing and purchasing history, as well as their interactions with a website or app, to suggest products that are most likely to interest them.

For example, platforms like Amazon use AI-powered recommendation engines that consider factors such as:

- Past purchases
- Browsing patterns
- Similar users' preferences
- Seasonal trends
- Price sensitivity

This allows customers to receive personalized suggestions that not only enhance their shopping experience but also drive higher sales for e-commerce businesses. Studies show that personalized product recommendations can significantly increase conversion rates and average order values.

2. Predictive Analytics for Inventory Management

AI is also transforming inventory management in e-commerce by predicting customer demand and optimizing stock levels. By analyzing past sales data, seasonality, and market trends, AI models can forecast future demand for products with remarkable accuracy.

This predictive capability allows e-commerce businesses to avoid stockouts and overstocking, ensuring that they have the right products available at the right time. For example, if AI detects a spike in demand for a particular product based on historical purchasing trends, it can automatically trigger restocking actions to avoid running out of inventory. Predictive analytics also help retailers optimize their supply chain, minimizing waste and maximizing operational efficiency.

3. Dynamic Pricing and Price Optimization

Dynamic pricing refers to the ability to adjust prices in real-time based on various factors such as demand, competitor prices, customer behavior, and market conditions. AI plays a crucial role in enabling dynamic pricing strategies by continuously analyzing vast amounts of data to identify patterns and opportunities for price adjustments.

For example, AI algorithms can identify when demand for a product is high and increase its price accordingly, or when a competitor lowers its price, triggering an automatic adjustment to stay competitive. This allows e-commerce platforms to optimize pricing strategies for maximum profitability while remaining competitive in the market.

4. Chatbots and Virtual Assistants

Customer service is a vital component of the e-commerce experience, and AI-driven chatbots are revolutionizing how businesses interact with customers. AI chatbots use natural language processing (NLP) and machine learning to understand and respond to customer inquiries, providing immediate support on product questions, order status, returns, and more.

These virtual assistants are available 24/7, ensuring that customers can always get the help they need, regardless of the time zone or business hours. By automating routine tasks, chatbots free up customer service agents to handle more complex queries and allow businesses to provide faster, more efficient service. Additionally, AI chatbots can be personalized, learning from previous interactions and continuously improving their ability to assist customers effectively.

5. Visual Search and Image Recognition

AI has also made significant strides in visual search technology, enabling customers to search for products using images rather than text. With the help of image recognition algorithms, AI can analyze and identify objects within an image, matching them to products in the retailer's inventory.

For example, if a customer sees an outfit they like in a magazine or on social media, they can upload the image to an e-commerce platform to find similar products available for purchase. This capability enhances the user experience by making it easier to find products, especially when customers don't know the exact name or details of an item. Visual search is also gaining popularity in mobile e-commerce, where customers can use their smartphones to take pictures and search for products in real-time.

6. Fraud Prevention and Security

Fraud is a major concern for e-commerce businesses, and AI is playing an increasingly important role in identifying and preventing fraudulent transactions. By analyzing transaction data, customer behaviors, and historical fraud patterns, AI models can flag suspicious activities in real-time.

AI-based fraud detection systems use techniques such as anomaly detection, behavior analysis, and machine learning to identify potential fraud and take immediate action. This includes blocking transactions, verifying customer identities, or alerting the relevant authorities for further investigation. By preventing fraud before it occurs, AI helps e-commerce businesses protect their customers, maintain trust, and minimize financial losses.

AI-Driven Personalization in E-Commerce

Personalization has become a key driver of customer engagement and loyalty in the e-commerce space. AI-powered personalization goes beyond just recommending products—it enables e-commerce businesses to deliver tailored experiences at every stage of the customer journey. Let's explore some of the most impactful ways AI is enabling personalization in e-commerce:

1. Personalized Content and Website Experience

AI can create personalized website experiences for individual users by adjusting content, product displays, and layouts based on their preferences and behavior. For example, an AI-driven e-commerce platform might change the homepage or product categories displayed based on what the customer has previously searched for or purchased.

By dynamically adjusting the user interface (UI) to match a customer's interests, e-commerce businesses can increase engagement and reduce bounce rates. This personalized experience makes customers feel valued and understood, which increases the likelihood of them returning to the website and making additional purchases.

2. Personalized Email Campaigns

Email marketing remains one of the most effective tools for engaging e-commerce customers. With the help of AI, businesses can personalize email campaigns based on customer behavior and preferences. For instance, AI can segment customers into different groups based on their purchasing patterns, and send them customized emails with product recommendations, promotions, or content that aligns with their interests.

By automating and personalizing email content, AI helps businesses deliver more relevant messages to customers, resulting in higher open rates, increased click-through rates, and ultimately, more conversions.

3. AI-Driven Customer Segmentation

Customer segmentation is an essential aspect of personalization. AI can segment customers based on various criteria, such as demographics, purchase behavior, browsing history, and engagement patterns. This segmentation allows e-commerce platforms to target specific groups with tailored offers and recommendations.

For example, AI may identify high-value customers who make frequent purchases and offer them loyalty rewards or exclusive discounts. Conversely, it may identify customers who haven't made a purchase in a while and send them personalized incentives to return and complete a purchase.

4. Personalized Search Results

AI can improve the search functionality on e-commerce platforms by delivering personalized search results based on a customer's previous interactions. This means that the more a customer engages with the site, the more the search engine learns about their preferences and can deliver results that are more aligned with their tastes.

For example, if a customer consistently browses for outdoor gear, the search engine will prioritize related products in future searches. Personalized search not only enhances the user experience but also increases the likelihood of a customer finding exactly what they're looking for, improving conversion rates.

Benefits of AI in E-Commerce Personalization

The integration of AI into e-commerce platforms provides numerous advantages for businesses and customers alike:

1. Enhanced Customer Experience

AI allows businesses to deliver highly personalized experiences, making customers feel understood and valued. By offering tailored recommendations, content, and interactions, AI improves the overall customer experience and fosters brand loyalty.

2. Increased Sales and Revenue

Personalization directly impacts conversion rates, average order values, and repeat business. By providing customers with products that match their interests and needs, AI drives higher sales and improves overall business performance.

3. Operational Efficiency

AI-powered automation in areas such as inventory management, pricing, and customer service enhances operational efficiency. Businesses can streamline processes, reduce manual intervention, and ensure that resources are used optimally.

4. Customer Retention and Loyalty

Personalized experiences foster stronger relationships between businesses and customers. When customers feel that a brand understands their preferences and offers tailored solutions, they are more likely to return and become loyal advocates.

Challenges in AI-Powered E-Commerce Personalization

Despite the benefits, AI-powered e-commerce personalization comes with its own set of challenges:

1. Data Privacy and Security

Collecting and analyzing vast amounts of customer data to deliver personalized experiences raises concerns about privacy. E-commerce businesses must ensure they comply with data privacy regulations, such as GDPR and CCPA, and protect customer data from breaches.

2. Algorithm Bias

If AI models are not properly trained or if they use biased data, the personalization algorithms may reinforce stereotypes or deliver inaccurate recommendations. Businesses need to regularly evaluate their AI models to ensure fairness and accuracy in the personalization process.

3. Complexity of Implementation

Implementing AI-driven personalization requires significant technical expertise and resources. Businesses need to invest in the right AI tools, data infrastructure, and talent to develop and deploy effective personalization strategies.

AI has become an indispensable tool in e-commerce, especially when it comes to personalization. By leveraging machine learning and other AI technologies, businesses can offer tailored shopping experiences, improve customer satisfaction, and drive higher sales. However, businesses must be mindful of challenges such as data privacy concerns, algorithm bias, and the complexity of implementation. When done correctly, AI-powered personalization can transform an e-commerce business into a customer-centric, data-driven powerhouse that not only meets customer needs but anticipates them, ultimately leading to long-term success in the competitive world of online retail.

14.4 AI in Smart Cities and Autonomous Vehicles

As the world continues to grow and urbanize, cities are faced with increasingly complex challenges in managing resources, infrastructure, and transportation systems. Traditional methods are no longer sufficient to meet the demands of modern cities, and the need for innovative solutions has never been more urgent. Artificial Intelligence (AI) is emerging as a transformative force in this realm, with its potential to revolutionize the way cities operate and how we navigate through them. AI's influence is also expanding into the realm of autonomous vehicles, which promise to reshape transportation systems, further enhancing the concept of smart cities.

This section explores how AI is deployed in smart cities and autonomous vehicles, highlighting its applications, benefits, challenges, and future impact. We will dive into specific examples of AI technologies, such as machine learning, computer vision, and Internet of Things (IoT) devices, and how they are helping create safer, more efficient, and sustainable urban environments.

AI in Smart Cities

Smart cities leverage technology to improve the quality of life for residents, optimize the use of resources, and address pressing urban issues such as traffic congestion, energy consumption, waste management, and public safety. AI plays a pivotal role in powering these cities, providing the tools necessary to analyze vast amounts of data in real-time and implement smart solutions that can automate and enhance city services.

1. Traffic Management and Congestion Reduction

One of the primary challenges in urban environments is traffic congestion. Smart traffic management systems powered by AI can optimize traffic flow, reduce accidents, and ease congestion. AI algorithms analyze data from traffic cameras, sensors, and GPS systems to predict traffic patterns and adjust traffic light timings in real-time, ensuring smoother flow. Additionally, AI can be used to identify bottlenecks, accidents, or other disruptions, and automatically reroute traffic to avoid delays.

For example, AI-driven smart traffic lights can prioritize emergency vehicles or public transportation to clear their paths, significantly improving response times. AI is also used to predict traffic congestion during peak hours, allowing authorities to implement dynamic pricing for toll roads or offer incentives for carpooling, reducing the overall number of vehicles on the road.

2. Energy Management and Sustainability

Sustainability is a key focus for smart cities, and AI plays a crucial role in optimizing energy consumption. AI-driven systems can monitor and manage energy use in real-time, making adjustments to lighting, heating, cooling, and electrical systems based on occupancy, weather forecasts, and usage patterns.

For instance, AI algorithms can control streetlights in response to pedestrian activity, dimming or brightening lights based on the number of people present, which conserves energy. In residential and commercial buildings, AI-based smart grids optimize energy distribution and identify inefficiencies, allowing cities to reduce energy waste and lower carbon footprints. Additionally, AI is used to monitor air quality and optimize the use of renewable energy sources, ensuring that the city's energy demands are met sustainably.

3. Waste Management and Recycling

AI is also revolutionizing waste management in smart cities. AI-powered robots and drones can be used to sort waste more efficiently, automating the recycling process and reducing the need for manual labor. Machine learning algorithms can be employed to analyze patterns in waste collection, predict the most efficient collection routes, and optimize waste disposal strategies.

For instance, AI sensors can detect when trash bins are full and notify waste management services in real-time, allowing for more timely and efficient pickups. Additionally, AI can be used to identify recyclable materials in waste streams, ensuring that recycling rates increase, and minimizing landfill usage. This not only saves money for municipalities but also promotes a cleaner, more sustainable environment.

4. Public Safety and Surveillance

AI-driven surveillance systems are increasingly being used to enhance public safety in smart cities. Using computer vision and pattern recognition, AI can monitor public spaces such as parks, streets, and transportation hubs for suspicious activities, helping law enforcement agencies to respond more quickly to potential threats.

AI systems can analyze video feeds from surveillance cameras in real-time to detect unusual behavior, such as crowds forming unexpectedly or individuals engaging in suspicious activities. This allows law enforcement to be proactive in preventing crimes or accidents. Additionally, AI can be used to optimize emergency response systems, ensuring that ambulances and fire trucks take the fastest routes to reach their destinations.

5. Smart Healthcare and Emergency Services

AI applications in healthcare are also vital to the functioning of a smart city. AI algorithms are being used to analyze health data, predict disease outbreaks, and provide insights into public health trends. Through connected health devices such as wearable sensors, AI systems can monitor the health of individuals in real-time, providing alerts when critical health events occur, such as heart attacks or strokes.

AI can help optimize the allocation of emergency medical services, ensuring that ambulances are deployed efficiently based on real-time data, such as the severity of calls or traffic conditions. In addition, AI can help hospitals predict patient admissions, optimizing resource allocation to ensure that hospitals are prepared for emergencies and reducing wait times for critical treatments.

AI in Autonomous Vehicles

Autonomous vehicles (AVs) are one of the most anticipated innovations in the field of AI, with the potential to drastically change the way we travel and interact with transportation systems. AVs, powered by AI, use a variety of technologies, including machine learning, computer vision, and sensor fusion, to navigate and make decisions without human intervention.

1. Self-Driving Cars

Self-driving cars, or autonomous cars, are perhaps the most well-known application of AI in transportation. These vehicles use AI-powered sensors, cameras, radar, and LiDAR (Light Detection and Ranging) to perceive their environment and make decisions, such as detecting pedestrians, recognizing traffic signals, and navigating roads. AI algorithms process this sensor data in real-time, enabling the vehicle to make safe and efficient driving decisions without human input.

For example, AI can enable a self-driving car to detect pedestrians crossing the street, identify cyclists, and avoid collisions by adjusting the vehicle's speed or path accordingly. Additionally, AI can enable vehicles to communicate with each other through Vehicle-to-Vehicle (V2V) communication, allowing them to coordinate their actions to improve traffic flow and reduce the risk of accidents.

2. Autonomous Public Transport

Beyond personal vehicles, AI is also being used to develop autonomous public transportation systems, such as buses, trams, and trains. Autonomous buses equipped with AI-powered sensors and cameras can navigate city streets and pick up passengers, reducing the need for human drivers. These AI-powered buses can operate on predetermined routes or dynamically adjust routes based on passenger demand, helping reduce congestion in busy urban areas.

Self-driving public transport systems could significantly lower costs for cities, improve safety by reducing human error, and provide greater accessibility for people with disabilities or those unable to drive. AI can also help optimize schedules and routes, ensuring that public transportation is more efficient and that vehicles are deployed where they are most needed.

3. AI in Traffic Safety for Autonomous Vehicles

While autonomous vehicles have the potential to greatly reduce traffic accidents, ensuring their safety is a top priority. AI plays a key role in improving the safety features of autonomous vehicles by enabling them to learn from real-world data, adapt to different driving environments, and avoid accidents. Through machine learning, self-driving cars can learn how to respond to a wide variety of driving situations, from inclement weather to unpredictable behavior by other drivers.

Additionally, AI enables autonomous vehicles to communicate with their surroundings, such as traffic lights, other vehicles, and infrastructure, helping them anticipate potential hazards and react in real-time to ensure the safety of passengers, pedestrians, and other road users.

4. Autonomous Vehicles and Smart City Integration

The deployment of autonomous vehicles will likely work in tandem with the growth of smart cities. In a connected smart city, autonomous vehicles can communicate with city infrastructure, such as traffic lights, road sensors, and parking meters, to optimize driving routes, reduce congestion, and ensure safety.

For example, AI could enable an autonomous vehicle to receive real-time traffic updates from the city's infrastructure, allowing it to adjust its route dynamically to avoid congestion or road closures. Furthermore, autonomous vehicles can be integrated with public transportation networks to create seamless travel experiences, where passengers can easily transition from self-driving cars to buses or trains without waiting for schedules or dealing with manual transfers.

Challenges and Ethical Considerations

While AI-powered smart cities and autonomous vehicles offer numerous benefits, they also present several challenges and ethical considerations:

1. Privacy and Data Security

The widespread use of AI in smart cities and autonomous vehicles generates vast amounts of data, much of which is sensitive in nature. For example, personal location data, video surveillance footage, and vehicle telematics data are all collected and processed by AI systems. Ensuring that this data is securely stored and that privacy is respected is a significant concern. Moreover, cities and companies need to comply with data protection regulations such as GDPR and CCPA.

2. Safety and Reliability

Although AI systems are becoming increasingly reliable, there are still concerns about their ability to operate safely in unpredictable environments. For autonomous vehicles, there is the risk of system failures, such as sensor malfunctions or algorithmic errors, which could lead to accidents. Continuous testing, validation, and updates are necessary to improve the reliability and safety of these systems.

3. Ethical Decision-Making in Autonomous Vehicles

AI systems in autonomous vehicles will need to make ethical decisions, such as in emergency situations when an accident is unavoidable. Programming these systems to make ethically sound decisions is a complex challenge. Developers must carefully consider how autonomous vehicles should respond to various moral dilemmas, balancing safety, fairness, and the well-being of all individuals involved.

AI's deployment in smart cities and autonomous vehicles promises to reshape urban life and transportation in the coming years. Through intelligent traffic management, energy optimization, waste management, and enhanced public safety, AI is transforming how cities operate, making them more efficient, sustainable, and livable. At the same time, autonomous vehicles have the potential to revolutionize transportation by providing safer, more efficient, and accessible mobility solutions.

However, the widespread adoption of AI in these domains must be approached with caution, as challenges related to data privacy, safety, and ethics must be carefully managed. The future of smart cities and autonomous vehicles is exciting, but it requires ongoing innovation, collaboration, and regulation to ensure that these technologies benefit society as a whole.

15. Challenges and Best Practices from AI Practitioners

Deploying AI models in real-world environments is a complex process filled with technical, operational, and strategic challenges. In this chapter, we explore the most common hurdles faced by AI practitioners, including scalability issues, model drift, infrastructure bottlenecks, compliance concerns, and cross-team collaboration challenges. Drawing from industry experts and experienced AI engineers, we outline best practices for successful deployment, covering topics such as MLOps automation, cloud and edge optimization, monitoring strategies, and ethical AI considerations. By understanding these real-world challenges and solutions, you'll be better prepared to deploy AI models efficiently, securely, and at scale, ensuring long-term success in production environments.

15.1 Scaling AI Deployments Effectively

Scaling AI deployments is a critical aspect of any AI project, particularly as organizations transition from prototypes or pilot models to full-scale production systems. While building and deploying an AI model for a small test case or initial use may be manageable, scaling it to handle large datasets, diverse inputs, and high user demand introduces numerous complexities. Achieving an effective and seamless scale requires a combination of robust engineering, the right infrastructure, strategic planning, and proactive management.

In this section, we will explore the key principles, strategies, and best practices for scaling AI deployments successfully. These strategies include optimizing models for performance at scale, addressing infrastructure challenges, managing costs effectively, and ensuring that scaling efforts are aligned with business objectives. Additionally, we will highlight some common pitfalls to avoid and share real-world examples of AI scaling across different industries.

1. Understanding the Scale of AI Deployments

Scaling an AI model is not just about making it "bigger" or running it on more machines. It involves ensuring that the model can handle significantly more data, operate under varying conditions, and maintain the same level of accuracy and reliability in a production environment. The scale can be defined in several ways:

- **Data Scale**: As data volumes grow, AI models need to process and analyze larger datasets in real-time or batch modes.
- **User Scale**: Scaling AI to serve more users concurrently, such as handling millions of queries per second, requires careful consideration of response times and load balancing.
- **Model Complexity**: More sophisticated models may have additional layers and parameters that require more compute power and fine-tuning to operate efficiently at scale.
- **Geographic Scale**: Scaling AI to serve users in different regions with varying network conditions, data privacy laws, and local requirements adds another layer of complexity.

2. Optimizing Infrastructure for Scale

A strong foundation of infrastructure is critical for any successful AI scaling effort. At scale, AI systems need to be highly available, performant, and resilient. The infrastructure must be flexible enough to handle unpredictable demands while ensuring the system runs smoothly.

Cloud vs. On-Premises Infrastructure

One of the first decisions to make when scaling AI is whether to deploy on the cloud or on-premises. Cloud platforms (such as AWS, Google Cloud, or Microsoft Azure) offer scalability and flexibility, allowing AI models to scale dynamically based on demand. This can be particularly advantageous when you're scaling quickly or don't want to invest in costly hardware upfront.

On the other hand, for organizations with stringent data privacy and security requirements, or those with large volumes of data that are impractical to store in the cloud, on-premises solutions may be a better option. On-premise infrastructure allows full control over data, hardware, and network traffic, but it can be costlier and less scalable without proper planning.

Distributed Computing and Parallelism

As the scale increases, many AI models may need to be trained or inferenced on massive datasets that exceed the memory and processing capabilities of a single machine. Distributed computing frameworks such as Apache Spark, Hadoop, and TensorFlow Distributed enable models to be trained across multiple machines or nodes in parallel, splitting the computational load and speeding up the training process.

When scaling AI, you can also leverage horizontal scaling, where additional machines (or nodes) are added to the infrastructure, and vertical scaling, where individual machines are upgraded to handle larger workloads.

Serverless Computing

For certain use cases, serverless computing can be an effective approach to scaling AI applications. Serverless frameworks, such as AWS Lambda or Google Cloud Functions, automatically scale AI services in response to demand without the need for managing servers manually. This can help minimize costs by only using resources when needed, which is ideal for bursty workloads or applications that experience sporadic usage.

3. Managing Model Efficiency and Cost

Scaling AI comes with the challenge of managing computational costs. As models are scaled up, they often require more powerful hardware (like GPUs, TPUs, or specialized AI accelerators) and more memory, all of which contribute to higher operational costs.

Model Optimization Techniques

To ensure cost-effective scaling, it is essential to implement model optimization techniques that reduce the computational cost without sacrificing performance:

- **Model Pruning**: Removing redundant neurons or weights from a neural network to reduce its size and improve inference speed.
- **Quantization**: Reducing the precision of the numbers used in the model's weights and activations, which can reduce memory usage and accelerate inference without a significant loss in accuracy.
- **Knowledge Distillation**: Training a smaller, more efficient model to replicate the performance of a larger, more complex model.

These optimization strategies help reduce the need for high-end hardware, making it easier and more cost-effective to scale AI models.

Elasticity and Auto-Scaling

Cloud platforms offer auto-scaling capabilities, where infrastructure resources are adjusted dynamically based on demand. This elasticity allows AI models to handle varying workloads without overprovisioning or underutilizing resources. For instance, during peak usage times, the cloud can automatically spin up additional virtual machines to handle increased traffic, ensuring that response times and system performance remain consistent.

4. Ensuring Reliability and Availability

As AI models scale, ensuring their reliability and availability is crucial to maintaining a seamless user experience. High-availability solutions, including redundant systems and failover mechanisms, are essential for keeping AI systems online and responsive.

Load Balancing

Load balancing is a technique that distributes incoming traffic across multiple servers to ensure that no single machine is overwhelmed by too many requests. For AI models, load balancing is particularly important for inference services that need to serve a large number of concurrent users, such as recommendation engines, chatbots, or search engines.

Load balancers intelligently route traffic to the least-loaded server or instance, reducing response times and preventing downtime due to server overload. Cloud-based load balancers also integrate with auto-scaling features to ensure that new instances are added when necessary to meet demand.

Redundancy and Failover

Building redundancy into AI deployments ensures that the system remains operational even if a particular component fails. Redundant systems, whether at the hardware or software level, provide backup resources to take over in case of failure.

For instance, in a cloud-based AI deployment, if one instance of a model fails, another instance can automatically take its place without interrupting the user experience. Failover systems help minimize downtime and maximize availability, ensuring that AI services are always accessible to users.

5. Ensuring Scalability in Data Pipelines

Effective scaling requires that the underlying data pipelines are also designed to scale. As the data volume grows, ensuring that data flows smoothly and efficiently to AI models for training and inference becomes more challenging.

Data Sharding and Partitioning

One strategy for scaling data pipelines is data sharding, where the data is split into smaller, more manageable chunks (or "shards") that can be processed in parallel. This reduces the load on any single system and ensures that the pipeline can scale as data volumes grow.

Data partitioning can also be used to distribute data across multiple storage systems or databases, allowing different parts of the dataset to be processed independently and simultaneously, speeding up data processing.

Real-Time Data Streaming

For AI applications that require real-time data processing, such as fraud detection or recommendation systems, real-time data streaming technologies like Apache Kafka or Amazon Kinesis can be employed to stream data directly into the AI system. These platforms can scale to handle massive volumes of data in real-time, enabling AI models to make immediate predictions based on the latest data.

6. Monitoring and Managing Scaled Deployments

Once AI systems are scaled, they need to be actively monitored to ensure that they continue to perform optimally. Effective monitoring provides insights into system performance, helps detect issues early, and ensures the system is operating at its best.

Key monitoring practices include tracking model performance metrics (such as accuracy, latency, and throughput), monitoring infrastructure health, and identifying potential bottlenecks in data processing or server load. Implementing alerting systems can notify teams when thresholds are crossed, enabling quick remediation of any issues.

7. Best Practices for Scaling AI Deployments

To scale AI deployments effectively, organizations should follow best practices that ensure both the technical and operational aspects of scaling are addressed:

- **Start small, scale incrementally**: Test your AI models in a limited scope before scaling to avoid unnecessary complexity.
- **Use modular architectures**: Design AI systems with modular components that can be scaled independently.

- **Maintain robust testing and validation**: Ensure that AI models are thoroughly tested and validated at every stage of scaling.
- **Focus on automation**: Use automated CI/CD pipelines, monitoring tools, and model management systems to streamline scaling processes.

Scaling AI deployments effectively requires a combination of the right infrastructure, optimization strategies, and proactive management. Whether scaling for data volume, user traffic, or geographic reach, a thoughtful approach to architecture and resources is necessary to ensure that AI models continue to perform well at larger scales. By addressing challenges related to infrastructure, performance, and reliability, organizations can unlock the full potential of AI at scale and deliver robust, high-quality AI services to users.

15.2 Lessons from AI Deployment Failures

AI deployment failures are inevitable in the journey toward mastering the integration of machine learning models into real-world applications. While failures can be seen as setbacks, they offer invaluable lessons that guide organizations in optimizing and refining their AI systems. In this section, we will explore some of the common reasons behind AI deployment failures and highlight the lessons that can be learned to prevent similar issues in future deployments.

1. Lack of Clear Business Objectives

One of the primary reasons AI deployments fail is the absence of clear business objectives. When AI models are developed without understanding the business needs or clear use cases, the deployment often leads to disappointing results. Models might perform well in a controlled environment or on research data but fail to deliver the expected value when exposed to real-world business scenarios.

Lesson Learned: Before beginning an AI deployment, it is critical to understand the problem the model is trying to solve. Define clear, measurable business outcomes and ensure that the AI model aligns with these objectives. Engaging with stakeholders early in the process to understand business needs can help ensure that the model meets user expectations and business goals.

2. Insufficient Data Quality or Quantity

AI models, especially machine learning algorithms, rely heavily on high-quality and diverse data to make accurate predictions. A common reason for deployment failures is the poor quality or insufficient quantity of data. This can result in inaccurate predictions, slow performance, or models that fail to generalize effectively to real-world scenarios. Data biases, noise, and missing values are just a few issues that can undermine an AI model's performance in production.

Lesson Learned: Data is the foundation of AI models, and poor data will lead to poor results. Therefore, organizations should focus on ensuring data quality, consistency, and diversity. Building strong data pipelines, data preprocessing steps, and data augmentation strategies will help ensure that the model is well-prepared for production environments. Additionally, investing in data governance and regular audits to eliminate biases can prevent ethical and legal issues down the line.

3. Overfitting to the Training Data

While overfitting is a well-known problem during model training, it can be especially problematic during deployment. Overfitting occurs when a model performs exceptionally well on the training dataset but struggles to generalize to new, unseen data. When models overfit, they may seem to perform well in pilot tests or on test sets but fail to make accurate predictions when exposed to real-world data.

Lesson Learned: Ensure that the model is thoroughly validated and evaluated using diverse datasets, including real-world data, before deploying it to production. Techniques like cross-validation, regularization, and careful selection of model complexity can help mitigate overfitting. Moreover, deploying models in stages, starting with smaller pilot deployments, can help identify overfitting or other issues before going live at scale.

4. Inadequate Infrastructure and Resource Management

Another common pitfall of AI deployments is inadequate infrastructure. When deploying an AI model into production, the infrastructure needs to be robust enough to handle the computational demands of the model, particularly if the model is large or complex. AI workloads often require high-performance computing resources, such as GPUs or TPUs, and cloud-based solutions or on-premises infrastructure that can scale efficiently.

Lesson Learned: Proper infrastructure planning is essential. Before scaling up an AI model for production, assess whether the hardware and cloud resources will meet the model's computational needs, both in terms of power and storage. Implement monitoring solutions to track resource utilization and scale infrastructure dynamically to accommodate fluctuating demands. Load balancing, auto-scaling, and resource optimization techniques are key to maintaining model performance at scale.

5. Poor Model Monitoring and Maintenance

Once deployed, AI models often face a variety of challenges related to performance degradation, data shifts, or model drift over time. A lack of ongoing monitoring can lead to missed opportunities to address these issues early, resulting in models that underperform or behave unpredictably in production. Without proper maintenance, models may become outdated or less effective as they are exposed to changing real-world data and environments.

Lesson Learned: Continuous monitoring of AI models is crucial after deployment. Organizations must track key performance metrics, such as accuracy, latency, and data drift, to detect any performance issues promptly. Implementing an automated model retraining pipeline or using MLOps practices can help ensure that the model stays up to date and performs optimally throughout its lifecycle. Regular audits and checks for model drift or bias are also necessary to maintain ethical standards.

6. Failing to Address Bias and Fairness

AI models are susceptible to biases in both their training data and their design. These biases can manifest in various ways, leading to unfair predictions or outcomes. For example, AI systems deployed in sensitive applications such as hiring, lending, or criminal justice have faced backlash for reinforcing societal biases present in historical data. If these biases are not properly managed, it can lead to negative real-world consequences and erode trust in the AI system.

Lesson Learned: Addressing bias and ensuring fairness in AI deployments should be an ongoing priority. This includes identifying and mitigating biases in training data, as well as implementing fairness and transparency measures during model development. Ethical considerations should be woven into the entire lifecycle of the AI project, from data collection to model deployment. Organizations should prioritize explainability, model transparency, and fairness audits to avoid unintended discriminatory outcomes.

7. Lack of Collaboration Between Teams

AI deployment often involves collaboration between various teams, including data scientists, engineers, business analysts, and IT professionals. A failure to establish effective communication and coordination between these groups can lead to misalignment, inefficiencies, and a lack of shared understanding of the deployment goals and expectations.

Lesson Learned: Cross-functional collaboration is key to a successful AI deployment. Organizations should foster open communication between business leaders, data scientists, engineers, and operations teams from the start. Regular meetings, shared documentation, and clear roles and responsibilities can help ensure that everyone is aligned and working toward the same goals. Encouraging knowledge sharing and collaboration will also facilitate faster issue resolution during deployment.

8. Underestimating the Complexity of the Deployment Pipeline

Building and maintaining an efficient deployment pipeline is often more complex than anticipated. Many AI deployments fail because organizations underestimate the complexity of integrating AI models into production systems, managing version control, and handling the continuous integration and delivery (CI/CD) processes. A poorly managed deployment pipeline can lead to delays, errors, and inefficiencies in delivering AI models to production.

Lesson Learned: Establish a well-defined deployment pipeline using DevOps or MLOps practices. Automate testing, version control, and deployment processes to ensure smooth transitions between development and production stages. Implementing a solid CI/CD pipeline and continuous testing strategy will help streamline the process of updating, retraining, and deploying models while reducing the risk of introducing bugs or performance issues.

9. Ethical, Legal, and Regulatory Challenges

Deploying AI in real-world applications often involves navigating a complex landscape of ethical, legal, and regulatory challenges. Many organizations fail to adequately address these concerns before deployment, leading to legal issues, regulatory fines, or public backlash. For instance, deploying AI models without proper consideration for data privacy laws (such as GDPR or CCPA) or ethical principles can result in significant liabilities.

Lesson Learned: Ensure that all AI models are developed and deployed in compliance with relevant ethical guidelines, data privacy regulations, and industry standards. Consult with legal teams, data protection officers, and ethics committees to ensure that AI deployment does not violate regulations or ethical norms. Implementing transparent practices, ensuring data privacy, and regularly auditing AI systems for compliance are essential for avoiding legal and reputational risks.

10. Unrealistic Expectations and Overhyped Promises

Finally, many AI deployments fail because of unrealistic expectations set by stakeholders. Overhyping AI capabilities, promising near-perfect results, or misrepresenting AI's potential can lead to dissatisfaction when the model doesn't meet these inflated expectations. It's crucial to manage expectations from the start and ensure that stakeholders understand the model's capabilities and limitations.

Lesson Learned: Setting realistic expectations is key to successful AI deployments. Engage stakeholders in conversations about the practical limitations and trade-offs involved in deploying AI models. Make sure that performance metrics, deployment schedules, and outcomes are clearly defined and based on achievable goals. Being transparent about what AI can and cannot do helps mitigate disappointment and ensures better alignment with business objectives.

AI deployment failures provide valuable learning opportunities. By carefully analyzing the reasons behind these failures, organizations can identify patterns, mitigate risks, and implement best practices that increase the likelihood of successful AI deployments in the future. From clarifying business objectives and improving data quality to addressing biases and implementing robust monitoring systems, these lessons will help ensure that AI models not only succeed in deployment but also continue to provide value long after they go live.

15.3 The Role of Cross-Functional Teams in AI Success

The successful deployment of AI models doesn't solely rely on the technical prowess of data scientists and engineers—it requires a cohesive, cross-functional team approach that incorporates various perspectives from across the organization. A cross-functional team is composed of individuals from different departments, each bringing unique skills, insights, and expertise to the table. In the case of AI deployment, these teams typically include data scientists, machine learning engineers, business analysts, product managers, operations teams, and legal or compliance experts.

In this section, we will explore the critical role that cross-functional teams play in the success of AI projects and how these teams collaborate to overcome the challenges of deploying AI models into real-world applications.

1. Aligning Business and Technical Goals

One of the most important roles a cross-functional team plays in AI deployment is ensuring alignment between the business objectives and the technical capabilities of AI models. Data scientists and engineers are often focused on the technical aspects of model development, but they might not always have an in-depth understanding of the business context in which the AI will be deployed. On the other hand, business teams are concerned with solving real-world problems, improving operations, or meeting customer needs.

Why It Matters: When business goals and technical goals are misaligned, AI deployment is at risk of failing to deliver meaningful results. For example, a model might perform well technically but fail to address the needs of the business or meet user expectations.

How Cross-Functional Teams Help: Cross-functional teams help ensure that AI projects are developed with business needs in mind. Product managers and business analysts collaborate with data scientists to define clear use cases, performance metrics, and KPIs that directly relate to business goals. These teams also ensure that technical limitations are communicated early, so the business understands what is achievable and what trade-offs need to be made.

2. Facilitating Communication and Knowledge Sharing

AI projects require an ongoing exchange of knowledge and information. Data scientists need insights into the business environment to tailor models to specific needs, while business teams rely on technical experts to understand the feasibility and constraints of deploying AI. Communication breakdowns between teams can lead to misunderstandings, delays, and suboptimal AI models that fail to meet expectations.

Why It Matters: In the absence of effective communication, teams may work in silos, leading to fragmented decision-making and inefficient workflows. Miscommunication about model performance, potential issues, or deployment timelines can lead to missed opportunities and costly errors.

How Cross-Functional Teams Help: Cross-functional teams foster an environment of collaboration, transparency, and mutual understanding. Regular meetings, shared documentation, and collaborative tools ensure that all team members are on the same page and aware of each other's progress and challenges. For instance, business analysts can provide feedback to data scientists on the practical implications of model outputs, while product managers can help ensure that the AI solution fits within the broader product ecosystem. These ongoing interactions are essential for continuous improvement and iterative development.

3. Addressing Ethical, Legal, and Regulatory Concerns

AI deployment is not just a technical challenge; it also requires addressing a complex set of ethical, legal, and regulatory considerations. Models can unintentionally perpetuate biases, violate privacy regulations, or have unintended consequences that may harm the organization's reputation or lead to legal repercussions. Cross-functional teams, particularly those that include compliance, legal, and ethics experts, are essential in navigating these concerns.

Why It Matters: Failing to address ethical, legal, or regulatory challenges early in the AI deployment process can lead to serious consequences. AI models that are biased, opaque, or non-compliant with data privacy laws can result in significant financial penalties, legal action, or loss of customer trust.

How Cross-Functional Teams Help: Legal and compliance experts within cross-functional teams work closely with data scientists and business leaders to ensure that models comply with relevant laws and regulations, such as GDPR or HIPAA. They can also provide guidance on data privacy, ensuring that sensitive data is handled appropriately. Ethics professionals help identify and mitigate biases in training data and models to ensure fairness and inclusivity. Having these experts involved early in the deployment process allows organizations to proactively address potential risks and maintain trust with customers and regulators.

4. Ensuring Scalability and Long-Term Success

AI deployment often involves scaling models to handle larger datasets, more complex use cases, or wider user bases over time. Cross-functional teams are instrumental in ensuring that AI solutions are not only scalable but also sustainable in the long term. For instance, engineering teams must work with business leaders to ensure that the infrastructure can support increased demand, while data scientists need to collaborate with product teams to adapt models to evolving business needs.

Why It Matters: Scaling AI models without proper planning can lead to inefficiencies, bottlenecks, and system failures. Additionally, a lack of foresight regarding long-term maintenance and updates can result in models becoming obsolete or ineffective.

How Cross-Functional Teams Help: Cross-functional teams help organizations design AI deployments that are scalable and adaptable to future requirements. Engineers ensure that the infrastructure (such as cloud services or on-premise servers) is capable of handling the increased computational load as the AI system scales. Data scientists work with business teams to monitor model performance and incorporate new features or data sources as business needs evolve. Together, these teams build AI solutions that not only meet current demands but are also flexible enough to grow and adapt to changing business landscapes.

5. Continuous Improvement and Model Optimization

Deploying an AI model is just the beginning—ongoing monitoring, evaluation, and optimization are necessary to ensure that the model continues to deliver value. Cross-functional teams are essential for identifying and addressing issues like model drift, changing user behavior, and new business requirements. By combining insights from different areas of expertise, teams can continuously refine and improve deployed models.

Why It Matters: If AI models are left unmonitored or unsupported after deployment, they may degrade over time, leading to poor performance or even failure. Ensuring the continuous success of an AI model requires ongoing collaboration and optimization.

How Cross-Functional Teams Help: Cross-functional teams are crucial in driving model optimization efforts. Data scientists and engineers monitor the model's performance, looking for signs of drift or degradation. Business analysts and product managers keep an eye on how the model is impacting business outcomes, providing feedback for improvements. Meanwhile, operations teams ensure that the infrastructure remains stable and efficient. By collaborating and sharing insights from their respective domains, cross-functional teams can ensure that AI models are continually updated and improved to maximize business value.

6. Fostering Innovation and Creativity

AI deployment can often benefit from a creative and innovative approach to problem-solving. Cross-functional teams bring together individuals with different perspectives, backgrounds, and expertise. This diversity enables them to think outside the box and approach AI challenges in novel ways.

Why It Matters: Innovation is essential in developing AI solutions that stand out in competitive markets. Teams that work in isolation may overlook potential improvements or creative solutions that could enhance the deployment's impact.

How Cross-Functional Teams Help: Cross-functional teams can brainstorm, experiment, and collaborate on novel AI approaches. Data scientists may work with business analysts to test new features or alternative model architectures. Engineers and operations teams can propose solutions to optimize model performance and scalability. Product managers can bring customer-centric insights, ensuring that the AI deployment meets user needs in creative and innovative ways. The result is a more effective, innovative, and successful AI deployment.

Cross-functional teams are integral to the success of AI deployment projects. By bringing together diverse expertise and perspectives, these teams can bridge the gap between business needs and technical capabilities, mitigate risks, ensure compliance, and foster continuous improvement. Involving a variety of stakeholders in the AI deployment process not only ensures that the model aligns with business goals but also enhances scalability, sustainability, and ethical standards. By fostering collaboration and open communication, cross-functional teams can unlock the full potential of AI technologies and create lasting value for organizations.

15.4 Strategies for Continuous AI Improvement

In the ever-evolving landscape of artificial intelligence (AI), deployment is only the beginning of a long journey toward creating models that consistently deliver value. AI models, just like any software system, need to be continuously improved to adapt to new data, changing user needs, technological advancements, and market shifts. As organizations scale and new challenges arise, the process of maintaining and enhancing AI performance becomes critical.

This section will discuss various strategies for ensuring the continuous improvement of deployed AI models, focusing on the iterative nature of AI systems and the importance of maintaining flexibility, responsiveness, and collaboration across all stages of the AI lifecycle.

1. Establishing a Feedback Loop from End Users

One of the most powerful ways to improve AI models is by establishing a direct feedback loop from the end-users or customers. Models that were trained on historical data might not always perform as expected in real-world applications, especially as users interact with the model and provide new inputs.

Why It Matters: User feedback provides valuable insights into how well the model is serving its purpose. It can reveal biases, edge cases, or performance issues that may not have been detected during initial testing. Without user input, it's challenging to understand the model's true impact on the business.

How to Implement:

- Collect data from user interactions with the AI system, including ratings, performance feedback, and usage patterns.
- Use this data to fine-tune models and identify areas for improvement.
- Implement A/B testing to measure the effectiveness of model changes and validate new iterations.

Having a feedback loop creates a dynamic improvement process where the model evolves based on actual usage, making it more effective and user-friendly over time.

2. Leveraging Continuous Integration and Continuous Deployment (CI/CD) for AI Models

To ensure AI models are always up to date and performing optimally, organizations should adopt a CI/CD pipeline. This pipeline allows for the automated and seamless deployment of updated versions of AI models, data, and code, helping to reduce the time between model training and deployment.

Why It Matters: Continuous deployment ensures that any improvements, bug fixes, or changes in business requirements are quickly reflected in the model, minimizing disruptions to the AI system's performance. It allows for a more agile approach to AI model management, with changes being tested and deployed in smaller, incremental steps.

How to Implement:

- Set up a CI/CD pipeline for your AI models using tools like Jenkins, GitLab CI, or CircleCI.
- Automate processes like model validation, testing, and deployment to reduce manual errors.
- Ensure that the pipeline includes monitoring and alerting mechanisms so that performance degradation or issues are immediately detected.

By using CI/CD for AI, organizations can streamline the process of updating models and ensuring their accuracy, reducing manual intervention and enhancing operational efficiency.

3. Monitoring Model Performance in Real-Time

Real-time monitoring of AI models is essential to detect issues before they escalate. Continuous performance monitoring allows teams to identify potential model drift, degradation in accuracy, or changes in data patterns that might negatively affect the model's output.

Why It Matters: AI models can degrade over time due to factors like changing user behavior, evolving data distributions, or shifts in the underlying problem space. Without continuous monitoring, it is difficult to spot performance issues early on, leading to reduced model effectiveness and business value.

How to **Implement**:

- Implement monitoring systems that track key metrics such as accuracy, precision, recall, or model drift in real-time.
- Use automated tools to log model predictions, error rates, and performance statistics.
- Monitor input data for anomalies or shifts that could indicate problems with the model's assumptions or behavior.
- Set up dashboards and alerts for immediate action when performance thresholds are breached.

Real-time monitoring gives teams visibility into how models are performing in production, making it easier to detect and fix issues before they affect users or business outcomes.

4. Retraining and Fine-Tuning with New Data

AI models are only as good as the data they are trained on. As new data becomes available, retraining and fine-tuning the models becomes essential to ensure that they stay relevant and accurate. Regular retraining allows models to adapt to changing conditions, new trends, and emerging patterns in the data.

Why It Matters: Data distributions can shift over time, leading to a phenomenon called "model drift." Retraining helps keep the model aligned with real-world data, ensuring that predictions remain accurate and reflective of current trends. Additionally, as businesses collect more data, retraining gives models access to fresh, high-quality datasets that can improve performance.

How to Implement:

- Set up a pipeline for automatically collecting and preprocessing new data, ensuring that it is labeled correctly and is of high quality.
- Periodically retrain models with updated datasets to incorporate the latest information and ensure that they reflect current trends.
- Use techniques like online learning or incremental learning, where the model is trained on new data as it arrives, to avoid the need for complete retraining.

Retraining and fine-tuning models with new data ensures that AI systems remain up to date and can continue to provide valuable insights and predictions.

5. Model Testing and Validation

Even after deployment, AI models should undergo continuous testing to ensure they maintain high performance. Testing helps identify bugs, evaluate edge cases, and validate that models are meeting the desired outcomes. In the context of AI, testing can also help uncover biases or unintentional consequences that might not be visible at first glance.

Why It Matters: Without robust testing, AI models could introduce errors, biases, or inconsistencies that affect the quality of predictions and business outcomes. Validation is especially important when the model needs to meet strict legal, ethical, or regulatory standards.

How to Implement:

- Conduct rigorous A/B testing, where two versions of the model are compared to see which performs better on real-world data.
- Use cross-validation techniques during the model's development to evaluate its generalizability and robustness.
- Test models regularly using real-world data to validate assumptions, edge cases, and performance metrics.
- Incorporate stress testing to evaluate how the model behaves under extreme or unforeseen conditions.

By maintaining a regular testing schedule, organizations can ensure that AI models stay reliable and perform as expected in production environments.

6. Collaborating with Cross-Functional Teams

AI improvement is not solely the responsibility of the data science or engineering teams. For sustained success, collaboration across business, product, and operations teams is necessary. Each department can provide valuable insights into how AI models are being used, whether they are achieving business objectives, and how they can be improved.

Why It Matters: Cross-functional collaboration ensures that the AI system is aligned with business goals and is adapted to changing user needs. It also promotes the identification of areas for improvement that might otherwise be overlooked.

How to Implement:

- Regularly communicate with product managers, business analysts, and domain experts to gather feedback on model performance.
- Set up cross-functional meetings to review performance metrics, discuss challenges, and identify potential improvements.
- Ensure that business teams understand the model's capabilities and limitations, which helps in making informed decisions about its evolution.

Collaboration fosters a continuous cycle of improvement by ensuring that all perspectives are considered and that the AI solution remains relevant to both users and business needs.

7. Incorporating Emerging Techniques and Technologies

The field of AI is rapidly evolving, with new algorithms, frameworks, and technologies being developed all the time. Keeping up with the latest advancements can lead to significant improvements in model performance, efficiency, and scalability.

Why It Matters: Emerging AI techniques such as transfer learning, meta-learning, and few-shot learning, as well as advancements in hardware like TPUs and GPUs, can significantly boost model performance. Ignoring these developments means missing out on potentially better solutions for optimizing or upgrading your AI models.

How to Implement:

- Stay informed about new research, tools, and techniques through academic journals, conferences, or industry blogs.
- Evaluate new techniques and technologies to see if they can improve the model's performance, reduce costs, or make it more scalable.
- Consider adopting newer frameworks or hardware accelerators to improve computational efficiency and reduce inference time.

By continuously exploring and integrating emerging techniques, organizations can maintain a competitive edge and ensure that their AI systems are leveraging the best available tools.

Continuous improvement is a cornerstone of successful AI deployment. The strategies outlined in this chapter—feedback loops, CI/CD pipelines, real-time monitoring, retraining, testing, cross-functional collaboration, and staying updated on emerging technologies—provide a comprehensive approach to ensuring that AI systems evolve over time and continue to deliver value. By maintaining an agile and responsive mindset and engaging multiple stakeholders in the process, organizations can maximize the impact of their AI models, enabling them to meet both current and future business needs.

16. The Future of AI Deployment

AI deployment is rapidly evolving, driven by advancements in automation, edge computing, federated learning, and AI-driven DevOps. In this chapter, we explore emerging trends that will shape the future of AI deployment, including serverless AI, real-time inference, self-learning models, and decentralized AI systems. We also discuss the impact of quantum computing, AI regulation, and ethical AI frameworks on deployment strategies. As AI becomes more integrated into critical applications, understanding these future trends will help practitioners stay ahead, ensuring that their AI solutions remain scalable, efficient, and aligned with industry innovations.

16.1 Emerging Trends in AI Deployment

The rapid advancement of artificial intelligence (AI) is transforming industries across the globe, and as AI continues to evolve, so do the ways in which it is deployed. As businesses increasingly rely on AI to drive innovation, efficiency, and growth, understanding the emerging trends in AI deployment is essential for staying competitive and leveraging the full potential of AI technologies. In this section, we will explore several key trends that are shaping the future of AI deployment, including new deployment strategies, the integration of AI with emerging technologies, and evolving infrastructure demands.

1. AI and Edge Computing: Deploying Intelligence Closer to the Data

Edge computing refers to processing data closer to where it is generated (e.g., on devices like smartphones, IoT sensors, and industrial equipment), rather than relying on cloud servers located far away. This trend is gaining traction as more businesses seek to deploy AI models that can process data in real-time and reduce the latency and bandwidth limitations of traditional cloud-based systems.

Why It Matters: Edge computing is especially useful for applications that require immediate decision-making, such as autonomous vehicles, industrial IoT, smart cities, and healthcare. By processing data locally, AI systems can make faster, more accurate predictions, while also reducing the reliance on cloud infrastructure.

How It's Shaping AI Deployment:

- **Real-Time AI Processing**: Edge AI allows models to process data instantly, which is critical for applications such as real-time fraud detection, autonomous navigation, and smart devices.
- **Bandwidth and Latency Reduction**: Edge AI minimizes data transfer to the cloud, reducing bandwidth requirements and ensuring low-latency communication.
- **Autonomous Devices**: Devices like drones, robots, and smart cameras are increasingly able to make autonomous decisions by running AI models on edge devices rather than relying on remote servers.

As AI models become more optimized for edge deployment, businesses will be able to unlock new capabilities in industries that require low-latency, real-time intelligence.

2. AI-Powered Automation in MLOps

MLOps (Machine Learning Operations) is rapidly evolving to include more automation, with an emphasis on continuous integration, continuous delivery (CI/CD), and end-to-end model management. With the growing complexity of AI systems and the need for frequent updates, automation in MLOps has become a critical trend for streamlining AI deployment pipelines and improving the efficiency of AI operations.

Why It Matters: AI models are continuously evolving, and automating the entire deployment process—from model training and testing to monitoring and retraining—can reduce human error, accelerate time-to-market, and ensure consistent model performance.

How It's Shaping AI Deployment:

- **Automated Model Retraining**: MLOps platforms are integrating automatic retraining systems to update models regularly, based on new data, without requiring manual intervention.
- **Continuous Monitoring**: Real-time monitoring and automated alerts help teams quickly identify when a model's performance deviates from expected thresholds, triggering automated responses, such as retraining or model updates.
- **CI/CD for Models**: MLOps automation enables the seamless deployment of models, reducing the risk of errors and downtime by automatically validating and deploying changes to AI models and algorithms in a controlled environment.

As MLOps evolves, AI deployment will become faster, more reliable, and more scalable, enabling businesses to maintain high-quality AI systems across all stages of the model lifecycle.

3. Explainable AI (XAI) and Ethical AI Deployment

As AI systems become increasingly integrated into critical decision-making processes, transparency and accountability in AI have gained significant attention. The emerging trend of Explainable AI (XAI) focuses on developing models that can provide understandable and interpretable results, ensuring that AI decisions can be traced and explained in human terms. This is particularly important in industries like healthcare, finance, and law, where decisions made by AI models must be justifiable.

Why It Matters: The demand for AI transparency is growing as organizations face increasing regulatory scrutiny and the need to address concerns around AI biases, fairness, and discrimination. XAI ensures that AI decisions can be trusted and are explainable to both stakeholders and end-users.

How It's Shaping AI Deployment:

- **Accountability and Compliance**: Transparent models are crucial for compliance with regulations such as GDPR and other privacy laws, where organizations must explain automated decisions made about users.
- **Bias Detection and Mitigation**: XAI allows businesses to identify and address biases in models that may unfairly affect certain groups, leading to more ethical AI deployment.
- **Trust in AI Systems**: By providing clear and interpretable explanations, XAI helps build trust with users and regulators, which is essential for widespread AI adoption.

The growing importance of explainability will drive AI deployment towards greater transparency, making AI more ethical and trustworthy across a variety of use cases.

4. Federated Learning: Decentralized AI Training

Federated learning is an emerging trend that enables the training of AI models across decentralized devices or data sources without the need to transfer sensitive data to a central server. Instead of gathering data in one location, federated learning allows AI models to be trained directly on local devices or edge nodes, and only the model updates (not the data itself) are sent back to the central server for aggregation.

Why It Matters: Federated learning addresses concerns around data privacy and security by keeping sensitive data on local devices, while still allowing AI models to learn from a wide variety of data sources. This is particularly important for industries that handle sensitive information, such as healthcare, finance, and telecommunications.

How It's Shaping AI Deployment:

- **Privacy Preservation**: By keeping data localized, federated learning reduces the risk of data breaches and minimizes the exposure of personal information.
- **Distributed AI**: Federated learning enables AI models to be deployed on a global scale, without requiring massive data centralization.
- **Collaborative Learning**: Organizations and industries can collaborate by sharing model updates rather than raw data, allowing for the creation of more robust models while respecting privacy concerns.

Federated learning is poised to revolutionize AI deployment, especially in applications where privacy and security are paramount.

5. AI in Autonomous Systems: Self-Deploying AI Models

As autonomous systems, such as self-driving cars and drones, become more prevalent, AI models are being designed to deploy themselves autonomously. This emerging trend involves developing models that can not only make decisions but also update and deploy themselves in real-time based on environmental changes or new data. These systems rely on continuous learning, real-time data processing, and advanced AI techniques to adapt to dynamic and unpredictable environments.

Why It Matters: Autonomous AI deployment is crucial for industries like transportation, logistics, and defense, where human intervention is not always feasible, and quick decision-making is essential for safety and efficiency.

How It's Shaping AI Deployment:

- **Self-Improving Systems**: Autonomous AI models can update themselves based on new observations and changes in the environment, ensuring optimal performance even in highly dynamic settings.
- **Real-Time Decision-Making**: Autonomous systems need to process data and make decisions in real-time, such as adjusting routes for self-driving cars or optimizing flight paths for drones.
- **Safety and Reliability**: These systems require robust AI models with built-in redundancy and continuous monitoring to ensure safe operations without human intervention.

Self-deploying AI is an exciting trend that brings immense potential for autonomous industries, reducing operational costs and enhancing safety.

The emerging trends in AI deployment reflect the growing complexity, scale, and diversity of AI applications across industries. From edge computing to federated learning, explainable AI to self-deploying models, these innovations are driving the next phase of AI deployment, where intelligence is deployed more efficiently, securely, and transparently. As organizations continue to explore these cutting-edge trends, they will unlock new opportunities, overcome challenges, and set the stage for a future where AI seamlessly integrates into everyday life and business operations. For businesses, staying ahead of these trends is essential to gaining a competitive advantage and ensuring long-term success in the AI-driven world.

16.2 Serverless AI and Cloud-Native AI Models

The world of artificial intelligence (AI) deployment is rapidly evolving, and two key trends that are reshaping the landscape are serverless AI and cloud-native AI models. Both concepts represent a significant shift from traditional deployment strategies and offer exciting new opportunities for businesses and developers. These technologies allow for more flexible, scalable, and cost-effective AI deployments, empowering organizations to innovate faster while minimizing the complexity of managing infrastructure.

In this section, we will delve into the concepts of serverless AI and cloud-native AI models, explore how they work, and examine their benefits and challenges in modern AI deployment.

1. What is Serverless AI?

Serverless computing is a cloud-native model where developers focus solely on writing code and defining the logic of an application, while the cloud provider manages the infrastructure. With serverless AI, developers can deploy machine learning models without worrying about provisioning, scaling, or maintaining servers.

In the traditional model of AI deployment, businesses need to allocate resources such as virtual machines (VMs) or containers to host models. These resources must be managed, scaled, and maintained, adding overhead and complexity. Serverless AI abstracts away these concerns, allowing AI models to be deployed and run without the need to manage the underlying infrastructure.

How It Works:

- In a serverless architecture, the cloud provider (e.g., AWS Lambda, Google Cloud Functions, or Azure Functions) automatically provisions compute resources only when an event or request triggers the AI model.
- The model is deployed as a function that responds to these events, such as a user request or data input.
- After execution, the resources are released, and you pay only for the actual compute time consumed during the execution of the function.

Why It Matters:

- **Cost Efficiency**: Since resources are allocated and charged based on usage, serverless AI can significantly reduce costs, especially for applications with unpredictable workloads or intermittent usage patterns.
- **Scalability**: Serverless AI automatically scales up or down based on demand, allowing for seamless handling of traffic spikes without manual intervention.
- **Simplified Management**: The serverless model abstracts away the complexities of server maintenance, allowing developers to focus on developing and deploying AI models rather than managing infrastructure.
- **Rapid Development**: Serverless platforms enable faster deployment and iteration of AI models, as there is no need for developers to configure or manage the underlying infrastructure.

Applications:

- **Real-time Predictions**: Serverless AI can be used for on-demand inference, such as real-time predictions for e-commerce recommendations or fraud detection.
- **Event-Driven AI Workflows**: Serverless platforms are ideal for triggering AI models based on specific events, like data ingestion, user actions, or sensor input in IoT applications.

Challenges:

- **Cold Start Latency**: Serverless functions can experience cold start latency, which occurs when there is a delay in spinning up the serverless environment before executing the model. This can be an issue for applications requiring low-latency responses.

- **Resource Limitations**: Serverless platforms typically have resource limits (e.g., memory, execution time), which may not be suitable for large-scale AI models or computationally intensive tasks.
- **Complexity in Model Size**: Deploying large AI models or deep learning models on serverless platforms may not always be efficient due to resource constraints.

2. Cloud-Native AI Models

Cloud-native AI models leverage the power of cloud infrastructure to create and deploy AI systems that are specifically designed to take advantage of cloud computing's scalability, flexibility, and accessibility. Unlike traditional AI models, which may be optimized for deployment on specific servers or data centers, cloud-native AI models are built to seamlessly integrate with cloud services and workflows.

How It Works:

- **Containerization**: Cloud-native AI models are typically packaged as containers (using technologies like Docker and Kubernetes), which are lightweight and portable units of software that include all dependencies needed to run the model.
- **Microservices Architecture**: AI models are broken down into smaller, independent services that can be scaled and deployed separately. Each microservice is responsible for a specific task in the model pipeline, such as data preprocessing, inference, or post-processing.
- **Cloud-Based AI Services**: Many cloud providers offer AI and machine learning services (e.g., Google AI Platform, AWS SageMaker, Azure AI) that allow businesses to deploy and manage models without worrying about the underlying infrastructure. These services provide end-to-end solutions for building, training, and deploying AI models in a cloud-native environment.

Why It Matters:

- **Scalability**: Cloud-native AI models can be easily scaled to handle large datasets and high volumes of requests, making them suitable for big data and high-performance applications.
- **Resilience**: Cloud-native AI models benefit from the inherent redundancy and fault tolerance of cloud environments, ensuring that models remain operational even in the event of failures or disruptions.
- **Seamless Integration**: Cloud-native models are designed to work well with other cloud services, enabling easy integration with databases, storage, data lakes, and other AI services.

- **Flexibility**: Cloud-native AI allows organizations to choose the best tools and frameworks for their needs, such as using TensorFlow for deep learning or scikit-learn for traditional machine learning, without worrying about hardware or software compatibility.

Applications:

- **Scalable AI for Enterprises**: Cloud-native AI models are ideal for businesses with rapidly growing data and traffic, such as large-scale recommendation systems, demand forecasting, and personalized content delivery.
- **Collaborative AI Development**: Cloud-native platforms facilitate collaborative AI development, enabling teams to work together on model training, version control, and deployment.
- **Multi-Cloud Deployments**: Cloud-native models can be deployed across multiple cloud environments (e.g., AWS, Azure, Google Cloud), ensuring flexibility and reducing the risk of vendor lock-in.

Challenges:

- **Data Privacy and Compliance**: As AI models in the cloud often process sensitive data, organizations need to ensure that they comply with data privacy laws and regulations (e.g., GDPR, HIPAA).
- **Cost Management**: While cloud-native models offer scalability, organizations must carefully manage their cloud resources to avoid unexpected costs, especially for large-scale AI applications with high processing demands.
- **Vendor Lock-In**: Relying on specific cloud providers for AI services may lead to vendor lock-in, which can limit flexibility and increase long-term costs.

3. The Synergy Between Serverless AI and Cloud-Native Models

While serverless AI and cloud-native AI models are distinct concepts, they complement each other in many ways. Cloud-native architectures provide a robust foundation for deploying AI models at scale, while serverless computing adds an additional layer of flexibility and cost-efficiency. Together, these trends allow businesses to build highly scalable, efficient, and resilient AI solutions.

How They Work Together:

- **Serverless Microservices**: AI models can be deployed as serverless functions within a cloud-native microservices architecture, combining the scalability of cloud-native models with the cost efficiency and flexibility of serverless computing.
- **Elastic Scalability**: Serverless functions, when combined with cloud-native AI, enable dynamic scaling based on demand. This allows businesses to handle fluctuating workloads without having to over-provision resources.
- **On-Demand AI:** The combination of serverless and cloud-native models allows for on-demand, event-driven AI deployment, making it ideal for use cases such as real-time predictions and AI-driven automation.

The emergence of serverless AI and cloud-native AI models is driving a paradigm shift in the way AI models are deployed, making it easier for organizations to scale, optimize, and manage their AI workloads. Serverless AI offers cost-effective and scalable solutions for applications with variable workloads, while cloud-native AI models leverage the full power of cloud infrastructure to provide robust, flexible, and resilient AI solutions. Together, these trends are helping businesses unlock new possibilities for AI deployment, enabling faster innovation, reduced infrastructure management overhead, and greater scalability.

As serverless and cloud-native technologies continue to evolve, they will play a pivotal role in the next generation of AI deployment, making AI more accessible, efficient, and impactful across industries. Understanding these trends will allow organizations to stay ahead of the curve and fully harness the potential of AI in the cloud.

16.3 Federated Learning and Decentralized AI

In recent years, federated learning and decentralized AI have emerged as powerful concepts in the field of artificial intelligence deployment. These innovative approaches address the growing concerns about data privacy, security, and the need for efficient AI model training without relying on centralized data storage. By enabling models to be trained collaboratively across distributed devices and systems, federated learning and decentralized AI are set to revolutionize the way AI models are trained, deployed, and maintained.

In this section, we will explore what federated learning and decentralized AI are, how they function, and the potential they hold for the future of AI deployment, particularly in industries where data privacy is critical, such as healthcare, finance, and IoT.

1. What is Federated Learning?

Federated learning is a distributed machine learning technique that allows AI models to be trained on decentralized data, which remains on the devices or local servers of the data owners. Unlike traditional machine learning, where data is collected and stored centrally for model training, federated learning keeps the data localized and only shares model updates (or gradients) across participating devices.

In essence, federated learning allows models to learn from data stored on devices such as smartphones, IoT devices, or edge servers, without the data ever leaving the local environment. This is a significant advantage in terms of privacy, data security, and reducing the need for large-scale data transfers.

How It Works:

- **Local Model Training**: Instead of uploading data to a central server, federated learning enables local devices (smartphones, laptops, etc.) to train the model on their own data.
- **Model Aggregation**: After training on local data, each device sends the model updates (gradients) to a central server, which aggregates the updates from multiple devices to improve the global model.
- **Privacy-Preserving**: The original data remains on the device, ensuring that sensitive information is not transmitted or stored in a centralized database. Only model weights or updates are exchanged.

Why It Matters:

- **Data Privacy and Security**: Federated learning addresses privacy concerns by ensuring that sensitive data remains on the user's device. It is particularly beneficial in domains like healthcare, where personal health data is highly sensitive.
- **Reduced Latency**: Federated learning can help reduce latency in AI applications by allowing models to learn and make predictions on local devices without waiting for data to be sent to a central server.
- **Efficiency**: The decentralized nature of federated learning enables AI models to be trained using data from a wide variety of sources without the need for large-scale data collection and transfer.
- **Cost-Effective**: By leveraging edge devices for model training, federated learning reduces the cost of cloud storage and data transfer.

Applications:

- **Healthcare**: Federated learning can be used to train AI models on medical data, such as patient records or imaging, while keeping the data on local hospitals' or healthcare providers' devices, ensuring privacy and compliance with regulations like HIPAA.
- **Mobile Applications**: Mobile devices can leverage federated learning to improve features like personalized recommendations, predictive text, and voice recognition, all while ensuring that user data stays private.
- **Autonomous Vehicles**: Federated learning can enable autonomous vehicles to learn from the vast amounts of data generated by each vehicle, improving their decision-making capabilities without sharing sensitive data across networks.

Challenges:

- **Communication Overhead**: Although federated learning reduces the need for large data transfers, sending frequent model updates can still result in communication overhead, especially with a large number of devices.
- **Data Heterogeneity**: Data on different devices may vary significantly in terms of quality and quantity, which can lead to challenges in training a robust and accurate model across diverse data sources.
- **Model Accuracy and Convergence**: Aggregating model updates from various devices can result in slower convergence and less accurate models, particularly when the devices' data is unbalanced or skewed.

2. What is Decentralized AI?

Decentralized AI refers to a broader approach where the control, training, and operation of AI models are distributed across multiple nodes or systems. Unlike federated learning, which typically involves central aggregation of model updates, decentralized AI removes the need for a central server entirely, operating on a peer-to-peer network.

In decentralized AI, each node in the network (which could be a device, server, or computer) participates in the AI process independently. The system can make decisions or process information without relying on a central authority or server.

How It Works:

- **Distributed Training**: Decentralized AI distributes the training of models across multiple nodes in a network, with each node contributing to the computation without relying on a centralized system.

- **Collaborative Decision-Making**: Instead of having one central server make decisions or predictions, decentralized AI models allow nodes to make decisions in a collaborative manner, using a consensus protocol or distributed algorithms.
- **Blockchain Integration**: Blockchain technology can be integrated into decentralized AI systems to ensure the integrity of the data and models and to provide a transparent and immutable record of decisions and transactions.

Why It Matters:

- **Eliminates Centralized Control**: By distributing the workload and decision-making across multiple nodes, decentralized AI reduces the reliance on centralized servers, which can be vulnerable to failures or attacks.
- **Resilience and Fault Tolerance**: The decentralized nature of these systems ensures that even if some nodes fail or go offline, the system can continue functioning without significant disruptions.
- **Enhanced Security**: Decentralized AI can enhance security by eliminating single points of failure and by using blockchain or other technologies to secure the model and data exchanges between nodes.
- **Fairness and Collaboration**: By operating on a peer-to-peer network, decentralized AI promotes fairness and ensures that each participating node has an equal say in the decision-making process, which is important in collaborative and multi-party environments.

Applications:

- **IoT Networks**: Decentralized AI is particularly suited for the Internet of Things (IoT) networks, where devices such as smart sensors, cameras, and vehicles can collaborate to process data and make decisions without relying on a central server.
- **Blockchain-Based AI**: In blockchain-based decentralized AI models, nodes (smart contracts) can train models, make decisions, and process transactions while ensuring transparency, trust, and security.
- **Autonomous Systems**: Decentralized AI can be used in autonomous systems like drones, robots, and self-driving cars, where each unit can independently make decisions and collaborate with others in a distributed environment.

Challenges:

- **Complexity in Coordination**: Coordinating the training and decision-making processes across decentralized nodes can be complex and may require advanced algorithms to ensure consistency and convergence.

- **Limited Resources**: Decentralized AI systems often operate on devices with limited computational power and storage, which may impact the performance of the AI models.
- **Security Concerns**: While decentralized AI can reduce the risks of centralization, it also opens the door to new security challenges, such as ensuring the authenticity of model updates and preventing malicious nodes from manipulating the system.

3. Benefits and Challenges of Federated Learning and Decentralized AI

Both federated learning and decentralized AI offer unique benefits, especially in contexts where data privacy, security, and collaboration are paramount. However, these approaches also present challenges in terms of coordination, model accuracy, and system complexity.

Benefits:

- **Privacy and Security**: Both approaches help ensure data privacy, which is critical in sensitive domains such as healthcare, finance, and government.
- **Scalability**: Federated learning and decentralized AI enable large-scale training across a variety of devices and systems without requiring massive infrastructure investments.
- **Collaborative AI**: These approaches foster collaboration across diverse systems, organizations, and devices, leading to richer, more diverse datasets and better-performing models.

Challenges:

- **Model Convergence**: Federated learning can struggle with achieving fast convergence, especially when the data across devices is heterogeneous. Similarly, decentralized AI models may face difficulty in ensuring consistent model updates without central coordination.
- **Resource Constraints**: The devices or nodes in federated or decentralized systems may have limited processing power or storage, which can limit the complexity of the models they can support.
- **Security and Trust**: Although decentralization offers security advantages, it also introduces challenges in verifying the authenticity of data and model updates, especially in federated learning environments.

Federated learning and decentralized AI are groundbreaking techniques that offer solutions to some of the most pressing challenges in modern AI deployment, particularly around data privacy, security, and scalability. By enabling AI models to be trained and deployed across distributed systems without centralizing data, these approaches are opening new possibilities for industries such as healthcare, finance, and IoT.

While these technologies hold great promise, they also present unique challenges in terms of model coordination, system complexity, and resource limitations. As research and development in federated learning and decentralized AI continue to evolve, we can expect these methods to play a central role in the future of AI deployment, creating more secure, private, and collaborative AI systems.

16.4 AI Regulation and Its Impact on Deployment

As artificial intelligence continues to become more integrated into various industries, its impact on society grows significantly. With AI driving advancements in healthcare, finance, transportation, and beyond, ensuring that its deployment is ethical, safe, and transparent is more important than ever. AI regulations, both existing and forthcoming, are central to this effort. They aim to govern the design, deployment, and use of AI systems to address concerns about safety, fairness, privacy, and accountability. In this chapter, we will explore the evolving landscape of AI regulation, how these laws impact AI deployment, and what businesses and organizations need to consider when deploying AI technologies.

1. Understanding AI Regulation

AI regulation refers to the set of laws, guidelines, and standards that govern how artificial intelligence should be developed, deployed, and used. These regulations are designed to ensure that AI systems are safe, ethical, and do not inadvertently cause harm. The regulatory landscape for AI is rapidly evolving, with different countries and regions developing their own frameworks. These frameworks can vary significantly in terms of scope, enforcement, and the degree of flexibility they offer for innovation.

For instance, the European Union has taken a pioneering stance with its Artificial Intelligence Act, proposed in 2021, which categorizes AI systems based on the level of risk they pose, such as high-risk systems in healthcare or transportation, and low-risk systems in areas like entertainment. Meanwhile, the United States has a more fragmented regulatory approach, with different federal agencies taking responsibility for regulating specific aspects of AI.

2. Key Areas of AI Regulation

AI regulation encompasses several important areas that impact how AI models are deployed. These regulations are designed to address a variety of concerns, including privacy, fairness, transparency, accountability, and security. Below are some of the primary focus areas of AI regulation:

a) Data Privacy and Protection

Data privacy is one of the most critical aspects of AI regulation. Many AI systems rely on vast amounts of data for training and operation. However, this data can include personal, sensitive information, making data privacy laws essential. Regulations like the General Data Protection Regulation (GDPR) in the EU and California Consumer Privacy Act (CCPA) in the U.S. set guidelines for how personal data should be collected, stored, and used.

For AI deployments, these regulations impact how models are trained and how personal data is handled. Organizations must ensure that AI systems comply with these privacy laws, especially when dealing with sensitive sectors like healthcare or finance, where data privacy is paramount.

b) Fairness and Bias Mitigation

AI systems can unintentionally perpetuate biases present in the data they are trained on. This can lead to unfair outcomes, particularly when models are used to make decisions in sensitive areas like hiring, lending, or criminal justice. AI regulations, such as the proposed EU AI Act, often include specific requirements for ensuring fairness and mitigating biases in AI models.

The regulation may mandate companies to perform regular audits to check for bias, use diverse datasets, and implement fairness metrics in their models. In this context, AI deployment must include mechanisms for identifying and mitigating biases that may arise from the model's design or training data.

c) Transparency and Explainability

As AI becomes more pervasive, understanding how and why AI models make decisions is critical to maintaining trust. Regulatory frameworks around the world are increasingly focusing on ensuring transparency and explainability in AI models. In the EU, for example, the AI Act mandates that high-risk AI systems should be explainable and that users must be provided with information about how the model makes its decisions.

Regulations like this impact AI deployment by requiring organizations to implement interpretability and explainability frameworks, particularly for applications where human decisions are influenced or replaced by AI systems, such as healthcare diagnostics, loan approvals, or criminal sentencing.

d) Accountability and Liability

Who is responsible when an AI system causes harm, makes an incorrect decision, or operates in a way that contradicts ethical guidelines? This is a central question in the field of AI regulation. Regulations often define the scope of accountability and liability for AI systems, especially for high-risk applications.

For example, in the EU, the AI Act outlines provisions for ensuring that organizations deploying AI systems are held accountable for their use and the impacts of their models. Organizations deploying AI models may be required to have a clear audit trail for their models, enabling regulators and affected parties to trace the origins and decisions made by the AI system. This can have significant implications on how AI models are deployed, monitored, and updated, ensuring organizations take full responsibility for their AI systems.

e) Safety and Security

AI systems can be vulnerable to attacks, including adversarial attacks that manipulate inputs to cause incorrect predictions. There are also concerns about the potential misuse of AI, such as the development of autonomous weapons or surveillance tools. AI regulations often address safety and security concerns by requiring organizations to implement rigorous testing, validation, and security measures for their AI systems.

The EU's proposed AI Act, for instance, classifies AI systems into categories based on the risk they pose, requiring high-risk AI systems to undergo stricter safety protocols. Regulations may require organizations to ensure that AI systems can handle unexpected inputs and behave predictably in real-world scenarios.

3. The Impact of AI Regulation on Deployment

AI regulations play a significant role in shaping how AI models are developed, tested, and deployed in real-world applications. Below are several key ways in which these regulations impact AI deployment:

a) Increased Development and Compliance Costs

Complying with AI regulations can increase the costs associated with developing and deploying AI models. Organizations may need to invest in additional resources to ensure that their models meet the necessary regulatory requirements, such as performing fairness audits, implementing security measures, and ensuring transparency. For example, organizations may need to hire legal and compliance experts, data scientists, and engineers to ensure that their models are aligned with data privacy laws and fairness guidelines.

b) Innovation and Flexibility in Deployment

While AI regulations are necessary to ensure ethical deployment, overly stringent or complex regulations can stifle innovation. Striking the right balance between regulation and innovation is crucial. Overly restrictive regulations could slow the pace of AI development and deployment, especially in rapidly evolving sectors like autonomous vehicles, healthcare, and finance.

Regulations that provide clear guidelines on responsible AI deployment, however, can enhance trust in AI and foster innovation. Knowing that AI models must meet certain standards may encourage companies to invest more confidently in developing AI solutions.

c) Global Variations in Regulations

One of the challenges faced by organizations deploying AI models globally is the variation in regulations across regions. While the EU has a comprehensive AI regulation framework in place, other regions, like the U.S. and China, have different approaches to AI regulation. This creates challenges for organizations that need to ensure compliance in multiple jurisdictions, particularly when deploying AI models globally.

To address this, businesses need to carefully evaluate the regulatory landscape in each region where they deploy AI models and ensure that their AI systems are compliant with local laws. This can involve modifying AI models or the deployment process based on regional requirements.

d) Impact on AI Adoption in Sensitive Sectors

Certain industries, such as healthcare, finance, and public services, are particularly sensitive to AI regulations. Strict regulations can slow the adoption of AI in these sectors, especially if the regulatory burden is heavy. However, the presence of clear regulatory guidelines can also provide reassurance to businesses and users, encouraging broader AI adoption in these critical sectors. For example, regulations in healthcare around data privacy (such as HIPAA in the U.S.) can facilitate the use of AI in medical diagnostics while protecting patient data.

4. Preparing for AI Regulation: What to Do Next

For organizations looking to deploy AI models, understanding and preparing for AI regulation is crucial. Here are some steps to ensure compliance and mitigate risks:

- **Stay Informed**: Keep abreast of evolving AI regulations in different regions and industries. Regularly consult with legal and compliance teams to understand the impact of regulatory changes.
- **Implement Ethical AI Practices**: Incorporate fairness, transparency, and accountability into the AI model development lifecycle. Ensure that models are interpretable and can be audited for compliance with ethical guidelines.
- **Focus on Data Privacy**: Take proactive steps to ensure that data privacy laws like GDPR and CCPA are followed during AI model training and deployment. Implement data anonymization and encryption techniques to safeguard sensitive information.
- **Adopt Robust Security Measures**: Invest in AI security to protect against adversarial attacks and ensure that deployed models are resilient and trustworthy.

AI regulation is a vital aspect of ensuring that artificial intelligence is deployed responsibly and ethically. As the regulatory landscape continues to evolve, organizations must stay informed and adapt to meet new guidelines while maintaining innovation. By addressing privacy, fairness, transparency, accountability, and security, AI regulation can ensure that AI models are deployed safely and effectively across industries, promoting trust and enabling the widespread adoption of AI technologies.

Bridging the gap between research and real-world applications, **Deploying A** **From Research to Real-World Applications** is your ultimate guide to su operationalizing AI. While many AI books focus on building models, this book t ͟ͅ you beyond research—teaching you how to deploy, scale, monitor, and maintain AI models in production environments.

From cloud-based solutions to edge AI, on-premises deployment, and MLOps automation, this book covers the full AI model lifecycle, ensuring your AI solutions remain scalable, efficient, and reliable. You'll explore practical case studies from industries like healthcare, finance, and autonomous systems, gaining valuable insights into real-world AI deployment.

By the end of this book, you'll have a clear roadmap for AI deployment, from optimizing model performance and setting up APIs to automating workflows and ensuring security. Whether you're a data scientist, ML engineer, or business leader, this book will equip you with the skills to turn AI research into impactful applications.

Take your AI projects beyond theory—deploy AI models with confidence! 🚀

Dear Reader,

Thank you for embarking on this journey with me through Deploying AI Models: From Research to Real-World Applications. Writing this book has been an incredible experience, and knowing that it can help you bridge the gap between AI research and real-world implementation is truly rewarding.

AI deployment is one of the most critical yet challenging aspects of artificial intelligence, and I deeply appreciate your time and effort in mastering this subject. Whether you're a data scientist, ML engineer, software developer, or AI enthusiast, your dedication to bringing AI solutions to life is what drives innovation and progress in this field.

I am incredibly grateful for your support—not just for this book but for the entire AI from Scratch series. Your curiosity, passion, and feedback inspire me to continue exploring and sharing knowledge.

I would love to hear about your AI deployment experiences, insights, and challenges. Feel free to connect, share your thoughts, and be part of this growing AI community.

Once again, thank you for being part of this journey. I hope this book empowers you to confidently deploy AI models and make a real-world impact.

Wishing you success in all your AI endeavors!

With gratitude,

Gilbert Gutiérrez

www.ingramcontent.com/pod-product-compliance
Lightning Source LLC
LaVergne TN
LVHW060120070326
832902LV00019B/3056